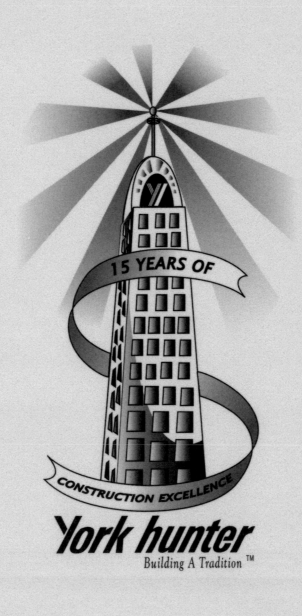

15 YEARS OF

CONSTRUCTION EXCELLENCE

York hunter
Building A Tradition ™

1372 BROADWAY, NEW YORK, NY 10018 TEL: 212 703-3700 EMAIL: INFO@YORKHUNTER.COM WWW.YORKHUNTER.COM

NEW YORK
A State of Mind

NEW YORK
A State of Mind

Introduction by **EDWARD I. KOCH**

rt Direction by **BRIAN GROPPE**

URBAN
TAPESTRY
SERIES
TOWERY
PUBLISHING, INC.

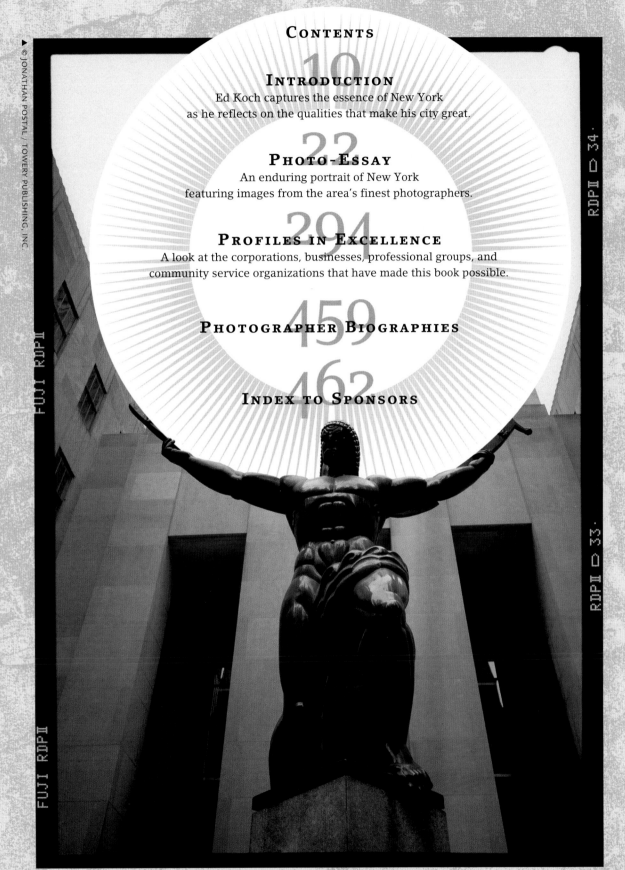

CONTENTS

INTRODUCTION
10
Ed Koch captures the essence of New York
as he reflects on the qualities that make his city great.

PHOTO-ESSAY
22
An enduring portrait of New York
featuring images from the area's finest photographers.

PROFILES IN EXCELLENCE
294
A look at the corporations, businesses, professional groups, and
community service organizations that have made this book possible.

PHOTOGRAPHER BIOGRAPHIES
459

INDEX TO SPONSORS
462

Library of Congress Catalog-in-Publishing information may be found on page 452.

BY EDWARD I. KOCH

BEING A NEW YORKER IS A STATE OF MIND. ANYBODY can become a New Yorker—if you live here for six months and at the end of the six months you find that you walk faster, talk faster, and think faster, then you're a New Yorker. ⚓ I was born in the Bronx, which means I'm one of the fewer than

50 percent of those living in New York City today who were born here. More than a majority came here from other cities in the United States and from other countries around the world. In fact, today that is actually the strength of New York City—this electricity that comes from a population that is so different than the rest of the United States because we have the sons and daughters of every country, of every state in the Union, who are in every level of our economy, including at-the-top leadership. So we get renewed by this constant influx of people who come to New York City from all over the world because they really believe, as Frank Sinatra has convinced us by singing so many times, "if you can make it here, you can make it anywhere."

When I speak around the country, I always mention the fact that my father and mother came to New York in the early 1900s; they were Polish Jews seeking to escape anti-Semitism and the wretched poverty they were living in. They had three children and each one was successful in the profession they selected— I became the mayor of the greatest city in the world. That fulfillment, of course, was not limited to me: Mario Cuomo, a son of Italian parents who came similarly looking for opportunities that weren't available to them in Italy, became governor of the Empire State, the greatest state in the Union. These are two of many examples of such successes. That's what's remarkable about the whole country, but particularly about New York City.

Take the Bronx, where I was born. First of all, it has one of the world's great thoroughfares: the Grand Concourse. The architecture— because the apartment houses were built in the 1920s and 1930s—is, in many cases, art deco. They are absolute gems, just wonderful to look at. They're now occupied overwhelmingly by black and Hispanic families who've moved into the homes of Jewish families who left in the 1960s and 1970s. Grand Concourse was predominantly Jewish when I was growing up, and the desire of every Jewish family was to move to the Grand Concourse because that meant you'd almost made it. But you'd really made it, if you were a Jewish family, if you moved

to the Upper West Side of Manhattan. And as those families moved out, Hispanic and black families looking to move from poverty areas plagued with crime began to move in. Later, beginning with the administration of John Lindsay, large numbers of families on welfare began to move in with city assistance. Today, the Bronx has a Hispanic plurality and a Hispanic borough president, Fernando Ferrer.

Now, what makes people who move here change—and they're all changed by the environment, by the discourse in the marketplace and at home and in the schools—is being subjected to the influences of so many different cultural traditions. What we in this city glory in is that our tradition is you should never forget who you are, where you came from, or where your parents came from.

THERE WAS A TIME WHEN CANDIDATES FOR PUBLIC OFFICE WOULD VISIT THE "THREE I'S"—ISRAEL, ITALY, AND Ireland—in other words, to bond with the Jewish, Italian, and Irish communities. Indeed, traditionally they were required to, if they were to have a chance of prevailing. Now that's no longer true. Now the bonding has a racial and ethnic context. The visits abroad now include Puerto Rico and the Dominican Republic, and, if you can afford it, South Africa. Nothing wrong with that. We glory in it. The city changes.

For example, there was a time when Little Italy dominated the Mulberry/Mott Street area off of Canal Street, going from Canal north to Houston Street. Now, because of the emigrant influx from Hong Kong—with the Chinese having left Hong Kong in large numbers, many of them coming to New York—Chinatown has overwhelmed Little Italy, and bought many of the Italian restaurants and buildings, reducing the size of Little Italy.

So where Chinatown before was basically Mott Street, now it has engulfed huge parts of Little Italy. And even though it's one of the oldest parts of town and the buildings are tenements—and I mean old tenements—real estate there is among the most expensive in town because the Chinese do like to live together here, and that area is still the dominant neighborhood for them. Although Flushing, in Queens, is expanding, and is now our most Asian borough in terms of population: Korean, Indian, Hindu, Pakistani, Chinese, Japanese . . . just wonderful.

A very nice but foolish councilwoman from that district was affronted by all the Asian language signs of the shops in parts of Flushing and introduced legislation in the city council to require that they also be in English—it was foolish. Ridiculous. She ultimately apolo-

gized. She was reelected, but a lot of apologies were required.

Astoria is another ethnic community that's amazing in its texture: It is overwhelmingly Greek. Two of my favorite restaurants are in Astoria; one's Greek, the other's Italian. Elias Corner has great fish prepared as only Greeks know how. The other one is Piccola Venezia. If either restaurant came to Manhattan, the prices would double and they would be huge successes. But they are huge successes in Queens—not cheap, but by comparison with Manhattan, very cheap. What is interesting about Piccola Venezia is that the people who own it are from Trieste, so they're Yugoslav or Italian. I think they would probably say they're Italian, but that is a special area. Trieste is very international—it was part of the Austro-Hungarian Empire, then part of the now former Yugoslavia, and now it's Italian, and so forth.

In Brooklyn, the largest new community is comprised of Russians. They first moved to Brighton Beach and now, as they become upwardly mobile, making their way up the economic ladder, they are moving to Manhattan Beach. Going to Brighton Beach to patronize the Russian shops, restaurants, and nightclubs is a great day of fun.

And the foods they've brought with them—they make Zabar's on the Upper West Side of Manhattan look puny! A hundred varieties of smoked fish and meats are just wonderful. The Russians are so modern looking, but still their products look old-world and very attractive. I mean, you just don't identify the Russians that way. While they beat us with *Sputnik*, they were also in some areas of daily life sort of primitive. For example, indoor plumbing did not exist in many parts of the country. But they're not primitive in their eating.

Another very large community in Midwood, Brooklyn, and much older than the Russian settlement of Brighton, is made up of Sephardic Jews. They have very large families, so they want—and do build—very large houses, mostly in the Midwood area, around Ocean Parkway. They have a lovely community, with a lot of synagogues that are beautiful with a Moorish/Arab look about them—Spanish, really—the original home of the Sephardic Jews before the Inquisition in 1492 when they were expelled unless they converted to Catholicism. They were welcomed by the sultan of Turkey, and other Muslim countries. ☞

J UST AS THE COMMUNITIES THAT COMPRISE NEW YORK ARE CONSTANTLY changing, so is the architecture of the city: Now it's modern, lots of glass and stone forming the skyscrapers that make up the city's commercial and residential buildings. Fortunately, we have landmark and zoning laws, which were tough to pass because the real estate developers didn't like them. These laws limited what they could do in terms of demolishing property and putting up some larger, grander (from their point of view), more expensive buildings. I belonged to one of the early groups—when I was a congressman and, before that, a city councilman. It was my passion, trying to stop the destruction of our great spaces, public and private.

For me, a special joy was the fact that when I was mayor, the landmarks law was argued before the U.S. Supreme Court in April 1978 by the chief appeals attorney, Leonard Koerner, whom I had appointed, and we won! Now, that has to be taken in the context of an earlier battle, which we lost. This was when the developer vandals tore down Penn Station, which had been compared by some as resembling in size the Baths of Caracalla—now famous ruins in Italy that were actually public baths under the Romans. It was a sin that they tore it down to build a skyscraper and the current version of Madison Square Garden. Almost everybody says that today. After Penn Station was torn down, we changed in the way we look at buildings. Now, of course, the real estate developers are contemplating tearing down Madison Square Garden, and I don't care if they do; it's not an architectural gem, it's just a very ordinary arena. Most buildings are not worthy of landmark description. But it was a sin to tear down the Baths of Caracalla at Penn Station, as we called it.

What is fascinating to me is something that happened only recently: the renovation of Grand Central Station, which is one of the most extraordinary public spaces in the whole world. There was an effort—I think it was in the early 1970s—on the part of the then owners of Grand Central to tear it down and build a skyscraper there. I was a congressman at the time, and a committee was formed to fight this. Jackie Kennedy Onassis was the chairwoman of the committee, and for me, a special memento of that fight was a photograph on, I think, the front page of the *New York Times*, of her, Bess Myerson, and myself walking down Park Avenue. As a result of her leadership, and a lot of people who joined her, we saved Grand Central Station.

But my favorite building, in terms of visiting it regularly—I go on a Sunday at least once every two weeks—is the Metropolitan Museum of Art. For one thing, I buy all my ties there; they have the best-looking ties in America, moderately priced, and the designs are real designs from furniture and tapestries and so forth from the museum's collection, and they have a much greater authenticity than the designs that are just simply thought up by tie designers, in my judgment. The museum itself in its collections is just extraordinary, and they're constantly changing the exhibits, so there's always something new to see, or you can just go back and see something you've already seen, and you see it with a new eye—because it's so vast. They also have wonderful reproductions of statues for sale. I have purchased almost every horse reproduction they offer; they now adorn my apartment.

The public has been changed in its philosophical conditioning: There was an effort in the late 1960s to prevent the Metropolitan Museum from building within the space that had been allocated to it in Central Park when it was first constructed. There were those who said, "No. What we want to do is disperse the collections throughout

GRAND CENTRAL
TERMINAL

the city." So there was an effort by a small group to place the Temple of Dendur—which we had been given by the government of Egypt—in a building on Canal Street. That would have been ridiculous. Fortunately, it never happened, and the Temple of Dendur is in the Met in its own specially built wing.

I ALWAYS LIKE TO TELL PEOPLE THAT IF YOU COMPARE OUR CITY WITH OTHER CITIES AROUND THE WORLD, then you will conclude that New York is not the most beautiful. I believe Paris is the most beautiful city because the architectural style is consistently glorious, and the French government keeps it that way. New York City's beauty comes from the diversity of its population and the skyscrapers.

The skyscrapers are here because of the special soil of Manhattan—more specifically, rock underneath Manhattan—that creates this extraordinarily firm foundation for skyscrapers. That's why New York is famous for its skyscrapers. The most beautiful buildings in the city, for me, are the Woolworth Building in downtown Manhattan across the street from City Hall, and the Chrysler Building, which is much more beautiful than the Empire State Building. It has that Buck Rogers look, that of the 21st century; it's futuristic in appearance, particularly in the building's top. It's art deco, and the very best example of that genre.

A large cluster of buildings that are very impressive to see are down at the Battery, at the foot of Manhattan Island—the best way to see them is by taking a boat ride, such as the Circle Line around Manhattan. They're these marvelous architectural gems, each different, but all modern, and cheek by jowl, complementing one another; many of them were built during the administration of John Lindsay. I also love the view of Manhattan from the Staten Island Ferry, which is now free—how many people have ever had a city provide anything free?

Speaking of Staten Island, there's a special community on the island called Snug Harbor. These buildings are Greek Revival and Victorian in architecture, and were built beginning in 1833 by Robert Richard Randall, who was interested in providing housing for retired seamen. As mayor, I worked with Staten Island community advocates to provide city funding to repair and rehabilitate this group of buildings, which will remind you in their visual impact of Williamsburg. The trustees have turned them into spaces where concerts and other public activities are held.

I THINK THE THREE MAJOR PLACE NAMES THAT ARE THE MOST FAMOUS around the world in referring to New York City are 42nd Street, Central Park, and Harlem. And all of them are having a revival.

Harlem is being reborn, with lots of construction and renovation of single-family town houses, which had been turned into rooming houses and are reverting now to their original use by black families. Harlem is a community that's 97 percent black. Some people might say, "Isn't that harmful?" No, it's not wrong. There are communities in New York City that are 97 percent Jewish, or Italian, or Hispanic, and then there are communities that are totally diverse in their demographic makeup.

The issue should always be: Are there legal or nonlegal restrictions that require you to live in a particular place, or prevent you from living where you would like to and can afford? That's wrong. But there is nothing wrong with freedom of choice. Lots of people like to live in a place that they perceive to be a cultural community and that includes racial, ethnic, and religious communities—places that they are comfortable with—and there's nothing wrong with that. Some black families who left Harlem and went to the integrated suburbs are coming back—these include the economic middle- and upper-middle-class families. We have a very strong black middle class. They are back buying town houses and renovating them, and that's just absolutely terrific.

And then there's Rockefeller Center. The law firm in which I'm a partner—Robinson, Silverman, Pearce, Aronsohn & Berman—is in the Rockefeller Center area. That phenomenal set of buildings is being renovated, bringing them up to date. That's what's wonderful about New York City—that it's constantly changing.

The operators of the complex are making Rockefeller Center more accessible for commercial businesses, putting in larger windows on the second floor, so that those second floors will be more attractive for commercial purposes and command greater rents.

Now, City Hall—where I had my office for 12 years; I'm the last of the three-term mayors because now we have term limitations—is another architectural gem. There are only three buildings that look like that in the whole United States. It was built in 1812, and when they built it, it was in the northernmost part of New York City, so you can see how small the city was then. It's really quite incredible when you think about it. So when they built it originally, the back of the building was left unfinished because nobody ever dreamed that anyone would look at the back of the building—now no longer true. But then the back of City Hall wasn't built from the same beautiful quarried

limestone that the front of the building was. That has since been rem-
edied. It's a wonderful building to work in: it's small, but just lovely. I
had only one cavil, and that related to an action by Robert Wagner,
my predecessor, who blocked off all the theretofore working fireplaces in the building.

I t's impossible to capture the spirit of this city without saying more about the food. I love ethnic
foods, and in New York you've got them to a fare-thee-well. Greenwich Village, for example, is like
Rome. You know in Rome, you can't get a bad meal if you go to any of the smaller Italian restaurants. If
you know where they are, you can always get a good, inexpensive meal. The Village in itself is extraordinary; we who live there like to talk about the fact that it's the only place in the borough of Manhattan
where you don't have a north/south grid system—instead, 4th Street crosses 11th Street. If you live in the
Village, you don't have a problem finding it. There are wonderful aspects of a neighborhood, and each
New York neighborhood has its own quirks and characteristics.

We also have some of the world's great restaurants, the five-star restaurants, like the Four Seasons or
Il Mulino. I think Il Mulino, on West 3rd Street, is the best Italian restaurant in the city. And then you have
restaurants in midtown Manhattan where the ambience is also just splendid. Trattoria del Arte, which is
on Seventh Avenue between 56th and 57th streets, has terrific food and a Madison Avenue crowd including the magazine and TV crowd. Or Orso on West 46th Street, which is a great place in the theater district.
It's very hard to get in, because it's a very small restaurant, but if you do eat there after the theater, you
will be eating with actors you may have just seen on the stage.

I remember sitting at a table at Orso with some friends of mine, and we were talking about the play
we'd just seen, which we did not like. Sitting at the next table was
Frank Langella, who's a great actor. Later, at our invitation, he joined
us at our table, and he said, "I was in agony because I could overhear
what you were saying, all the negative comments about a play, and I
thought it was my play." We hadn't been discussing the play he was
in, but I thought it was rather wonderful, conveying as it did the un-
derstandable insecurity and sensitivity of actors.

Then there's the Oyster Bar, in the bowels of Grand Central Station, which recently underwent a $200 million renovation. The restau-
rant has the biggest seafood menu in America and the owner, Jerome
Brody, is a wonderful restaurateur. Another great restaurant, attracting local personalities and tourists with its special ambience—that of
a French bistro—is Balthazar, on Spring Street in SoHo.

SoHo is an area to walk around—it has wonderful little boutiques
and it's just a great walking area. SoHo sounds like it's a real name,
but it means South of Houston Street (SO: south, HO: Houston Street).
Real estate developers adopted it as an acronym because it copies
London's SoHo district. Then came NoHo—North of Houston Street—
and TriBeCa—the Triangle Below Canal Street. These are all wonderful revitalized areas in downtown Manhattan, where many people are
living in lofts developed out of factory and other commercial buildings
long in disuse. ☛

EVERY INTERNATIONAL CITY HAS A ZOO, AND OURS IS ONE OF THE BEST, if not the best. When I was mayor, there was a visit to the city by the then prime minister of the People's Republic of China. I was working very closely with the Wildlife Conservation Society that runs the Bronx Zoo, and they told me they wanted a panda. So when the prime minister came, I said, through an interpreter, "Could we speak alone?" He said we could, so I said, "Mr. Prime Minister, I am going to be running for reelection shortly, and if I could get a panda, I'm a shoo-in. Can you help me get one?" "We don't give pandas anymore," he responded. "But Mr. Prime Minister, you gave two to San Francisco," I said. "Oh," he said. "Yes. But we only lent them." I said, "That's fine, I am happy to have one or two on loan." Later, when I escorted him to his car, I said, "What, if anything, can I tell the people of my city about a panda, Mr. Prime Minister?" He replied cryptically, "I think you can tell people it is quite possible that New York City will have a panda." And we did. And I was reelected.

I was happy to turn over the Central Park Zoo to the same Wildlife Conservation Society; the old zoo had kept animals in cages, including lions and tigers. The new one is totally different. They have a polar bear exhibit—with Gus, probably the only polar bear who needed a psychiatrist. Poor Gus, he couldn't stop swimming in a monotonous pattern. But the psychiatrist cured him. The polar bear and the penguins are still the two biggest draws at that zoo.

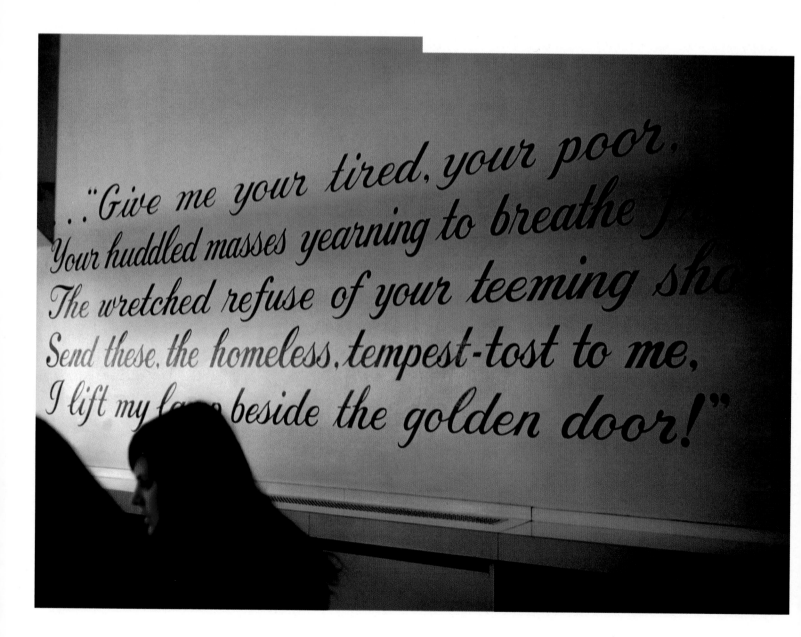

I MENTIONED AT THE START THAT, TO ME, WHAT MAKES NEW YORK CITY special is the constant influx of emigrants—from other parts of the country and the world. Let me tell you a story. It takes place on St. Patrick's Day—the parade is wonderful; it's the biggest, most joyous in the city and maybe the whole world. Its only competition in size and joy is the Puerto Rican Day Parade. I remember my first St. Patrick's Day Parade, in 1978. I had appointed a police commissioner, Bob McGuire, and he was my first appointment—the police commissioner is the most important appointment a mayor makes, in terms of public perception. When I announced the appointment to the press, I said, "Ladies and gentlemen, my appointment for police commissioner is Bob McGuire." The dean of the press corps, Gabe Pressman, said, "So, Mr. Mayor, more of the Irish Mafia?"—meaning the police commissioner is always Irish. I, looking shocked, put my hand on Bob McGuire's shoulder and I said, "Bob! You told me you were Jewish!" Then he put his hand on my shoulder and said, "No I didn't, Mr. Mayor. I told you I looked Jewish."

Bob and I had our first march together on St. Patrick's Day, leading the Emerald Society—they are the police band, and use only bagpipes and drums. We're waiting to take off with the band when suddenly an elderly woman comes running toward us—she must have been in her mid-70s—she rushes to Bob, who is a wonderful man, very modest, and still remains a friend, and when she embraces him, he turns quite red in embarrassment. Then she says, in a very thick brogue, "Oh, the P.C., the P.C."—meaning the police commissioner—and he, wanting to break out of her embrace, said, "Madam, let me introduce you to the mayor." She says, "Oh, the mayor. Glory be to God. Now I can die." I thought—then and now—"only in New York." ✒

AS THE STATUE OF LIBERTY HELD UP her torch to welcome them in, an estimated 12 million immigrants entered the United States through Ellis Island between 1892 and 1954. For many of them, the first test of citizenship came atop the so-called Stairs of Separation (OPPOSITE), where officials watched for any signs of huffing and puffing that might indicate physical weakness— and possibly deportation. Today, the steps of New York are far less ominous and much more inviting.

LWAYS WORTH THE PRICE OF admission, New York City has a ticket for everything—movies, theater, music, sports, you name it. But the best deal in town remains the $1.50 subway token, which sends customers reeling through turnstiles, ready to ride the more than 714 miles of track to anywhere in the city.

F ORTUNES ARE MADE AND LOST, ALL
in the hope of moving on up in
New York's financial district, where
Wall Street, the Federal Reserve
Bank, the World Trade Center
(OPPOSITE BOTTOM), and the Nasdaq
building (RIGHT AND OPPOSITE TOP)
reside.

KING KONG SCALED IT, BUT FEW skyscrapers can touch it. The Empire State Building, completed in 1931, remains a universally recognized landmark, though even at 1,454 feet, it is no longer the tallest building in the world, or in the city, for that matter. More than 79 million people have visited its observatory decks to view the city from on high.

S KYSCRAPERS DEFINE THE NEW YORK City skyline. Erected in 1902, the Flatiron Building (TOP), a triangular-shaped fixture a mere six feet wide at its point, forever defines the legendary corner where Broadway, Fifth Avenue, and 23rd Street intersect. Working southward toward SoHo (New Yorker lingo for "south of Houston Street"), this mile-and-a-half strip of Broadway has been dubbed Silicon Alley with the influx of high-tech businesses looking to rival their West Coast counterparts.

ONCE A THRIVING CENTER FOR vice and crime (pickpockets were a specialty), Times Square has been transformed into a shrine to corporate America and is quite the media assault on the senses. The Sony JumboTron broadcasts network television to the square, while blinking neon advertising takes center stage. Tourists, business-people, aspiring actresses and actors—such as Richard Dreyfuss circa 1977's *The Goodbye Girl* (ABOVE)—all converge at this historic intersection of 42nd Street, Seventh Avenue, and Broadway.

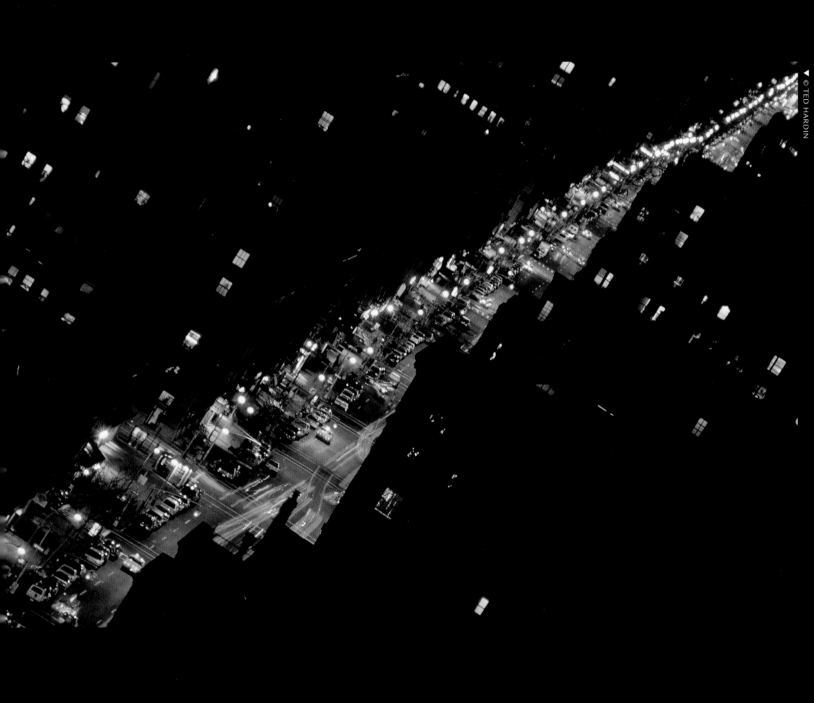

highlight of architect Philip
Johnson's deconstructivist period.
The elderly architect continues to
keep offices within its glossy walls.

SOMETIMES THE LINES OF REALITY grow a bit blurry in New York, a wavy reflection of the city's constant movement.

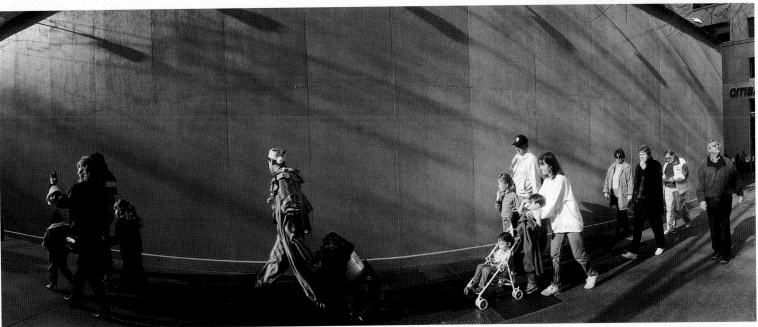

PERHAPS MORE THAN ANY CITY, New York is a walking person's paradise. Keeping in step with the forever-in-a-hurry crowd is another matter. Fifth Avenue from sunup to sundown is not a place to lollygag (OPPOSITE).

ITH SOME 11,000 TAXIS LICENSED each year, hailing a cab in New York is typically one of the easier tasks—so popular, as a matter of fact, that it's become an art form.

ORLD-RENOWNED WALL STREET
symbolizes the world of finance
and houses several of its venerable
financial institutions, including the
New York Stock Exchange (OPPOSITE),
founded in 1792. Only a half mile
long, the block also offers several
historical museums, among them
Trinity Church at Broadway and
Federal Hall National Monument.

N 1792, A MERE 24 BROKERS traded under a tree at 68 Wall Street, beginning what would become the world's largest stock market. Today, a seat on the New York Stock Exchange can cost up to $1 million, and, with more than 3,000 companies to report on, networks such as CNN and CNBC feed a bullish business culture that has reached new heights in popularity.

IF YOU CAN MAKE IT HERE, YOU can make it anywhere, the song claims. Though known for their brusque manner, New Yorkers share a genuine sense of optimism— where the raging bull inspires the belief that the markets will rise. And while dreams are often realized here, a prudent speculator knows how to differentiate between a golden opportunity and a curbside hustle.

N EW YORKERS ARE A LAW ABIDING bunch. The city's crime rate has dropped over the past few years by a reported 43 percent, allowing locals the leisure to let down their guard from time to time. Once a

haven for drug dealers and petty crime, Bryant Park (ABOVE) was closed in the late 1980s, but was reopened in 1992 and reclaimed as a spot for midtown workers to relax.

HOW IS IT POSSIBLE THAT IN A city where residents regularly use public transportation, parking spaces are at such a premium? Though on the decline—down from 13 million annually in the early 1990s to only around 9 million in recent years—summonses are still swiftly dispatched, making towing one of New York's more lucrative industries. Violators (or victims, depending on your perspective) cough up more than $100 a piece to retrieve their cars from the pound.

AUTOMOBILES DO HAVE THEIR place in New York City—just not necessarily on the streets. For those who don't want to take a chance on misinterpreting one of the city's 566,000 parking signs, lots are readily available. But you'll pay a price: around $15 for two hours or $25 for a full day.

F YOU CHOOSE TO MOTOR THROUGH the Big Apple, at least do it in style. Vintage cars and vanity license plates match wits with murals and other vehicle motifs across the city.

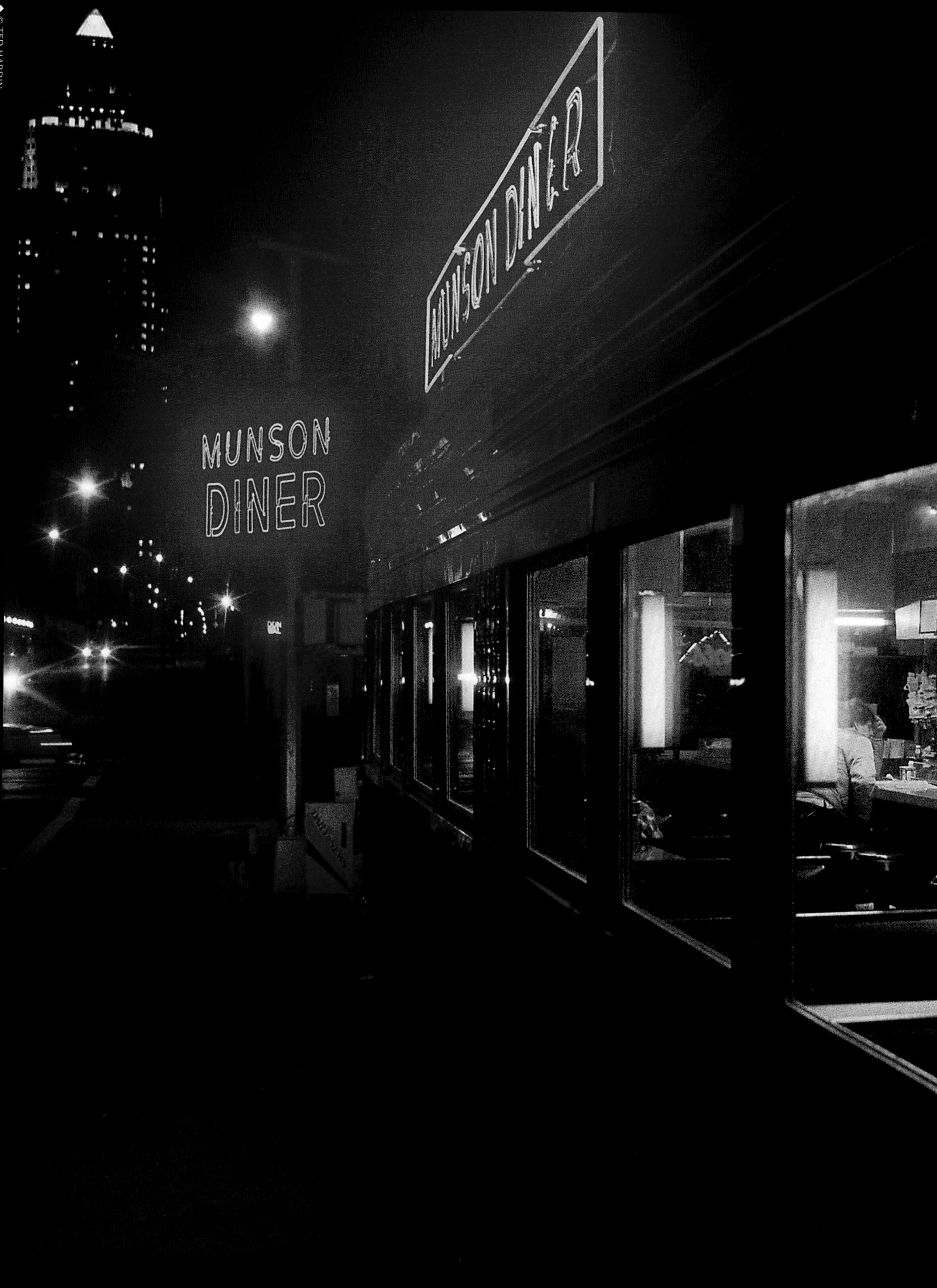

◆ © TED HARDIN

THE OLD RAILROAD CAR THAT is the Munson Diner, located at 11th Avenue and 49th Street, is best known for its 1950s-style Formica bar and tables, and linoleum floors. The 80-seat eatery recalls a simpler time in American cuisine—even if its own menu is a bit more varied than greasy burgers and strong coffee. In a fitting tribute, newspaper columnist Jimmy Breslin highlighted the diner during the opening and closing credits of his short-lived ABC late-night television show *Jimmy Breslin's People*.

F ROM GOURMET TO AROUND-THE-corner, New Yorkers flip over all types of pizza. Thankfully, due to the city's strong culinary heritage, nearly all of the local pies are worth trying at least once—and most, far more than that.

ALL NATURAL

Y OU'D HAVE TO BE SOFT IN THE head not to appreciate the savory smells of New York, which—like the city itself—are strong and varied. Nothing defines the day-to-day experience as well as the pushcart. An estimated 4,000 licensed vendors sell everything from hot dogs to falafel to pretzels to pickles.

Nᴇᴡ Yᴏʀᴋ'ꜱ ᴇᴛʜɴɪᴄ ᴅɪᴠᴇʀꜱɪᴛʏ guarantees an excellent opportunity to sample all types of fresh and unusual cuisines. The Fulton Fish Market at the South Street Seaport (ᴏᴘᴘᴏꜱɪᴛᴇ ʀɪɢʜᴛ) is the largest fish market in the country.

But opportunities also await in the other boroughs, whether it's squid at Elias Corner in Astoria, Queens (ᴏᴘᴘᴏꜱɪᴛᴇ, ᴛᴏᴘ ʟᴇꜰᴛ), or "delicious" cow foot (ʙᴏᴛᴛᴏᴍ ʀɪɢʜᴛ), available at a West Indian neighborhood deli in Brooklyn.

Manhattan's South Street Seaport and the nearby South Street Seaport Museum (PAGES 70-71) recall New York's history as a natural harbor. The seaport today attracts more than 10 million visitors annually to shop and view its extraordinary maritime sights. Several boats are available to tour the area, including *W.O. Decker*, a 30-foot-long wooden tugboat built in 1930.

New York's origins as a seaport city have resulted in an array of international influences from spices to similarly aromatic flower bouquets. It's hard to beat locally grown apples, however, for a flavor that will really send your taste buds soaring.

H. J. MILLS
INDERHOOK
NEW YORK

© JONATHAN POSTAL / TOWERY PUBLISHING, INC.

© TED HARDIN

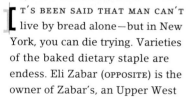

I T'S BEEN SAID THAT MAN CAN'T live by bread alone—but in New York, you can die trying. Varieties of the baked dietary staple are endless. Eli Zabar (OPPOSITE) is the owner of Zabar's, an Upper West

Side grocery that features fresh bread and more than 300 types of cheeses. The store's hectic atmosphere (BOTTOM LEFT) is considered part of its charm, and the movie *You've Got Mail* cast it as the deli

where lead actors Tom Hanks and Meg Ryan shop for their delicacies. For something solid to slap between two slices, check out Fretta Bros. meats (BOTTOM RIGHT).

N E W   Y O R K

ANY A NEW YORKER HAS BEEN driven crazy by the city's exacting pace, which seems, on occasion, to have gone to the dogs. Sometimes though, the local nuttiness can bring a welcome smile.

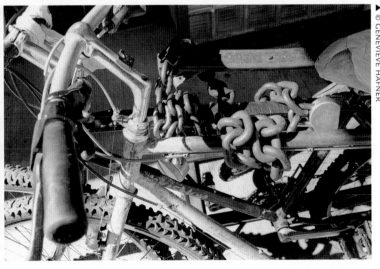

DESPITE SINCERE EFFORTS, THERE simply isn't any way to secure everything in a city the size of New York, where rusty locks and chains, wrought iron cages, and gratings are as commonplace as the bagel.

WHILE RITZY DEPARTMENT STORES line Fifth and Madison avenues, some of the best deals can be had on the streets. Outdoor antique fairs, such as the one in Chelsea (RIGHT), have bargains galore for the smart shopper. Individuals also sell their personalized lines of goods, from handwoven to handcrafted. But buyer beware: Fake and stolen items are extremely common as well.

OLD-TIME TRADES, SUCH AS SILVER-smithing and garment tailoring, have their experts, but New York has become more noteworthy for its high-profile entertainment business. Roger Sadowsky (BOTTOM LEFT) makes guitars and customizes instruments for an impressive clientele that includes Paul Simon and Bruce Springsteen. Silvercup Studios in Long Island City, Queens (TOP), is where commercials and Hollywood blockbusters—such as *When Harry Met Sally*; *The Godfather, Part III*; *Working Girl*; and, most recently, HBO's hit show *The Sopranos*—are shot.

Ticker tape parades have become routine to New Yorkers. The NHL's Rangers, whose now-retired Wayne Gretzky (BOTTOM RIGHT) is the league's all-time leading scorer, won their fourth Stanley Cup for the 1993-1994 season.

© ODETTE LUPIS

The New York Yankees have a storied history, racking up 25 World Series championships, including back-to-back sweeps in 1998 and 1999. Team members' names are synonymous with baseball, from center fielder Bernie Williams (BOTTOM RIGHT) to five-time Cy Young Award winner Roger Clemens (BOTTOM LEFT).

SPORTS COMPLEXES ARE LOCATED throughout the metropolitan area. Yankee Stadium in the Bronx— the House That Ruth Built—remains one of the most famous and historic addresses in sports (OPPOSITE), while Giants Stadium (TOP), part of the Meadowlands Sports Complex in nearby New Jersey, plays host to two NFL teams—the Giants and the Jets.

EW YORKERS HAVE AN INSATIABLE
appetite for sports. Basketball
remains a prime favorite, whether
it's the NBA's Knicks (RIGHT), the
WNBA's Liberty (OPPOSITE, BOTTOM
RIGHT), or perennial crowd favorite
the Harlem Globetrotters (OPPOSITE,
BOTTOM LEFT). The corner of Sixth
Avenue and Fourth Street in the
West Village is a hot spot for min-
gling with talent scouts, out in force
at the Cage (OPPOSITE TOP) to scout
the city's up-and-coming stars.

EXTREME SPORTS—BICYCLE STUNT riding, sky surfing, wake boarding, sport climbing, rock riding, and the list goes on—are the latest athletic variation for the young and limber. New Yorker Eitan Kramer (OPPOSITE LEFT) has competed as an in-line skater in events sponsored by ESPN, while Ryan Jacklone (OPPOSITE RIGHT) is known for pioneering the Houston Twist and the Misty Flip, two difficult acrobatic moves.

GROWING UP IN AN URBAN AREA, where the way you look often reigns supreme, can present its challenges. Still, most students find the time to apply themselves to their studies, like the graduates of Manhattan Comprehensive Night and Day High School (OPPOSITE).

KEEPING IN TOP PHYSICAL CONDI-tion provides New Yorkers with that extra punch they always seem to have. Personal trainers, including Delores Muñoz (TOP), make a living teaching others how to keep fit. Heavyweight fighter Gerry Cooney, though no longer actively boxing, still strikes a menacing pose remi-niscent of his career (OPPOSITE).

© ODETTE LUPIS

ON YOUR MARK, GET SET, GO. Started in 1970, the New York City Marathon today attracts more than 31,000 participants, who begin the race at the Verrazano-Narrows Bridge in Staten Island and hope to finish 26.2 miles and five boroughs later in Central Park.

DRAMA

ROMANCE

I T'S NOT UNUSUAL TO SEE celebrities on the streets of New York City, and some of them might even be working. George Clooney (OPPOSITE) was on the run from the bad guys in 1997's *The Peacemaker*, the first feature film for DreamWorks SKG, the movie-music-TV juggernaut of Steven Spielberg, Jeffrey Katzenberg, and David Geffen.

F ROM CITY HALL TO THE FEDERAL courts, the New York government scene is covered. The law and Robert M. Morgenthau (OPPOSITE) are virtually synonymous in the area. Appointed U.S. attorney by President John F. Kennedy in 1961, Morgenthau went on to become New York County's district attorney in 1975.

As home city to what is arguably the world's most famous symbol of freedom–the Statute of Liberty–New York strives to offer justice for all.

NEW YORK

O N St. Patrick's Day in New York, everybody's Irish. But the festive celebrations don't stop there. From Hong Kong to Brazil to the Dominican Republic to the Caribbean, everyone takes to the streets and waves his or her flag high (PAGES 106-109).

NEW YORK

A STATE OF MIND

EVERYTHING IN NEW YORK IS done on a super scale. While its heroes may be little more than blow-up balloons at the heart of the Macy's Thanksgiving Day Parade, the Chrysler Building (OPPOSITE), completed in 1930 with its futuristic stainless steel and art deco architecture, is very much the real thing.

I N ART AS IN REAL LIFE, GAY New Yorkers have come out. But it wasn't always so. In 1969, a police raid at a noted homosexual meeting place—the Stonewall Inn in Greenwich Village—turned into a riot. The next year, a Gay Pride parade was organized to raise awareness for the rights of gay citizens, and now, 30 years strong, it is one of the city's most celebrated parades, incorporating gay police officers, motorcyclists, war veterans, and others expressing their individuality and solidarity.

New York's annual Puerto Rican Day Parade, held to honor the accomplishments and culture of Puerto Ricans everywhere, includes in excess of 11,000 participants, some 100 floats, and more than 2 million viewers standing alongside Fifth Avenue between 44th and 86th streets. Worldwide percussionist giant Tito Puente (TOP) was on hand for the 1999 parade, as were scores of belly dancers.

© JONATHAN POSTAL / TOWERY PUBLISHING, INC.

W HAT WALL STREET IS TO finance, Greenwich Village's Bleecker Street is to literature and music. Long the subject of song and poem, the street once embod- ied the creative essence of the Village. These days, performers keep the artistic spirit alive in venues from the subway to Wash- ington Square Park.

WHEN IT COMES TO THE STATUE of Liberty, everybody gets in on the act. Although Colbar Art, Inc. manufactures officially sanctioned, polyresin-and-marble-dust miniatures of the landmark, other, more individualized, impressions abound.

122

T HE HEAT FROM HER TORCH notwithstanding, Lady Liberty can do little to melt away the snow from the city's many sidewalks (PAGES 120-121). For viewing pleasure, however, it's hard to beat the gentle slopes of Central Park, idyllic under a blanket of white (OPPOSITE AND ABOVE).

O PENED IN 1932 AS PART OF Rockefeller Center, the recently renovated Radio City Music Hall remains a historic theater that presents a variety of performances.

The Radio City Christmas Spectacular, featuring the Rockettes, entertains some 1.1 million holiday visitors a year, an even more amazing feat when you consider

the club has only 5,901 seats. The show runs for eight weeks, with six back-to-back performances on weekends, testing the endurance of the 250-member cast and crew.

ANTA CLAUS ALWAYS COMES to town when the town is New York City. And it's just a rumor, but he's said to frequent a quaint Chinatown establishment year-round—incognito, of course.

N A TRADITION DATING BACK more than 150 years, Chinatown explodes in celebration of the Chinese New Year. The dragon dance (OPPOSITE) caps the parade celebrating the festive occasion.

LIFE IS A GAS FOR BIKE MESsengers coursing the New York City streets. For firefighters, the threat is a little more serious. Some 11,000 of them battle an estimated 1,000 fires a day.

MORE THAN 100 MILES OF steam pipes, resting two to 30 feet underground, supply heat and power to New York's build- ings. The escaping steam also provides a dramatic foreground for the Chrysler Building and bluesman Leon Thomas.

TRASH DISPOSAL IS A HOT TOPIC in New York these days as city officials grapple with ways to get rid of some 13,000 tons a day of the stuff. Keeping the complex web of city services running smoothly is enough to put anybody in the dumps.

THE INDUSTRIAL LANDSCAPE is an inevitable by-product of a bustling metropolis. So is the garbage itself. Residential garbage is hauled off every day on barges, destined for other states that reluctantly accept New York's trash. With the closing of local landfills, the crisis of where to put unwanted refuse steadily increases.

As part of its *Extreme Shopping* program, QVC offered folks the chance to adopt the Brooklyn Bridge for $25,000 a year, a twist on the old joke that the bridge is for sale. The funds went to pay for trash pickup and graffiti removal. Opened in 1883, the historic structure—made with 3,500 miles of steel wire—connects Brooklyn, the most populous borough in New York, to Manhattan.

WINDOW WASHERS OF AMERICA take note: The Jacob K. Javits Convention Center (OPPOSITE), opened in 1986, has more than 16,000 panes of glass. Part of the World Financial Center, the co- lossal Winter Garden (ABOVE) stands 120 feet tall and features 16 palm trees inside, along with an unobstructed view of the Hudson River.

N 1626, PETER MINUIT "BOUGHT" Manhattan Island for about $24 from folks he thought owned it. At the time, Native Americans lived throughout the rural land—hard to believe these days when a view from a midtown apartment confirms the ceaseless urban development. New York's bucolic past is immortalized in sculpture and architecture across the city.

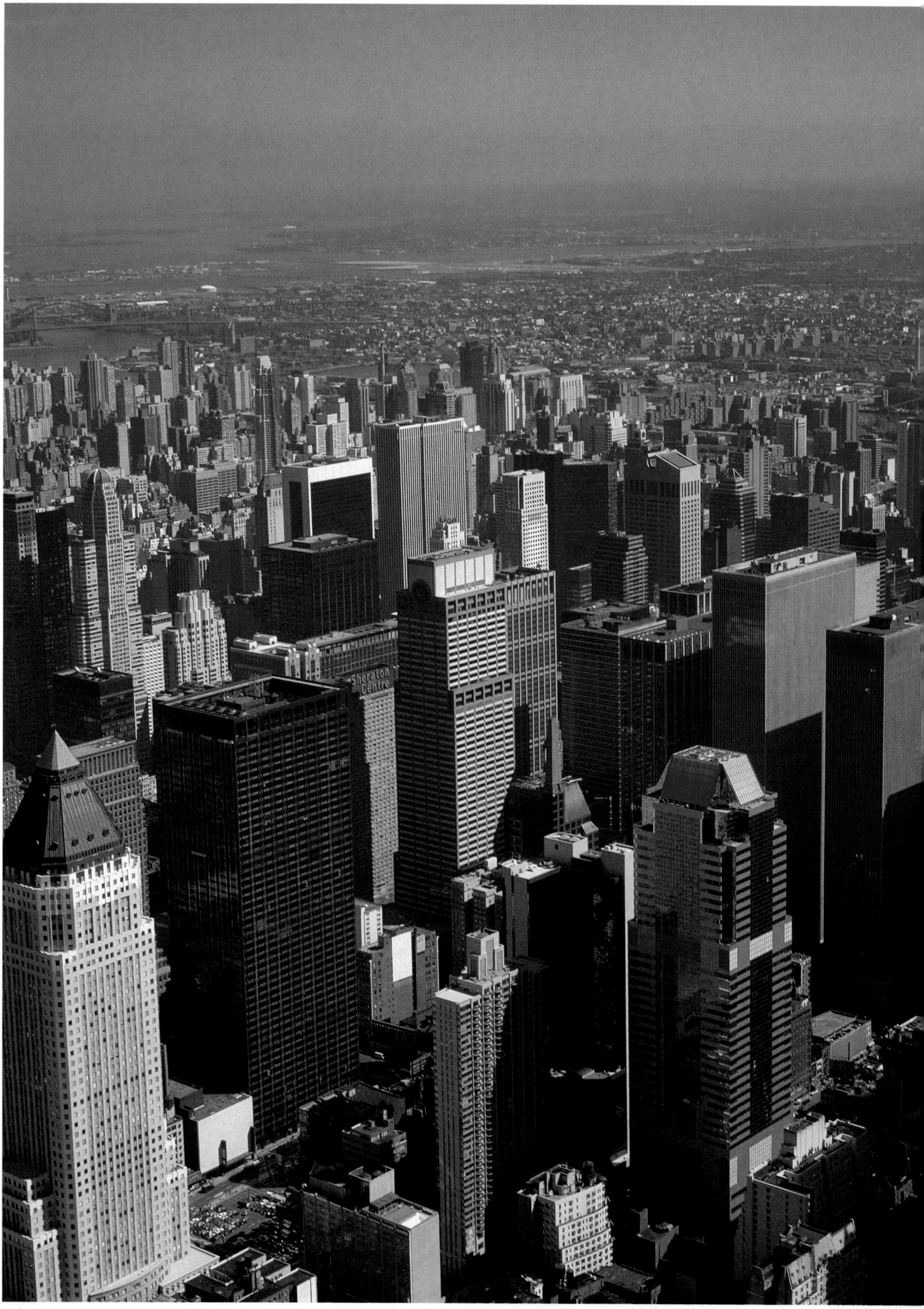

▲ © STAN RIES

THE VIEW FROM ON HIGH CAN
be invigorating or frightening,
depending on your perspective.
Dan Purcell (TOP), an ironworker
with Local 40, clearly rises to the
occasion of his job, as do those in
charge of restoring the Fountain
of Abundance, located in the
Grand Army Plaza.

WHOEVER SAID NO ONE GETS A free ride? When fathers and their children get together, a bit of palling around is the order of the day.

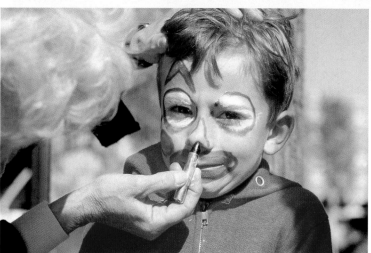

© ODETTE LUPIS

The CITY GOES TO GREAT lengths to entertain its youth, from the Children's Museum of Manhattan (OPPOSITE, BOTTOM RIGHT) to the braille-equipped nature path signs of Flushing, Queens, (BOTTOM RIGHT). In the great out-of-doors known as Central Park, the familiar characters of *Alice in Wonderland* and a giant bubble help keep young imaginations stimulated.

COLORFUL PUBLIC ART AND advertising carry a message to New Yorkers of all shapes and sizes. The distinctive style of artist Keith Haring (TOP RIGHT AND BOT- TOM RIGHT) took on many shapes and forms during the years he was alive.

NEW YORK'S YOUNG ARTISTS often take their works to the streets (PAGES 160-163). Lower East Side artist Dan Witz (BOTTOM RIGHT) has consistently turned to the boarded-up windows and various surfaces of the city to display his works (TOP AND BOTTOM LEFT). Esther Pearl Watson and Mark Todd also hone their craft within the city's confines. Watson has done illustrative pieces for the *New York Times*, *Time*, and *Fortune*, and has published a children's book called *Talking to Angels*. Todd's work has appeared in numerous publications, including the *New Yorker* and *GQ*. His corporate clients include Sony, Warner Bros., and Polygram Records.

© DAN WITZ

162

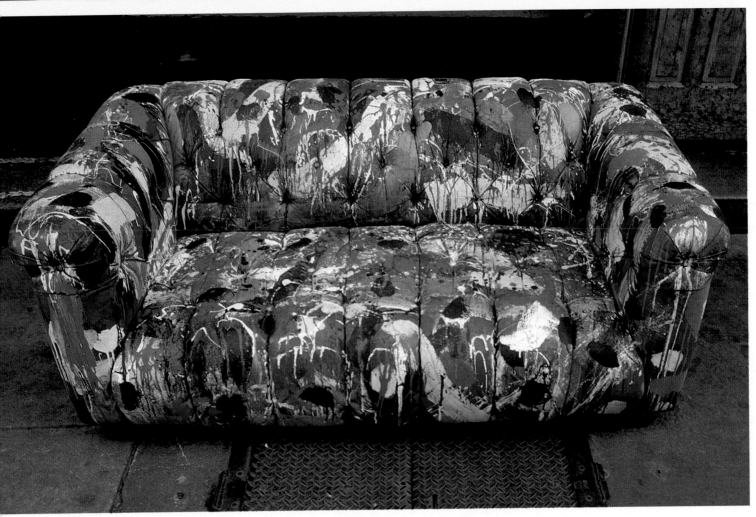

EVEN THE ARCHITECTURE IN NEW York gets loud. Frank Lloyd Wright designed the Solomon R. Guggenheim Museum's trademark spiral (TOP), only to have a 10-story tower added on to double the space. Jean Dubuffet's *Group of Four* *Trees* sits in the Chase Manhattan Plaza (BOTTOM LEFT), and Ivan Chermayeff's red sculpture at Nine West 57th Street was designed to put the address on the map. And, boy, does it ever.

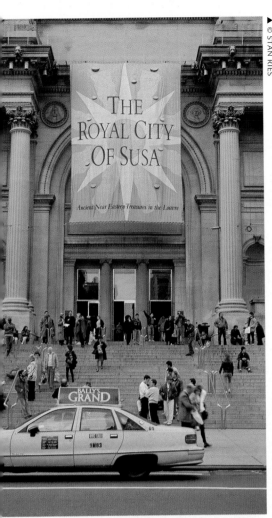

© STAN RIES

One of the most comprehensive museums in the world, the Metropolitan Museum of Art is an overwhelming experience for even the most seasoned visitor. Outside, on its steps, rest the tired, if not the poor; inside, stunning collections are on display.

© PATRICK BATCHELDER

© BUD LEE

FAMOUS NAMES AND THEIR WORKS abound outside the museum setting as well. Pablo Picasso's *Bust of Sylvette* (BOTTOM LEFT) sits near New York University and a sculpture by Auguste Rodin (OPPOSITE TOP) graces the rooftop garden at the Metropolitan Museum of Art. True masters of their craft, Andy Warhol (OPPOSITE, BOTTOM LEFT) and Salvador Dalí (BOTTOM RIGHT) once walked along the city streets.

ADISON AVENUE MEETS Greenwich Village: The cult of personality skewers the line between pop art and advertising. *Village Voice* columnist and E! Entertainment Television contributor Michael Musto (OPPOSITE CENTER) keeps the beat for the latest gossip, feeding the publicity machine for those who are famous for being famous.

See

N EW YORKERS THRIVE ON EXCESS stimuli, the more surreal the better. Signs reminding folks to "see" and "think"—advertising execs call this ambient media—flash past in the blink of an eye, although no one blinks at seeing a statue of George M. Cohan riding the bus or the Statue of Liberty taking a ferry ride.

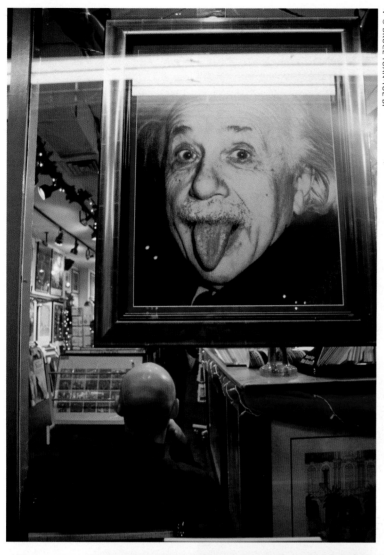

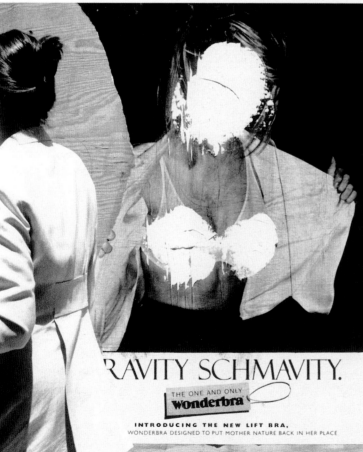

GRAVITY SCHMAVITY.

THE ONE AND ONLY
wonderbra

INTRODUCING THE NEW LIFT BRA,
WONDERBRA DESIGNED TO PUT MOTHER NATURE BACK IN HER PLACE

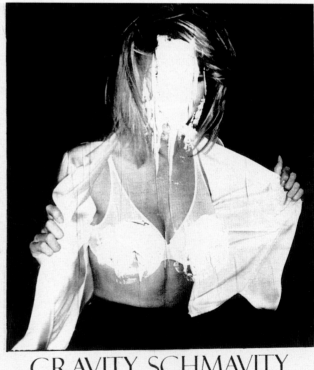

GRAVITY SCHMAVITY.

THE ONE AND ONLY
wonderbra

INTRODUCING THE NEW LIFT BRA,
AN EVERY DAY WONDERBRA DESIGNED TO PUT MOTHER NATURE BACK IN HER PLACE

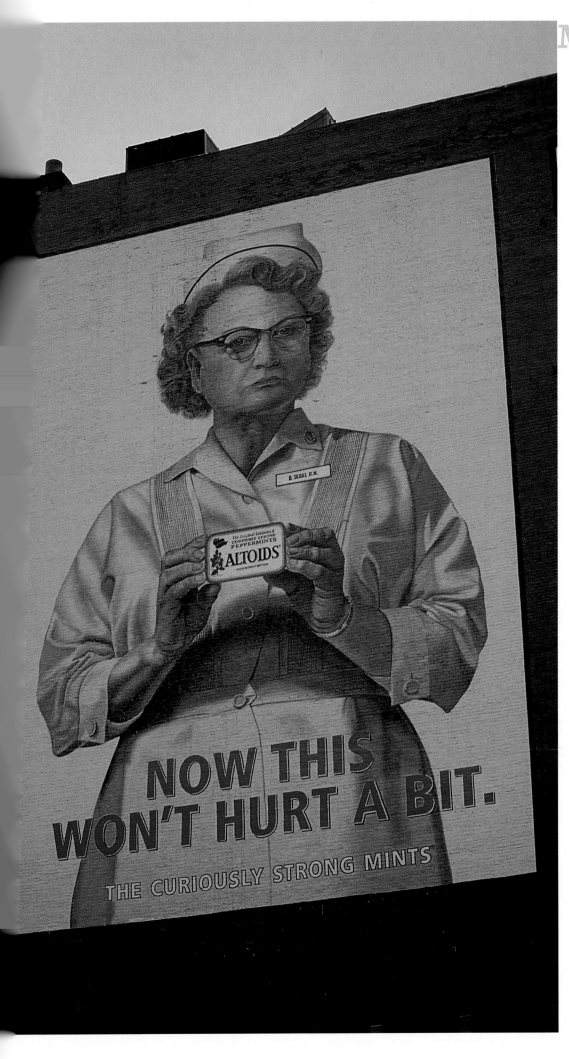

ona Lisa, Mona Lisa, men have . . . played you? Not exactly the right words to the song made famous by Nat King Cole, but in New York, perhaps a chorus of "Anything Goes" might be more fitting.

And while fallout shelters may be a thing of the past, reminders still abound of what brought them into being (PAGES 176-177).

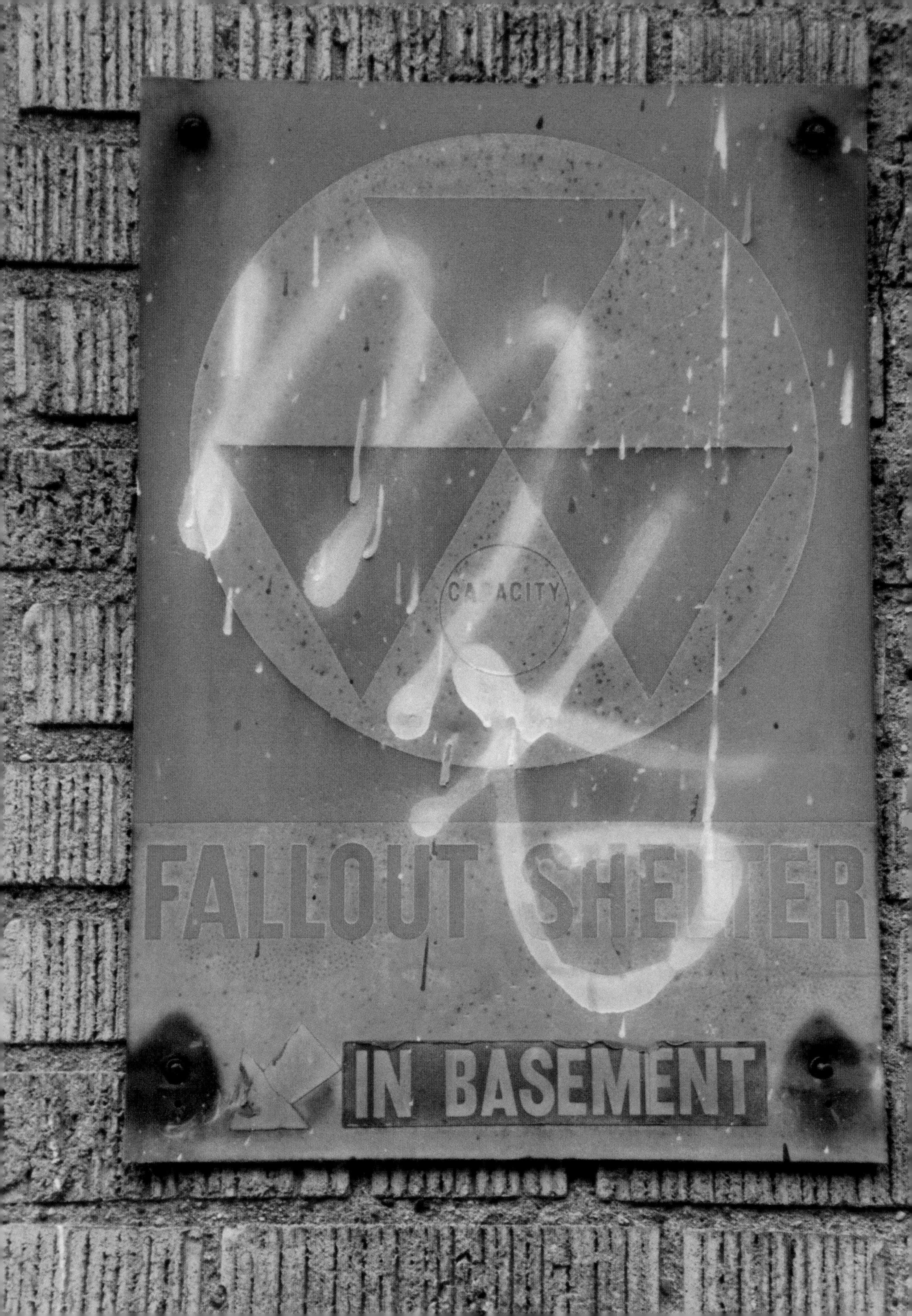
CAPACITY
FALLOUT SHELTER
IN BASEMENT

THE UNITED STATES MILITARY
Academy at West Point is
located about an hour north of
New York City. Between 800 to
1,000 cadets graduate each year,
celebrating on the historic campus
covered with powerful monuments
to great men who served the country well. One such distinguished
West Point graduate was General
Douglas MacArthur (OPPOSITE
LEFT), who was number one in his
1903 graduating class, and at 50,
was the youngest chief of staff in
U.S. history.

LIKE THEIR NEIGHBORS AROUND the country, New Yorkers are patriotic types. In addition to the fireworks that grace the city's skies on occasion, the *Intrepid* Sea-Air-Space Museum, a World War II aircraft carrier docked at Pier 86, has been transformed into an incredible floating display of the country's aviation and marine past.

THE PLAQUE UNDER THE STATUE
of St. George slaying the dragon
(ABOVE AND OPPOSITE RIGHT) states
"Good Defeats Evil." A gift from
the former Soviet Union that rests
inside the United Nations garden
near 47th Street, the piece is made
from the wreckage of U.S. and
Soviet nuclear missiles. In Central
Park, a statue pays tribute to
Wladyslaw Jagiello (OPPOSITE LEFT),
grand duke of Lithuania from 1377
to 1401, and king of Poland from
1386 to 1434.

NEW YORK STATE HAS SOME OF the toughest gun control laws on the books and many reminders of what has been lost. Two proponents of nonviolence, both of whom were assassinated, have their special place in the city. A statue of peace activist Mahatma Gandhi stands in Union Square Park (RIGHT); John Lennon is remembered at Strawberry Fields in Central Park (OPPOSITE BOTTOM), only blocks from the site of his slaying; and at the United Nations headquarters, the barrel of a bronze handgun remains knotted forever in a dramatic sculpture.

ERCHED ATOP A WORLD WAR II
monument in historic Battery
Park, a giant bronze eagle keeps
watch over eight granite slabs
etched with the names of 10,700
servicemen lost at sea.

A VIBRANT PRIMROSE IN THE peaceful surroundings of the Bronx Zoo proves to be a suitable landing strip for two delicate butterflies.

A SOLDIER AMONG SOLDIERS, Ulysses S. Grant is buried, along with his wife, in Grant's Tomb (RIGHT). Honoring all of those who fought for their country, the Soldiers' and Sailors' Memorial Arch in Prospect Park serves as a reminder of the great sacrifices families made for their country. In Queens, the living mix with the dead, in keeping with the continuum of life (PAGES 190-191).

NEW YORK'S MANY PLACES OF worship help shed light on the trials and tribulations of everyday living.

The intimidating Gothic structures of Riverside Church (opposite) and St. Patrick's Cathedral are at the same time architecturally and spiritually inspiring. Funded by John D. Rockefeller, Riverside Church was completed in 1930, taking three years to construct. The church's 74-bell carillon and 12,000-pipe organ are among the world's largest. St. Patrick's Cathedral, one of the best examples of American Gothic church architecture in the United States, was begun in 1858, formally opened in 1879, but didn't celebrate its first mass until 1906.

[N 1654, JEWISH REFUGEES FROM Brazil came to America and established the first New York synagogue. German and Russian Jews came later and occupied much of the Lower East Side. Today, the Jewish faith remains very strong and visible throughout all of New York City.

CONFUCIUS

EASTERN RELIGIONS MIX HANDILY with Madison Avenue-inspired culture in New York City, where a Buddhist temple can support both its attending members and a scenic cigarette billboard.

NEW YORK'S SHRINES AND TRIButes abound, particularly in heavily populated Catholic areas such as Little Italy (OPPOSITE), where homage is paid to Saint Anthony, the patron saint of lost things.

To "GO WITH GOD" TAKES ON many meanings in a city as diverse as New York, where the expression could call for quiet reflection or simple ascendance to a higher goal.

As emphatic as they might be, the signs that paint the town in New York sometimes still fall on deaf ears. At their more poignant, they can reflect a great divide (PAGES 206-207).

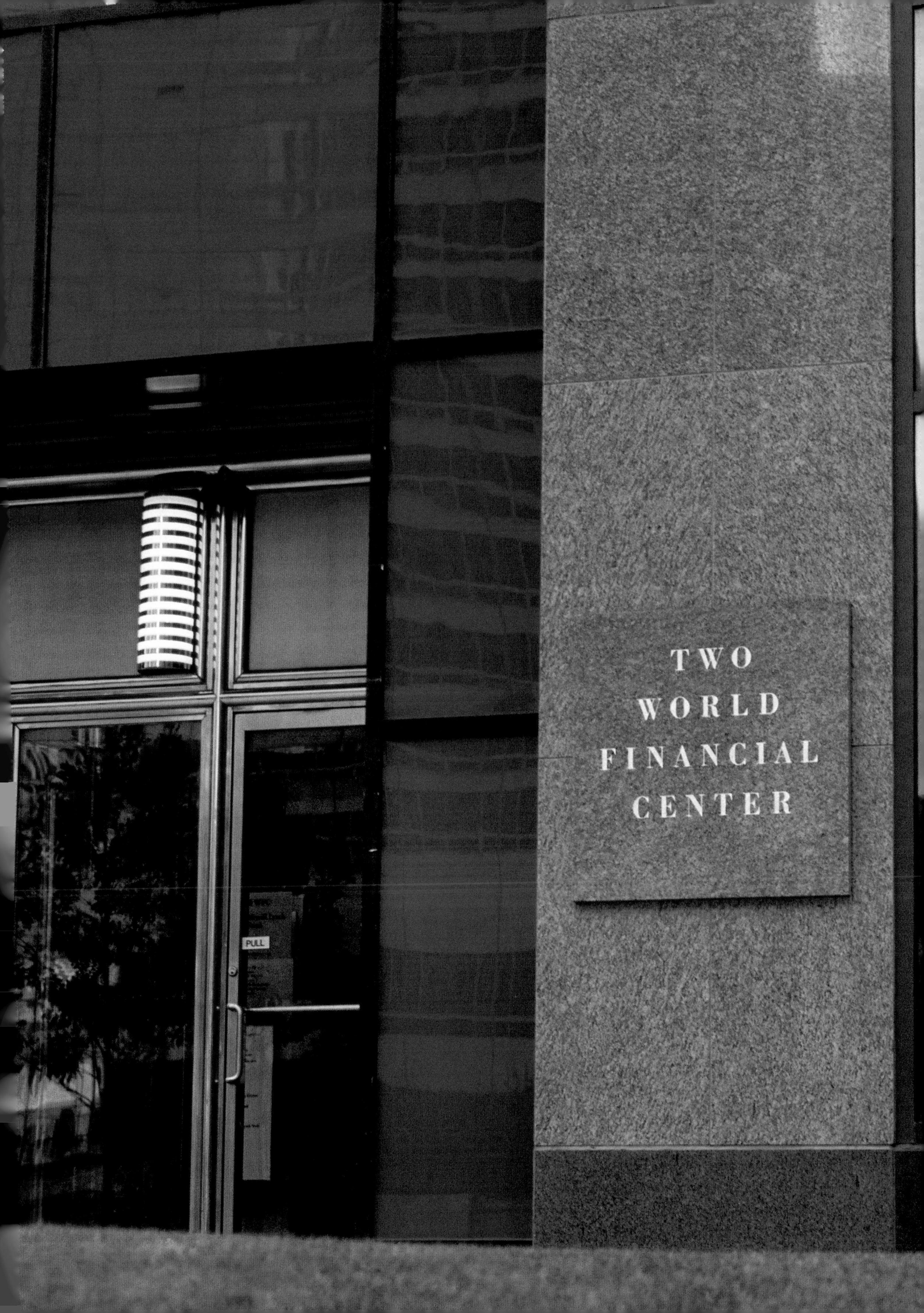
TWO
WORLD
FINANCIAL
CENTER
PULL

THE ORB OF MUCH OF THE
world's monetary activity lies
in New York's financial district.
Deals brokered here affect the rich
and the poor both near and far.

MAJESTIC IN ANY WEATHER, the World Trade Center is a home away from home for some 50,000 workers who daily inhabit the 110-story twin towers.

EW YORK OPULENCE IS NO better signified than by the buildings named after two of its most successful real estate tycoons. Harry Helmsley and Donald Trump are responsible for reshaping much of the way New York looks. Trump Tower remains an exclusive address with high-end boutiques and residences. The 34-story Helmsley Building was sold several years after Helmsley's death by his widow, Leona, whose tax evasion charges put her in a less than favorable light.

H IGH CUISINE HAS MANY HOMES in New York. From the Trump Tower restaurant (BOTTOM LEFT) to the American and Italian creations of Union Square Cafe co-owner and chef Michael Romano (TOP LEFT) or the French delicacies of La Fourchette chef Marc Murphy (TOP RIGHT) and Lutèce chef Eberhard Mueller (OPPOSITE), there's a menu to satisfy any palate. And what better way to top off a good meal than with Godiva chocolates?

MANY OF NEW YORK'S DEPRESSION-era buildings are adorned with statuary and detail that hark back to the art deco style so popular during that period. Paul Manship's 1934 creation *Prometheus* (OPPOSITE) watches over the Fifth Avenue entrance to Rockefeller Center, a 19-building complex named after its developer, oil magnate John D. Rockefeller.

Time has flown since Grand Central Terminal opened its doors in 1913. Once the main transportation hub for New York City, the renovated facility today still handles some 550 trains daily. The main concourse is a spectacle to behold, with its tall ceiling and 60-foot-high windows, shedding romantic light on the commuters passing through.

© JONATHAN POSTAL / TOWERY PUBLISHING, INC.

ERE'S LOOKING AT YOU, KID. While many native New Yorkers avoid eye contact, there are a few long-standing faces that never turn away, including Frank W. Woolworth (OPPOSITE, BOTTOM LEFT) and Puck (OPPOSITE TOP), a statute that stands over the Puck Building downtown. Now a place for fashion shoots and fancy parties, the building was erected in 1885 to house the editorial offices of the satiric magazine *Puck* (and much later, *Spy Magazine*).

© STEPHEN F. HARMON

U RBAN DWELLERS HAVE AN
extra sense of closeness: communicating by fire escape or by
good old-fashioned yelling.

New Yorkers are fiercely proud of their neighborhoods—of which there are countless varieties. Park Slope (OPPOSITE) became a highly desirable spot in Brooklyn once the Brooklyn Bridge was opened in 1883. Today, the area remains impressive for both its varied housing stock and its ethnic diversity. St. Luke's Place (TOP LEFT) is a short but storied block in Greenwich Village. Writer Theodore Dreiser and poet Marianne Moore were two of its famous literary residents.

CITY GARDENING REQUIRES creativity and perseverance, but with a bit of imagination, even the smallest of balconies becomes a colorful bouquet. Community gardens, nurtured by groups such as the Brooklyn Bears (LEFT), have sprung up for some 20 years on city property that was otherwise abandoned. More recently, to the dismay of urban gardeners, the city has been reclaiming the lots for development.

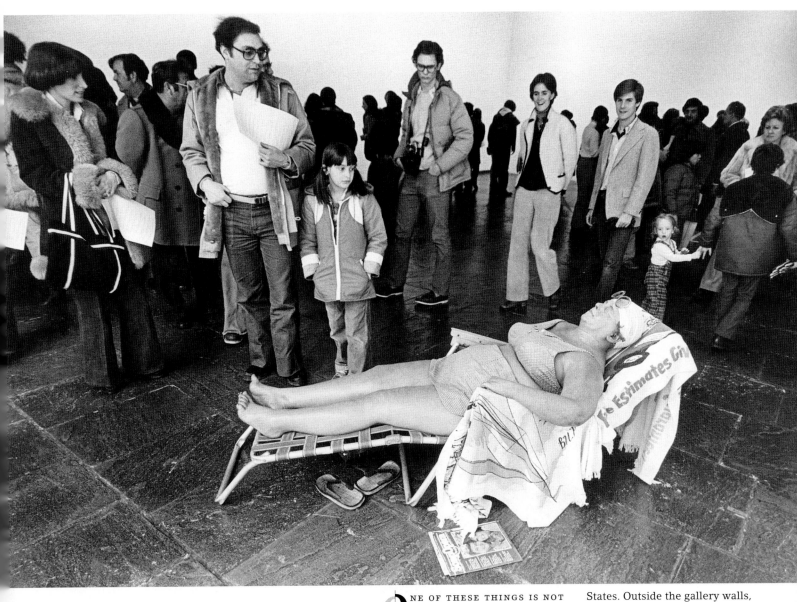

ONE OF THESE THINGS IS NOT like the other. The ultrarealistic work of Duane Hanson (ABOVE) has fooled many a discerning eye in exhibitions across the United States. Outside the gallery walls, if you can't make it to the beach to sun with the mermaids, any bright stairwell should do.

If it's New Year's Day, those must be members of the Coney Island Polar Bear Club on the beach. Each January 1 since 1903, dressed in their swimming attire, club members plunge into the icy waters of the Atlantic Ocean. The preseason swim is nothing for the Central Park Zoo's Gus, who "bearly" notices the "aqua colda."

T HE GENERAL POPULACE IS getting all fired up these days over tattoos. Michelle Myles of Daredevil Studio on the Lower East Side is just one of many artists citywide who can render a man illustrated.

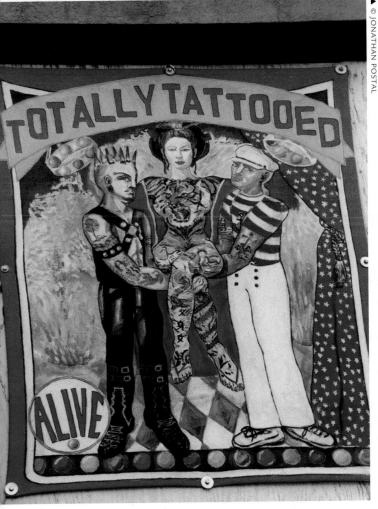

A STATE OF MIND

THE AMERICAN MUSEUM OF
Natural History (OPPOSITE) is
just one of many unique venues
in New York where our past is on
display. If it's today's animal life
you're interested in, species from
faraway lands—such as gavials
from India—call the Bronx Zoo
home (THIS PAGE).

236

WHEN IT COMES TO RUNWAY fashion, New Yorkers don't monkey around. Well, actually, sometimes they do. Walt Disney Studios supported the video release of its *Summer of the Monkeys* with a show at the Fashion Cafe, where the works of distinguished designers were modeled by some prestigious primates (OPPOSITE, TOP LEFT).

AKE NO MISTAKE, NEW YORK is a fashion capital. From the funky shops in SoHo (OPPOSITE TOP) to the upscale, uptown crowd at Bergdorf Goodman and Estée Lauder (LEFT), variety is key to New York shopping life, where you can get sartorial advice first-hand from designer Betsey Johnson (OPPOSITE BOTTOM) at her Seventh Avenue shop.

E LABORATE, STYLISH EASTER bonnets are the rule for the Easter Parade in front of St. Patrick's Cathedral on Fifth Avenue.

New York's hot spots are getting into the swing of things. In the 1990s, clubs everywhere have seen a revival in swing dancing, featuring zoot suits, crinoline skirts, cocktail dresses, and the music of Glenn Miller, Benny Goodman, and Louis Prima.

UPPER CLUBS HAVE REPLACED discos as favorite nighttime hangouts in New York. Enjoying the evening at Tatou, a hopping midtown supper club, are "Lo-Fi" Lee Bennett Sobel (OPPOSITE) and wife, Shawn "Hi-Fi Honey" Sobel, who head up Lo-Fi Entertainment, a company specializing in all things retro from booking swing bands to publishing a magazine for moderns.

© JONATHAN POSTAL / TOWERY PUBLISHING, INC.

© JONATHAN POSTAL / TOWERY PUBLISHING, INC.

F OUNDED IN 1978, DONALD Byrd/The Group has become one of the city's premier contemporary dance organizations. Relying on the talents of numerous skillful dancers, the troupe has delighted New York audiences as well as national ones, particularly with its annual presentation of *The Harlem Nutcracker*.

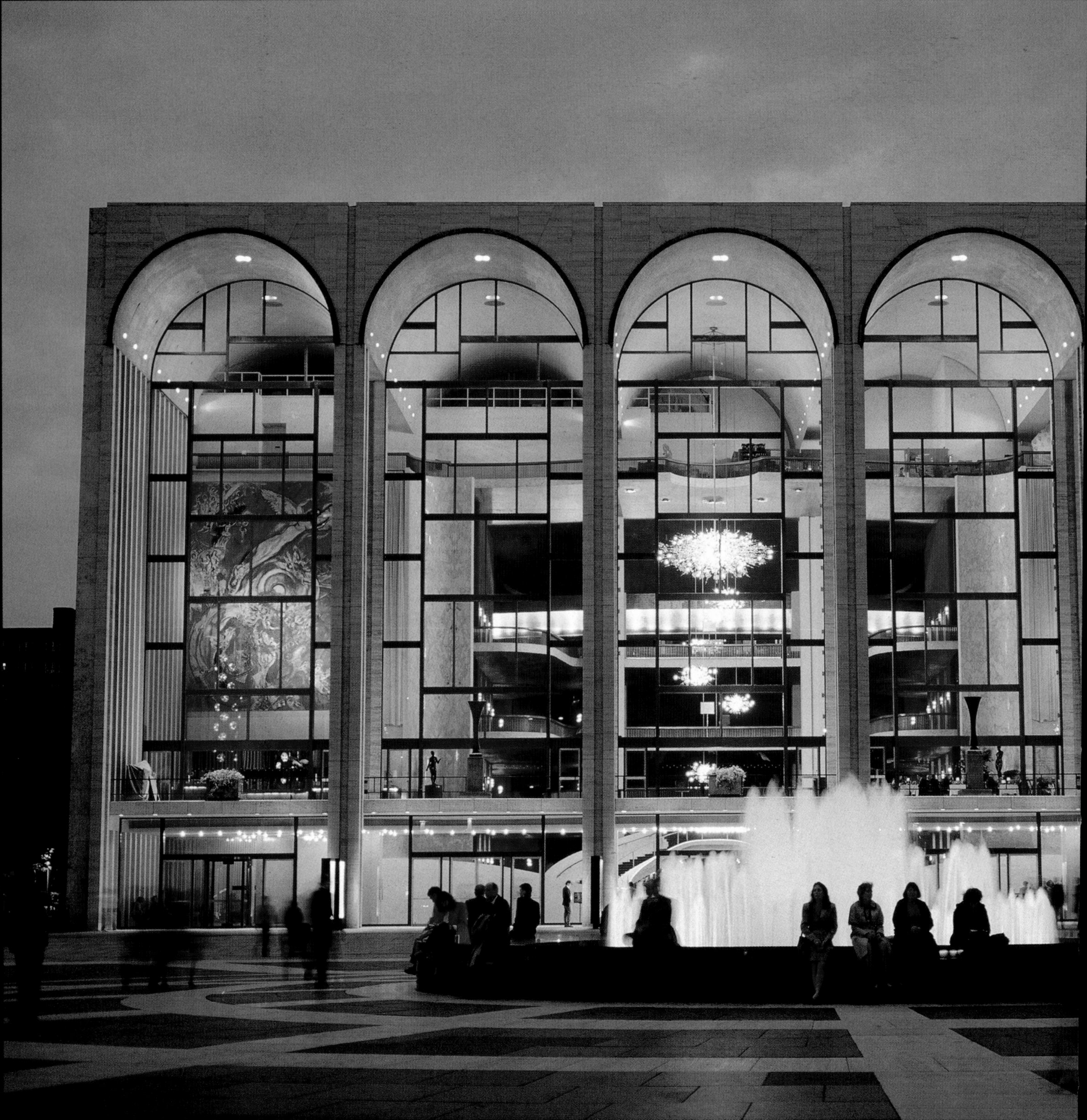

© DAVID FORBERT

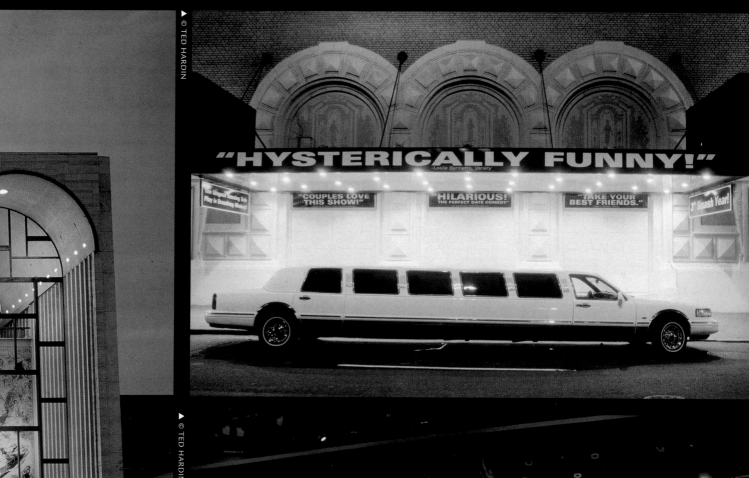

FROM OPERA TO THEATER, THE best and the brightest are drawn to New York's rich cultural heritage. The murals of Marc Chagall can be seen through the windows of the Metropolitan Opera House at Lincoln Center (OPPOSITE), host to the Metropolitan Opera and the American Ballet Theatre. And nobody is laughing at the success of British-born set designer Tony Walton (BOTTOM), although he seems to be having a pretty good time as the winner of three Tony Awards, an Oscar, and an Emmy for his work on productions such as *Guys and Dolls*, *All That Jazz*, and *Death of a Salesman*.

T HEY SAY THE NEON LIGHTS are bright on Broadway, and—for once—they are right. Dancers Elizabeth Parkenson and Scott Wise share a little of the Great White Way with patrons of New York's Hogs & Heifers Saloon. The duo appears in *Fosse*, a tribute to legendary choreographer and director of musical comedy Bob Fosse, whose credits include *Sweet Charity*, *Damn Yankees*, *Cabaret*, and *Pippin*.

ROCK MUSIC CAN BE HEARD IN a variety of New York venues, ranging from the distinguished Carnegie Hall (OPPOSITE TOP) to CBGB (TOP) in the Bowery. CBGB's owner Hilly Kristal (BOTTOM) wasn't having much success with the country bluegrass and blues that the club intended to showcase when the Ramones, a leather-jacketed band from Queens, came through the doors and ushered in the punk era. One by-product of the movement was David Byrne (OPPOSITE BOTTOM) and his band, Talking Heads.

A VAST OCEAN OF PERSONALITIES pool together to lend New York its character. Mo B. Dick (OPPOSITE, TOP LEFT) is the founder of Club Casanova, a drag king review where women appear as men. And while Theo Kogan (OPPOSITE, TOP RIGHT) might have a man's first name, she's the leader of the all-woman punk rock band the Lunachicks. Former computer hackers Mark Abene (OPPOSITE, BOTTOM LEFT, ON LEFT), aka Phiber Optik, and business partner David Buchwald are now two of the principal partners in Crossbar Security, Inc., a firm specializing in helping corporations protect themselves from getting hacked.

NEW YORK REMAINS HOME TO an eclectic array of musicians. Marc Anthony Thompson took a shot at a solo career in L.A., but it was New York's music community that gave him a warm reception. He now records as Chocolate Genius—whom he describes as "Don Rickles meets Jimi Hendrix" —for V2 Records. Gary Lucas (OP-POSITE), on the other hand, was inspired by the music of Captain Beefheart, joining his Magic Band in the early 1980s. Lucas has since played with Leonard Bernstein, Iggy Pop, Jeff Buckley, John Zorn, and poet Allen Ginsberg, among others.

P OOL IS A GAME OF SKILL AND few know that more than Francine Crimi (OPPOSITE), the only female master billiards instructor in the world. Crimi teaches future pool sharks at American Billiard School.

IF YOU LOVE A MAN IN UNIFORM, New York has plenty of quaintly attired gentlemen looking to hold the door, hail a cab, sign for packages, and even draw a horse and carriage for you.

The Chelsea Hotel on 23rd Street has always been a haven for artists. Writers such as Vladimir Nabokov and Arthur Miller called the seedy hotel home. Canadian poet Leonard Cohen wrote the song "Chelsea Hotel #2" about his tantalizing relationship there with Janis Joplin. Keeping pace with today's New York is novelist Jonathan Ames, who writes about sexual deviation in his novel *The Extra Man* and also chronicles sordid affairs in his *New York Press* "City Slicker" column.

New York's jazz heritage is kept alive by the musicians and scholars who live in the area. Disc jockey and record producer Phil Schaap (OPPOSITE) has an encyclopedic knowledge of the music, and broadcasts popular radio programs daily from Columbia University's WKCR. Living legend and jazz bassist Milt Hinton has played with the likes of Cab Calloway, Count Basie, and Louis Armstrong, and remains one of the most recorded jazz musicians in the world.

SUMMER IN THE CITY IS A TIME
for incredible sights and sounds,
featuring some of the best live
performances in the country.
Music can be heard throughout
the season at the JVC Jazz Festival
in Bryant Park (OPPOSITE), on an
afternoon in Dante Park (TOP),
and in Central Park (BOTTOM),
where the New Hype Jazz Band
takes the stage.

N EW YORK CITY WINTERS CAN be frigid, snow-covered affairs, so once springtime hits, folks take to the outdoors for strolling or dining alfresco. For food Italian style, local epicures turn to Pó, where Chef Mario Batali is known for serving up a feast in any kind of weather.

Central Park is 843 acres of green land set in the heart of Manhattan Island. Filled with scenic spots for painting and reflecting, the park has become synonymous with the city itself.

CONSERVATORY GARDEN AT
the north end of Central Park
consists of three formal areas that
include yew hedges, Siberian crab
apple trees, wildflowers, and thousands of perennials.

THE TREES OF CENTRAL PARK belie the fact that New York is a concrete jungle. One great place to escape to is the roof of the Metropolitan Museum of Art (OPPOSITE), where a little sun and a lot of the *New York Times* will have you thinking you're sitting on top of the world.

AST SHADOWS TELL THE STORY of a great city, steeped in history and rich in promise (PAGES 276-279).

IEWED FROM THE AIR, THE full magnitude of New York's overwhelming scope becomes more and more apparent.

FIVE BOROUGHS COVERING MORE than 300 square miles. Keeping connected is challenging in New York, but there is one constant that ties the city together: For its more than 7 million people, living here is truly a state of mind.

NEW YORK
Profiles in Excellence

A LOOK AT THE CORP-
ORATIONS, BUSINESSES,
PROFESSIONAL GROUPS,
AND COMMUNITY SERVICE
ORGANIZATIONS THAT
HAVE MADE THIS BOOK
POSSIBLE. THEIR
STORIES—OFFERING AN
INFORMAL CHRONICLE
OF THE LOCAL BUSINESS
COMMUNITY—ARE AR-
RANGED ACCORDING
TO THE DATE THEY
WERE ESTABLISHED IN
THE NEW YORK AREA.

ALLTEL Information Services ✎ Amalgamated Bank of New York ✎ American Airlines, Inc. ✎ American Warehousing/American Stevedoring ✎ Bellevue Hospital Center ✎ Benetar Bernstein Schair & Stein ✎ Berenson & Company LLP ✎ Bloomberg L.P. ✎ BlueStone Capital Partners, L.P. ✎ Bridge Information Systems ✎ Bristol-Myers Squibb ✎ Bristol Plaza ✎ Cadwalader, Wickersham & Taft ✎ The Chase Manhattan Corporation ✎ CIBC World Markets ✎ Citipost ✎ City University of New York ✎ Computer Generated Solutions, Inc. ✎ Condé Nast Publications ✎ Covenant House ✎ D'Arcy Masius Benton & Bowles ✎ Data Industries Ltd. ✎ Document Express, Inc. ✎ The Doneger Group ✎ EarthWeb ✎ Empire Blue Cross and Blue Shield ✎ Executive Health Group ✎ Fashion Institute of Technology ✎ First American Title Insurance Company of New York ✎ Fitzmaurice & Company, LLC ✎ The Four Seasons ✎ Gibney, Anthony & Flaherty, LLP ✎ Gotham, Inc. ✎ GVA Williams ✎ Health Capital ✎ Holland & Knight LLP ✎ IBJ Whitehall Financial Group ✎ Inter-Continental Hotels of New York ✎ International Flavors & Fragrances, Inc. ✎ Intimate Brands, Inc. ✎ Jacobi Medical Center ✎ JLC Environmental Consultants, Inc. ✎ KeySpan Energy ✎ Ladenburg Thalmann & Co. Inc. ✎ Lazare Kaplan International Inc. ✎ Lillian Vernon Corporation ✎ Maimonides Medical Center ✎ Manhattan East Suite Hotels ✎ Memorial Sloan-Kettering Cancer Center ✎ MultiPlan, Inc. ✎ New York City Health and Hospitals Corporation ✎ New York Life Insurance Company ✎ New York Mercantile Exchange ✎ New York State Metropolitan Transportation Authority ✎ NYC & Company ✎ NYU Medical Center: New York University School of Medicine, NYU Hospitals Center ✎ Our Lady of Mercy Healthcare System ✎ Parsons School of Design ✎ Pfizer Inc ✎ Platinum Television Group ✎ PricewaterhouseCoopers ✎ Revlon ✎ Structure Tone Inc. ✎ The Trump Organization ✎ United Nations Development Corporation (UNDC) ✎ U.S. Trust Corporation ✎ Viatel, Inc. ✎ Watson Wyatt Worldwide ✎ The Williams Capital Group, L.P. ✎ Willis ✎ WNBC ✎ YMCA of Greater New York ✎ York Hunter ✎ Young & Rubicam Inc.

1736 BELLEVUE HOSPITAL CENTER

1792 CADWALADER, WICKERSHAM & TAFT

1799 THE CHASE MANHATTAN CORPORATION

1830 HOLLAND & KNIGHT LLP

1841 NYU MEDICAL CENTER: NEW YORK UNIVERSITY
SCHOOL OF MEDICINE, NYU HOSPITALS CENTER

1845 NEW YORK LIFE INSURANCE COMPANY

1847 CITY UNIVERSITY OF NEW YORK

1849 PFIZER INC

1852 YMCA OF GREATER NEW YORK

1853 U.S. TRUST CORPORATION

1872 CIBC WORLD MARKETS

1872 NEW YORK MERCANTILE EXCHANGE

1876 LADENBURG THALMANN & CO. INC.

1884 MEMORIAL SLOAN-KETTERING CANCER CENTER

1888 OUR LADY OF MERCY HEALTHCARE SYSTEM

Bellevue Hospital Center

To say that Bellevue Hospital Center is the oldest public hospital in the country doesn't convey the tradition and history of a hospital that is recognized around the world for the excellence of its care. When the president of the United States or any visiting dignitary comes to New York, Bellevue is the destination in case of illness or accident, though this alone doesn't really explain the quality of cutting-edge medicine found there.

Listing significant firsts in medical education and treatment doesn't convey the depth and breadth of innovation that has changed the face of medicine.

Quoting the staggering numbers of people that Bellevue treats each year—75,000 emergency visits, 26,000 admissions, 476,000 outpatient calls—can't truly illustrate the commitment to care for anyone needing medical attention.

Telling the story of how Bellevue has helped New York through epidemics of yellow fever, typhus, cholera, tuberculosis, and polio; how it treated those injured in riot and war; or how it receives wounded police and firefighters—even these stories don't express the unique partnership between Bellevue and the city.

No Potential Patients Turned Away

Bellevue's mandate to serve all people is responsible for the level of care it delivers and for the impact it has had on medical practice. When someone walks through its doors, Bellevue brings the benefit of more than two and a half centuries of innovative and compassionate care.

No matter how critical the illness, or devastating the accident, Bellevue will attend to them. Regardless of status or stature, insurance or bank account, no one is turned away. If a new treatment or procedure must be developed, the caring professionals at Bellevue will apply the resources necessary to handle it. If they have to deal with contagion or unknown factors, Bellevue

BELLEVUE HOSPITAL HAS HELPED NEW YORK THROUGH EPIDEMICS OF YELLOW FEVER, TYPHUS, CHOLERA, TUBERCULOSIS, AND POLIO.

Iospital will do whatever is nec-
ssary to treat and heal people
vhom others have refused to
andle.

No matter the circumstances,
Bellevue's caregivers will provide
he best care available.

FROM THE EARLIEST YEARS

Bellevue Hospital Center traces its
roots to a six-bed infirmary in New
York City's first almshouse in 1736,
the site of today's City Hall. Described in the minutes of the
Common Council as a "House of
Correction, Workhouse and Poor-
house," the building sheltered
vagrants, alcoholics, orphans,
paupers, the infirm, the insane,
and the aged. The medical infirmary was to "be suitably furnished for an infirmary and for no
other use whatsoever."

Through the decades, the hospital provided the growing area
with a variety of public health services, subject to the direction and
politics of the city. After a number
of relocations and expansions, it
was officially named Bellevue
Hospital in 1825. And in 1847,
the establishment of a permanent
medical board composed of outstanding physicians served to create an identity independent of
the city, and set the hospital on a
course of growth and achievement.

Bellevue Hospital is internationally known as a Level I
Trauma Center and microsurgical
reimplantation center. Bellevue is
also a receiving hospital in the
nationally designated categories
of cardiac, neurological, toxico-
logical, neonatal, and psychiatric
emergencies, and serves as a
designated 911 receiving station.

On a national scale, a number
of Bellevue's innovative programs,
such as geriatrics and child life
programs, are emulated in other
U.S. hospitals, and the center continues to serve as a role model for
other public hospitals in its response to the AIDS epidemic,
homelessness, tuberculosis, and
drug abuse.

A HISTORY OF FIRSTS

Throughout its 263-year history,
Bellevue has been a pioneer in
the fields of public health, medical education, and social work
services. No hospital in the coun-

try has been responsible for as
many firsts as Bellevue.

In 1856, it was the first to use
a hypodermic syringe; in 1861,
Bellevue established the first
liaison between a hospital and a
medical college; and in 1867, it
opened the first outpatient department in the United States. In 1869,
Bellevue pioneered the first hospital-based ambulance service in
the country; and in 1873, it founded
the first American School of Nursing based on Florence Nightingale's
plan. In 1874, Bellevue started
the nation's first children's clinic;
in 1876, the nation's first emergency pavilion. In 1878, it had
the first pathology course in a
U.S. medical college, and in 1884,
the hospital opened the first laboratory for teaching and researching pathology and bacteriology.
In 1892, Bellevue introduced the
diphtheria antitoxin. The first
appendectomy at a U.S. hospital
was performed at Bellevue in 1887.

Beginning the 20th century,
Bellevue established the nation's
first ambulatory cardiac clinic in
1911. The year 1923 brought the
first U.S. child psychiatry inpatient
unit. Bellevue also pioneered in-
sulin shock therapy for treatment

of mental illness in 1936. The first
cardiopulmonary laboratory in
the world, establishing the process of cardiac catheterization,
was created by Bellevue in 1940—
a procedure that garnered the
hospital a Nobel Prize in 1956.

In 1947, Bellevue began the
first nonmilitary rehabilitation
unit in a general hospital. Active
immunization for serum hepatitis
B began in 1971 at Bellevue. The
Micro-Surgical Replantation Center for New York City was established in 1982, and the Level I
Trauma Center in 1983. Bellevue
was designated a Head and Spinal Cord Injury Center in 1988,
and in 1990, began an accredited
Emergency Medicine Residency
Program.

Since 1970, Bellevue has been
the flagship hospital of the New
York City Health and Hospitals
Corporation, the nation's largest
municipal health care system.
The 1,200 beds of today's hospital dwarf the original six. None-
theless, the basic commitment to
the belief that anyone, regardless
of race, religion, nationality, or
ability to pay, is entitled to quality health care has not changed
during the past 263 years.

TO SAY THAT BELLEVUE HOSPITAL
IS THE OLDEST PUBLIC HOSPITAL
IN THE COUNTRY DOESN'T CONVEY
THE TRADITION AND HISTORY OF
A HOSPITAL THAT IS RECOGNIZED
AROUND THE WORLD FOR THE
EXCELLENCE OF ITS CARE.

CADWALADER, WICKERSHAM & TAFT

As the nation's oldest law firm, Cadwalader, Wickersham & Taft enjoys a special place in the history of New York. Established in 1792, Cadwalader boasts more than 200 years of continuous service to many of the country's most prestigious institutions. The firm has participated in many of the most significant social, economic, and legal issues accompanying the growth of the United States.

GLOBAL REACH

Today, Cadwalader is a pre-eminent international law firm, combining its rich history with forward-thinking dynamism. Its influence has expanded all around the world, serving clients with interests in Europe, South America, and the Pacific Rim. Cadwalader has offices in Washington, D.C., Charlotte, and London, in addition to its New York headquarters.

Cadwalader's clients range from the most sophisticated and powerful global investment banks, financial institutions, corporations, and insurance companies to wealthy individuals, not-for-profit organizations, and health care institutions. The firm's legal services have always responded to an increasingly sophisticated economy by providing progressive strategies and solutions to complex legal and business issues.

Eight practice groups, with more than 400 attorneys, now serve the firm's clients worldwide: Capital Markets, Corporate, Financial Restructuring, Health Care/ Not-for-Profit, Litigation, Project Finance, Real Estate, and Tax & Private Client. The firm's recent growth in the mergers and acquisitions arena is a testament to Cadwalader's solemn commitment to continue to broaden its scope and dimension.

HISTORY OF GROWTH

Cadwalader's rich history began in 1792 when John Wells, an orphan from Otsego County, New York, started a law practice in Manhattan. As Wells' career flourished, his opinions were increasingly sought on major public issues. In 1818, he established a partnership with George Washington Strong, combining their skills to forge, in the words of Strong, "a monstrous deal of business—more than any office in the state."

When Wells died in 1823, a marble portrait bust was commissioned in his honor by his peers. They dedicated this statue "to the man who elevated and adorned their profession by his integrity, eloquence, and learning." The statue still stands today in the vestibule of St. Paul's Chapel.

By 1878, Charles Strong, a descendent of the late George Washington Strong, was heading the firm. He was joined by John L. Cadwalader, who had served as assistant secretary of state. The firm, then named Strong & Cadwalader, catapulted into the elite ranks of firms representing major corporations.

In 1883, George W. Wickersham, an antitrust expert, joined the firm. In 1909, he interrupted his practice to serve as the U.S. attorney general under President William Howard Taft. Taft's brother, Henry W. Taft, had joined Strong & Cadwalader in 1889. His antitrust experience won him an appointment in 1907 as special assistant to the U.S. attorney for the Southern District of New York to supervise the government's case against the American Tobacco Company. Taft also became a member of the Salvation Army Advisory Board, an organization that remains a valued client to this day.

In 1914, the firm adopted its current name of Cadwalader, Wickersham & Taft. Through two world wars and the Great Depression, Cadwalader continued to play a major role in U.S. history. It handled two of the most publicized cases of the time: the Gloria Vanderbilt custody case and the copyright infringement suit involving *Gone With the Wind*.

Cadwalader made history in 1942 when it elected Catherine Noyes Lee as the first female partner of a major Wall Street firm. Six more women lawyers joined the firm during World War II.

By the early 1960s, Cadwalader's practice included complex tax matters, shipping industry finance, mergers and acquisitions, international finance, and trademark cases, as well as litigation, real estate, general corporate work, and trust and estates.

Cadwalader's litigation practice continued to expand in the 1970s. The firm handled such high-profile cases as *Tavoulareas v. The Washington Post*, the Agent Orange class action suit, the Dalkon Shield class action suit, and the *Fund of Funds* case.

A BUST OF JOHN WELLS, FOUNDER OF CADWALADER, WICKERSHAM & TAFT, CAN BE SEEN IN THE VESTIBULE OF ST. PAUL'S CHAPEL AT BROADWAY AND VESEY STREET.

JOE VERICKER

Securitization, the creation of financial products, became the firm's largest practice area in the 1980s. Cadwalader pioneered the creation of mortgage- and asset-backed securities, including pass-through certificates, guaranteed mortgage certificates, and collateralized mortgage obligations. The firm also established a leading commodities practice and developed a major swaps and derivatives practice that is rivaled by few other firms.

Local Roots

Despite its global reach, Cadwalader remains loyal to its roots with a deep commitment to community service, including pro bono work and generous support of charitable causes.

Cadwalader cares about the quality of life of its diverse workforce of 900 employees, lawyers, and support staff. It became the first major law firm to allow its workers casual dress throughout the summer. The firm's workforce also benefits from the latest in technological support.

Cadwalader also sponsors a 25-member chorus; a monthly Book Club discussion in its unrivaled library; attorney social gatherings; and book, craft, and tech fairs, as well as an array of intramural sports teams. Its summer associates are treated to the best of New York life, including Broad-

way shows, movie premieres, and Yankees games.

From its role as one of the major ship financing law firms to its place today as an internationally diversified law practice,

Cadwalader continues to meet each new challenge with infinite energy and enthusiasm. As one partner said on the eve of the millennium: "We're 207 years old and growing younger every day."

THE CHASE MANHATTAN CORPORATION

As THE CHASE MANHATTAN CORPORATION LOOKS FORward to the millennium, the company is celebrating its own bicentennial. The passage of 200 years includes the combination of more than 100 predecessor organizations and the progressive transformation of Chase into one of the world's preeminent global financial services firms. Since the founding in 1799 of its earliest predecessor firm, The Manhattan Company, Chase has played a fundamental role in the expansion of industry and trade, first in the United States and then internationally.

A TRADITION OF MEETING CUSTOMERS' NEEDS

The company was formed originally to provide water that was pure and wholesome in response to an outbreak of yellow fever that had raised concerns about New York's water supply. Chase's roots are deep under the sidewalks of New York where hollowed tree trunks served as pipes to transport the water. The company's charter was later amended to include banking. During the financial panic of 1857, when most banks suspended the practice of redeeming paper banknotes for gold, The Chemical Bank (a predecessor) continued its redemption policy. This action helped stabilize the financial markets, established an example for other firms, and earned Chemical the nickname Old Bullion. In 1861, when the Civil War began, The Hanover Bank (another predecessor) joined with other banks in New York, Boston, and Philadelphia to float a loan to the government.

Chase has also vigorously supported the development and prosperity of the communities it serves. In the 1880s, that meant funding construction of the Brooklyn Bridge, the world's first steel-wire suspension bridge – as innovative a project then as any multibillion-dollar financing that Chase is leading today.

A TRACK RECORD OF PROVIDING INNOVATIVE SOLUTIONS

Pumping pure water . . . manufacturing iron and brass wire . . . making alum, blue vitriol, and other drugs and chemicals . . . these were the capabilities of Chase's earliest predecessors, which – before the Free Banking Act of 1838—formed banks as offshoots of industrial organizations. Chase predecessors, among other things, entered the lending business after instructing company officers to provide a list of businesspeople who "merit discounts and can safely be trusted (1805); introduced the concept of "reaching out to small businesses and people of average means" (1905); formed one of the earliest bank security affiliates to underwrite, distribute, and manage large securities (1917); formed a special lending unit to serve public utilities (1932) and established a petroleum department (1936); issued "scrip drafts" to provide customers with credit for purchases in stores, a precursor to modern-day credit cards (1946); set up an international advisory committee, drawing members from businesspeople around the world, to provide counsel on the company's increasing global activities (1965); pioneered the syndicated loan market (1980s); accomplished the largest interstate banking merger at that time with Chemical Banking Corporation's acquisition of Texas Commerce Bank (1987); engineered the historic merger of two money center banks (Chemical Banking Corporation and Manufacturers Hanover Trust Company) at the forefront of the merger

oom (1992); led the convergence of commercial and investment banking (1992 and beyond); and announced the merger of the new Chemical with The Chase Manhattan Corporation, to create the new Chase (1995). Today, Chase combines the best of commercial and investment banking, offers world-class information and transaction processing services, and has a leading U.S. retail franchise. All of its businesses are bolstered by formidable technology capabilities that support the needs of consumers, wealthy individuals and families, entrepreneurs, small businesses, multinational corporations, financial institutions, and governments.

COMMITMENT TO THE COMMUNITIES CHASE SERVES

Chase has an unwavering commitment to strengthen the diverse communities it serves and has been rated outstanding under the Community Reinvestment Act—the highest possible rating awarded by the Federal Reserve Bank of New York.

Chase is the top bank lender for affordable housing and retail development in lower-income communities in the New York region, including lead bank lender for Harlem USA-the largest single investment to date by the Upper Manhattan Empowerment Zone. Chase is a leader in Small

Business Administration (SBA) Lending, making more SBA loans than any other financial institution last year in the New York district and earning SBA's highest lender award, the Pinnacle Award, for the third consecutive year.

Chase has a broad range of volunteer programs involving more than 15,000 employees, family members, and retirees. The firm was the recipient of the 1998 March of Dimes President's Award for its nationwide performance in the March of Dimes Teamwalks. Chase employees have a long history of giving to numerous charitable organizations, including the United Way and the United Negro College Fund (UNCF), and of donating blood. Chase is the only company that has ever won all four Summit Awards—United Way of America's highest tribute for corporate community involvement. The 1998

employee United Way campaign raised $8 million. The company has supported the UNCF since its inception in 1944 through grants, scholarship programs, and employee donations. Chase is proud to have more than 50 UNCF graduates among its employees.

TWO HUNDRED YEARS FORWARD

For the past 200 years, Chase has put its strength and financial expertise to work, building deep and enduring relationships around the world. The ability to foresee and move with confidence in new directions is part of the Chase heritage. The result is an asset of unlimited value: a reputation for integrity and trust that spans generations and sets Chase apart as the world enters the new millennium, and as the company moves into its third century of growth and prosperity.

HOLLAND & KNIGHT LLP

OLLAND & KNIGHT LLP RECENTLY MADE LEGAL HIStory. With the selection of Martha Barnett as the American Bar Association's president-elect, Holland & Knight is the first law firm in America to have two ABA presidents. This is an impressive reflection on the quality of the people in the firm, and

THE MAGNIFICENT MARBLE LOBBY AT 195 BROADWAY, HOME TO THE NEW YORK OFFICE OF HOLLAND & KNIGHT LLP, IS LOCATED IN DOWNTOWN MANHATTAN'S HISTORIC DISTRICT. CONSTRUCTED BETWEEN 1915 AND 1922 AND INSPIRED BY THE GREEK PARTHENON, THIS BUILDING ONCE HOUSED THE AT&T WORLD HEADQUARTERS.

a tribute to the quality of the law practiced at Holland & Knight.

Barnett will be responsible for leading the significant, 450,000-member ABA into the next century and no doubt will have an impact on the practice of law, as did Chesterfield Smith, the firm's chairman emeritus who served as ABA president in the 1970s.

Smith is a leader who is greatly respected for instituting significant reforms in the legal establishment. He led efforts in promoting women and recruiting minorities into the legal profession, and, along with Managing Partner Bill McBride, was responsible for making Holland & Knight one of the first law firms in the country to do significant pro bono work. He believed that the law should first be viewed as an institution for the public good, and second as a place to make a living—a principle that continues to guide Holland & Knight today.

LEADERSHIP IN THE LAW

A full-service commercial law firm, Holland & Knight is among the 20 largest law firms in the world with more than 850 attorneys throughout 19 offices in the United States and Mexico City, with representative offices in Buenos Aires, Brazil, and Tel-Aviv, Israel, providing global representation in more than 55 practice areas.

The firm is comprised of five primary departments: Business Law; Litigation; Public Law; Real Estate, Environmental, and Land Use; and Ancillary Professional Services, which was established in 1997 and delivers comprehensive consulting, problem-solving, and decision-making services designed to identify and respond to issues before they lead to unforeseen lawsuits, business hardships, and exposure to unnecessary risks.

The firm's clients are diverse and their business interests range in scope from local to international. They include financial institutions, utility companies, insurance companies, domestic and foreign governments, the maritime industry, transportation, aircraft manufacturers, a variety of media enterprises, passenger cruise lines, foreign aircraft companies and carriers, construction companies, real estate developers,

entertainment, intellectual property, telecommunications, most of the phosphate mining and manufacturing companies in Florida, citrus producers and other agricultural enterprises, trade associations, and many other companies, institutions, and individuals. Additional information about the firm is available at its Web site, www.hklaw.com.

Holland & Knight traces its origin to two separate firms; one dates from the 1880s and the other from the early 1900s. Spessard L. Holland, a former Florida governor and U.S. senator founded one firm; Peter O. Knight an early business and civic leader in Florida, founded the other. The two firms merged to form Holland & Knight in 1968. That firm then merged with the New York firm Haight, Gardner, Poor & Havens in 1997.

A HISTORY OF COMMUNITY SERVICE

Over the years, Holland & Knight has developed a reputation as one of the most active pro bono firms in the country. Each year, the firm contributes about 3 percent of its billable hours to pro bono work—the equivalent of approximately $7.5 million. In addition, Holland & Knight formed the Women's Initiative in 1995 to develop the professional and economic opportunities of all women lawyers. The firm also administers the Holocaust Remembrance Project, which sponsors an annual writing contest to commemorate the Holocaust. Opening Doors for Children is another project sponsored by the firm, which improves the lives of children from birth through high school.

"For this firm, just being a good lawyer is not sufficient," says Smith. "You must be a lawyer who does good things."

URING THE CIVIL WAR, A NEW YORK LIFE INSURANCE Company agent crossed battle lines, under a flag of truce, to pay a claim to a needy widow and family. This indelible moment in history remains as valid a depiction of the company's commitment to its clients today as it did then. While the company—the number one producer of life insurance in the United States—has expanded its services beyond life insurance, its focus has never wavered. Its one overriding purpose is to be there for its customers in their time of need.

HISTORICAL ROOTS

New York Life was founded on April 12, 1845, as the Nautilus Insurance Company. Its first president was James DePeyster Ogden and its chief actuary was Pliny Freeman. The company's first secretary, Lewis Benton, bought the first policy with a face amount of $5,000. The fledgling insurer's total assets at the time were approximately $17,000. In 1849, Nautilus was renamed New York Life Insurance Company, and it would go on to become one of the world's largest and soundest financial institutions.

Over the years, the company's agents have included successful people from all walks of life, including politics, law, literature, and the military. It has insured American men and women from pioneers, farmers, and mill workers to leaders of industry and government, including nine U.S. presidents. It not only has provided enhanced business services in the wake of earthquakes, tornadoes, floods, and hurricanes, but also has led humanitarian efforts to help the victims. It was the first major life insurer to focus its resources on AIDS research and prevention. Today, through its Nurturing the Children program, New York Life is helping youngsters across the nation through charitable donations and by fostering volunteerism among its agents, employees, and retirees.

A GIANT AMONG INSURANCE COMPANIES

New York Life is an extremely successful Fortune 100 company, maintaining operations in all 50 states through a network of employees and agents. In addition to life insurance, annuities, and long-term care coverage, it offers asset accumulation products, such as mutual funds and institutional money management. It serves nearly 4 million individual policyholders with whole life, universal life, and term insurance, as well as fixed and variable life insurance and annuity products. The firm's asset management area has more than $55 billion in assets under management in three primary investor markets: retail mutual fund buyers, company and individual retirement plans, and institutional investors.

New York Life also is active and successful in a number of special markets. Group Membership Association underwrites and administers group life, health, and disability insurance for large professional associations. NYLIFE Administration manufactures and markets long-term care insurance. And AARP Operations underwrites, administers, and direct-markets life insurance to that organization's 32 million members. Through its international subsidiary, New York Life also offers insurance and asset accumulation products and services to emerging-market nations abroad. The company also owns a controlling interest in Express Scripts, Inc., one of the largest full-service pharmacy benefit management firms in the nation.

Today, the company that opened its doors in 1845 with $17,000 now has consolidated assets of more than $90 billion and assets under management of nearly $123 billion.

NEW YORK LIFE INSURANCE COMPANY'S HEADQUARTERS IS LOCATED ON MADISON AVENUE (LEFT).

DURING THE CIVIL WAR, A NEW YORK LIFE INSURANCE COMPANY AGENT CROSSED BATTLE LINES, UNDER A FLAG OF TRUCE, TO PAY A CLAIM TO A NEEDY WIDOW AND FAMILY. THIS INDELIBLE MOMENT IN HISTORY REMAINS AS VALID A DEPICTION OF THE COMPANY'S COMMITMENT TO ITS CLIENTS TODAY AS IT DID THEN (RIGHT).

NYU Medical Center: New York University School of Medicine, NYU Hospitals Center

FOR ANY ACADEMIC MEDICAL CENTER, THE QUALITY OF care is only as good as the quality of experience, research, education, and practice that goes into it. At New York University (NYU) Medical Center, the care is exceptional because of the people and facilities that comprise this internationally renowned institution.

It starts with the New York University School of Medicine, one of the nation's leaders in medical education, and its history of more than 150 years of excellence in patient care, scientific research, and the education and training of physicians. In addition, the school includes the Post-Graduate Medical School, and the School of Medicine's Skirball Institute of Biomolecular Medicine. NYU Hospitals Center and Health System includes Tisch Hospital, Rusk Institute of Rehabilitation Medicine, Hospital for Joint Diseases, and NYU Downtown Hospital. Each of NYU's institutions is respected as being among the most dedicated, patient-oriented care facilities in the world.

In 1998, NYU Hospitals Center and Health System became a full clinical partner with Mount Sinai Hospital, creating the clinical partnership known as Mount Sinai NYU Health. Through this historic agreement, two of the premier medical centers in the nation joined together to provide an even stronger base of medical research and clinical care. Six hospitals comprise the core organization—Tisch Hospital, Rusk Institute of Rehabilitation Medicine, Hospital for Joint Diseases, NYU Downtown Hospital, Mount Sinai Hospital, and Mount Sinai Hospital of Queens. Mount Sinai NYU Health also includes affiliations with the two schools of medicine (NYU School of Medicine and Mount Sinai School of Medicine) and more than 40 clinical affiliates throughout the New York City region.

THE ROOTS OF CARE

The NYU School of Medicine's history dates back nearly two centuries, and includes many innovations that have helped to shape American medicine. The original and distinguished faculty of the Medical College of the University of New York, founded in 1841, included Valentine Mott, probably the foremost surgeon of his day, and John Revere, the youngest son of patriot Paul Revere and the medical school's first chairman of medicine. The present School of Medicine was created by the later merger, in 1898, of the two independent

medical schools, Medical College of the University of New York, and Bellevue Hospital Medical College. In 1935, the name of the school was changed to New York University School of Medicine.

The Mission of a Medical School, a prospectus written by the faculty of the school early in the 20th century, is as meaningful and guiding today as it was then. It states: "The mission of a medical school is threefold: the training of physicians, the search for new knowledge, and the care of the sick. The three are inseparable. Medicine can be handed on to succeeding generations only by long training in the scientific methods of investigation and by the actual care of patients. Progress in medicine, which is medical research, must look constantly to the school for its investigators and to the patient for its problems, whereas the whole future of medical care rests upon a continuing supply of physicians and upon the promise of new discovery. The purpose of a medical school, then, can only be achieved by endeavor in all three directions— medical education, research, and community care—and they must be carried on simultaneously, for they are wholly dependent upon each other, not only for inspiration, but for their every means of success."

Today, the school has approximately 4,500 faculty members and an annual enrollment of more than 650 students. More than 1,000 major biomedical projects are funded by government and nongovernment sources annually, with $100 million in funded research projects. Faculty members are attending physicians at Tisch Hospital, Rusk Institute, Bellevue Hospital Center, and Hospital for Joint Diseases.

RESEARCH, DEVELOPMENT, AND PRACTICE

Throughout its history, New York University School of Medicine has been an integral part of the history of American medicine. In 1854, the first successful resection of a hip joint was performed by NYU's Dr. Lewis A. Sayre, the first professor of orthopedic surgery in the United States. Twelve years later, NYU opened the first outpatient clinic in the nation. And in 1884, NYU established the Carnegie Laboratory, the first facility in the country devoted to teaching and research in bacteriology and pathology.

Over the years, many NYU School of Medicine alumni and Medical Center research scientists have won honor and fame for their individual achievements. In 1889, for example, Dr. Walter Reed discovered the mosquito transmission of yellow fever. Throughout the 1930s, Drs. Homer Smith, William Goldring, and Herbert Chasis pioneered the study of the kidneys, providing the original

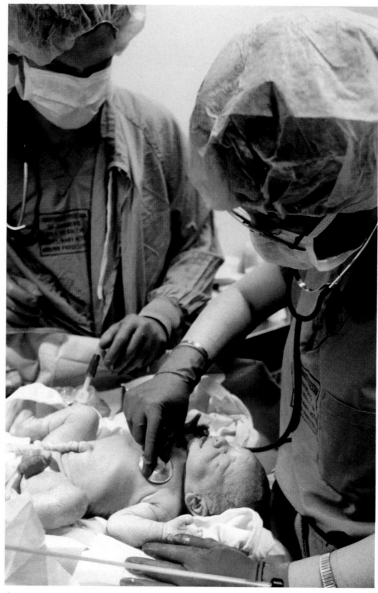

two co-receptors on the surface of the immune cells that play a vital role in the way that HIV infects cells. In 1998, Dr. Harold Koplewicz opened the NYU Child Study Center, one of the most comprehensive centers for childhood mental disorders in the United States.

Today, the school continues to dedicate itself to continuing it mission by providing a rich atmo sphere for scholarship, research and care. NYU faculty understan that the students, as their succes sors, should not merely replace but surpass their expertise and accomplishment. They are committed to the concept of the physician-scientist and the mission of creating the environment to attract those who are and will become the top in their fields. Furthermore, the institution is determined to stay ahead of the major events and trends shaping contemporary medicine, such as the revolution in molecular biology and medical technology; the need to find a balance between rising health care expectations and the finite limits on resources the explosive growth in biomedical information; and patients' increasing involvement in directing their own care.

A Nucleus of Clinical Care

The NYU School of Medicine and the NYU Hospitals Center and Health System work together, providing the resources necessary to continue their legacy of world-class research, education, and patient care. The NYU Medical Center houses a host of facilities, each committed to the academic mission they share, and to the imperative need to apply the most current research and advanced patient care practices.

With approximately 700 beds, the Tisch Hospital is an acute care general hospital that annually admits about 30,000 patients from the community and around the world. Founded in 1882 as the New York Post-Graduate Hospital, it became part of the NYU Medical Center in 1947; it was rebuilt on its present site in 1963, and renamed the Tisch Hospital in 1990. The central component of clinical care at NYU Medical Center, the

framework for understanding the physiology of human kidney function and the pathophysiology of the kidneys in hypertension and nephritis. In 1933, Dr. William S. Tillett conducted groundbreaking studies of enzymes involved in blood clotting; his work led to the development of streptokinase, a drug used to combat heart attacks.

During the World War II years, NYU-trained Dr. Julius Axelrod worked with faculty members in the Medical School's malaria research program, for which he was later awarded the Nobel Prize in medicine. Dr Jonas Salk, M.D., Class of 1939, developed the first polio vaccine in 1955. Dr Albert Sabin, Class of 1931, introduced the live-virus oral polio vaccine in 1961. Drs. Saul Krugman and Louis Cooper developed the rubella vaccine in 1965. Dr. Frank C. Spencer was the first to experimentally propose the use of the

internal mammary artery in bypass surgery in 1967, and performed the first clinical operation with Dr. George Green in 1969.

Dr. Joseph G. McCarthy pioneered craniofacial reconstruction on an infant born with severe facial deformities in 1974. NYU scientist Dr. Alvin Freidman-Kein presented the first evidence linking a rare cancer, Kaposi's sarcoma, with immune deficiency in a distinct population of homosexual men in 1981, a key step in identifying AIDS. In 1994, Dr. Joseph Schlessinger devised a model, called dimerization, for growth factors to communicate their messages to a cell's nucleus, an important contribution to the understanding of cell signaling, a process transforming the study of cancer. In 1996, Drs. Fred Valentine and Roy Gulick led the landmark study of a potent triple-drug therapy to combat AIDS. In 1997, Dr. Dan Littman identified

Tisch Hospital is a major center for specialized procedures in cardiovascular services, neurosurgery, AIDS, cancer treatment, reconstructive surgery, and transplantation. The hospital's role as a major teaching facility and referral center reflects its use of the latest technology and health care protocols for the most complicated disease situations. An important part of Tisch is its Cooperative Care Unit, the first of its kind in the nation. Each room at the unit has two beds, one for the patient and the other for a family member or friend serving as a care partner.

The School of Medicine's Rita J. and Stanley H. Kaplan Comprehensive Cancer Center is the site of basic and clinical research in virtually every key area of oncology, including melanoma, breast, ovarian, prostate, brain, and gastrointestinal cancer therapy. One of the school's ma-

jor research resources is its Nelson Institute of Environmental Medicine, where scientists examine the prevention, early diagnosis, and treatment of environmentally related diseases. NYU School of Medicine is also home to one of 13 National Institutes of Health-designated Centers for AIDS Research, with one of the nation's largest programs of clinical trials evaluating drugs to treat both HIV infections and HIV-related cancer.

The Rusk Institute of Rehabilitation Medicine, a facility with 170 beds, is the country's first and largest university rehabilitation center for treatment, training, and research in physical disabilities for both adults and children. It was founded in 1947 by Howard A. Rusk, M.D., often called the father of rehabilitation medicine. There are nearly 3,000 inpatient and nearly 56,000 outpatient visits at Rusk each year.

The Hospital for Joint Diseases is one of the nation's premier hospitals for treating orthopedic, rheumatological, and, more recently, neurological movement disorders for adults and children. With 220 beds, it treats more than 11,000 patients surgically each year, and has more than 63,600 outpatient visits.

NYU Downtown Hospital is a 330-bed facility offering comprehensive medical, surgical, pediatric, obstetric, and gynecological services for the communities of lower Manhattan. It is known for its innovative community programs, such as the Chinese Community Partnership for Health and the Downtown Heartsavers Program, which offers educational programs about heart disease and treatment for the Wall Street financial community.

The NYU Hospitals Center and Health System and NYU School of Medicine also maintain affiliations with select institutions for a variety of joint academic and clinical programs, including Bellevue Hospital Center, Department of Veterans Affairs Medical Center in Manhattan, Lenox Hill Hospital, North Shore University Hospital, Gouverneur Diagnostic and Treatment Center, Jamaica Hospital, and Chinatown Health Clinic.

Together, the NYU School of Medicine and Medical Center provide the resources necessary for superlative patient care, medical education, and research.

FRED VALENTINE, M.D., AND HIS COLLEAGUES AT NYU MEDICAL CENTER LED THE LANDMARK STUDY SHOWING THAT COMBINATION THERAPY WITH THREE DIFFERENT DRUGS CAN TRANSFORM HIV INFECTION INTO A MANAGEABLE LONG-TERM DISEASE FOR MANY PATIENTS.

NYU MEDICAL CENTER IS A MAJOR TEACHING FACILITY AND REFERRAL CENTER WHERE PHYSICIANS EMPLOY STATE-OF-THE-ART TECHNIQUES AND TECHNOLOGY TO OFFER UNSURPASSED PATIENT CARE.

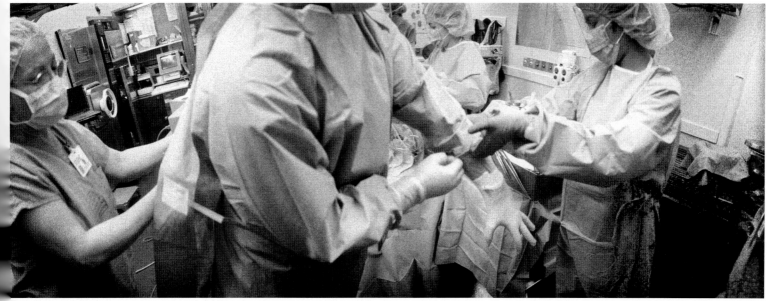

CITY UNIVERSITY OF NEW YORK

What makes CUNY remarkable is the quality of the education given every day to every student at this public university. More CUNY graduates went on to earn Ph.D.'s than graduates of Harvard, Columbia, and New York universities combined between 1983 and 1992.

A SMART PLACE TO LEARN

CUNY, with an annual operating budget of more than $1 billion, is a comprehensive center for higher learning. Within New York City, it comprises 10 senior colleges, six community colleges, one technical college, a graduate school, a law school, and a medical school, and offers more than 300 different individual degree programs.

With a full-time teaching faculty of approximately 5,600 and 90 research centers and institutes,

WITH A FULL-TIME TEACHING FACULTY OF APPROXIMATELY 5,600 AND 90 RESEARCH CENTERS AND INSTITUTES, CITY UNIVERSITY OF NEW YORK (CUNY) IS ONE OF THE NATION'S MAJOR RESEARCH INSTITUTIONS.

CUNY is one of the nation's major research institutions. On its faculty are world-renowned talents, thinkers, artists, and experts whose diverse contributions build the university and extend virtually every domain of learning and service: the arts, letters, sciences, engineering, technology, management, economics, and the professions, including education, law, and medicine.

The quality of the university has been recognized in many ways. The latest report from the National Research Council ranked more than one-third of the university's doctoral programs among the top 20 programs nationwide, and the arts and humanities programs collectively ranked 16th in the nation. Faculty members from the university have received fellowships from the National Endowment for the Humanities, National Endowment for the Arts, Rockefeller Foundation, National Institutes of Health, National Science Foundation, John Simon Guggenheim Memorial Foundation, MacArthur Foundation, and American Council of Learned Societies, among many others.

In addition to awards from the National Institutes of Health, National Aeronautics and Space Administration, and National Science Foundation, CUNY faculty have received prestigious support from the Carnegie Corporation and the Ford and Kellogg foundations.

TODAY, CUNY ENROLLS CLOSE TO 200,000 STUDENTS IN DEGREE-CREDIT PROGRAMS. ITS STUDENT BODY—AMONG THE MOST DIVERSE IN THE NATION, WITH 115 NATIVE LANGUAGES SPOKEN BY STUDENTS FROM 164 COUNTRIES—IS REPRESENTATIVE OF THE RICH CULTURAL TEXTURE OF NEW YORK.

GRADUATES OF CUNY HAVE BE-
COME LEADERS IN VIRTUALLY EV-
ERY FIELD—FROM SCIENCE TO THE
ARTS, GOVERNMENT TO PHILAN-
THROPY, BUSINESS TO MEDICINE.

Seven Faculty members have won MacArthur Foundation Fellowships, including a poet, a physicist, a historian, a scholar of Tibetan culture, a mathematician, and two anthropologists.

THE STUDENTS AND THE CITY

CUNY traces its beginning to 1847 and a municipal referendum authorized by the state legislature to determine if the people of New York City were willing to underwrite the cost of an institution of higher education open to the children of the rich and poor together. The Free Academy, created as a result of that vote, later became the City College of New York. In 1870, Hunter College was founded to educate women, and became the first free normal school in America.

Today, CUNY enrolls close to 200,000 students in degree-credit programs. Its student body—among the most diverse in the nation, with 115 native languages spoken by students from 164 countries—is representative of the rich cultural texture of New York. Although 91 percent are residents of New York City, almost half were born outside the continental United States.

The students who come to CUNY are a particularly hardworking group. They come to learn, often while working a full-time job, to enhance the quality of their life through education. Fifty-nine percent of the undergraduates work and go to school simultaneously; nearly 42 percent of the undergraduate students attend part-time; 150,000 additional students enroll in adult and continuing education programs; 42 percent of the undergraduate students are 25 years of age or older; and one-quarter have children.

"The City University of New York has historically taken hundreds of thousands of motivated New Yorkers to the highest level of success in business, government, science, education, and the arts," says Chancellor Matthew Goldstein. "Thousands of bright, dedicated students are ready to make the same climb today."

The local return on the city's investment in CUNY is high: Fully 80 percent of CUNY's graduates continue to live and work in New York City. This creates a valuable work pool that attracts and maintains businesses in the area, and ensures a substantial stream of dollars spent in the city and a career-long stream of taxes paid by the graduates.

REMARKABLE ALUMNI

Perhaps no measure of a university's success, however, is more telling than the contributions of its alumni. Graduates of CUNY have become leaders in virtually every field—from science to the arts, government to philanthropy, business to medicine. Eleven of the school's alumni have won Nobel Prizes—among the highest number won by any public university— for discoveries ranging from the biochemistry of communications in the nervous system to the mathematics of market equilibrium.

The university also counts among its alumni Jonas Salk, the discoverer of the polio vaccine; Colin Powell, the first African-American to become chairman of the Joint Chiefs of Staff; and Jerry Seinfeld, comedian and television superstar.

"CUNY has been the touchstone for many people who have enriched our lives," says Goldstein. "Men and women who have created art and music, provided leadership at crucial periods in our nation's history, opened vistas in science, founded new businesses, and literally saved lives."

PFIZER INC

GLOBAL, RESEARCH-BASED PHARMACEUTICAL COMPANY

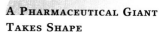

Pfizer Inc has always been dedicated to discovering and developing innovative, value-added products designed to help people enjoy healthier and more productive lives. Its history is a chronicle of a small fine-chemicals business founded in 1849 that has become one of the world's premier pharmaceutical companies.

"At Pfizer, we have a tradition of conquering uncharted territory," says William C. Steere Jr., chairman and CEO. "The history of Pfizer is the story of a great humanitarian enterprise. It is a story of great science, impressive commitment, and remarkable people. Again and again, we've defined ourselves by taking on challenges that no one else was able to tackle. And our spirit of enterprise has led to amazing achievements."

SEEKING OPPORTUNITY IN THE NEW WORLD

Pfizer's enterprising spirit was evident from the start. Its founders, cousins Charles Pfizer, a chemist, and Charles Erhart, a confectioner, who had emigrated to the United States in the late 1840s from Ludwigsburg, Germany, soon recognized the young nation's growing need for chemicals. With money borrowed from Pfizer's father, they set up shop in a red brick building in the Williamsburg section of Brooklyn.

A harbinger of things to come, the cousins' first breakthrough was a formulation of santonin, a treatment for parasitic worms that was effective but intensely bitter. They made the drug more palatable by blending it with almond-toffee flavoring and shaping it into a candy cone. The product was an immediate hit. Buoyed by this success, the company began to diversify. Within 10 years, Pfizer was manufacturing more than a dozen other chemicals and preparations, including borax, camphor, and iodine. The company continued to grow, broadening its product portfolio throughout the 19th century and gaining a reputation for high-quality products, technical expertise, reliability, and customer focus.

In the early decades of the 20th century, citric acid, which Pfizer had begun manufacturing in 1880, became its most popular product. In perfecting the fermentation process used to produce citric acid, Pfizer developed an expertise that later enabled it to successfully mass-produce penicillin, an achievement that laid the foundation for Pfizer's transformation from a chemical company into a pharmaceutical giant.

A PHARMACEUTICAL GIANT TAKES SHAPE

In 1928, the discovery of penicillin by British bacteriologist Alexander Fleming offered real hope in the battle against infection, but penicillin was difficult to extract and impossible to preserve. After a year's research, Fleming shelved his discovery in frustration. A decade later, a team of scientists at Oxford University rediscovered Fleming's work and revived research into the disease-killing mold. Although there was increasing evidence of penicillin's effectiveness, the British, who came under bombardment during World War II, were unable to carry out the necessary research.

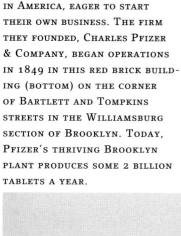

IN THE MID-1840S, COUSINS CHARLES PFIZER (LEFT) AND CHARLES ERHART (RIGHT) ARRIVED IN AMERICA, EAGER TO START THEIR OWN BUSINESS. THE FIRM THEY FOUNDED, CHARLES PFIZER & COMPANY, BEGAN OPERATIONS IN 1849 IN THIS RED BRICK BUILDING (BOTTOM) ON THE CORNER OF BARTLETT AND TOMPKINS STREETS IN THE WILLIAMSBURG SECTION OF BROOKLYN. TODAY, PFIZER'S THRIVING BROOKLYN PLANT PRODUCES SOME 2 BILLION TABLETS A YEAR.

hey turned to America for ssistance.

In 1941, Pfizer responded to ιe U.S. government's appeal ιat urged American industry to ·y to find a way to mass-produce enicillin—the world's first wonder ·ug. Working with scientists ·om Columbia University, Pfizer egan conducting experiments ·ith penicillin using surface fer- ιentation in glass flasks, but the ιitial yields were exceedingly low.

In the fall of 1942, Pfizer tried ·radically different approach: eep-tank fermentation, based ·n the process the company had erfected for the production of ·tric acid. But this attempt posed ·normous risks because it meant ιat Pfizer would have to curtail ·roduction of citric acid and other ·ell-established products while ·cusing on the development of enicillin.

Realizing the critical need ·or penicillin during wartime, ·fizer's senior management team ·ok the leap and purchased a ·acant ice plant near its Brooklyn ·lant. Employees worked around ·he clock to convert it and to per- ·ect the complex production pro- ·ess. Within four months, the ·orld's first penicillin plant not ·nly was up and running, but ·lso was producing five times ·nore penicillin than originally ·rojected.

With a need for massive quantities of this new drug, the U.S. government authorized 19 additional companies to use Pfizer's deep-tank fermentation techniques. Despite their access to Pfizer's technology, none of them came close to matching Pfizer's level of production or quality. In fact, Pfizer became the world's largest producer of penicillin, responsible for provid- ing 90 percent of the penicillin carried ashore by Allied forces at Normandy on D day, and more than 50 percent of the drug used by the Allies during the rest of the war. Pfizer's innovative think- ing and pioneering spirit helped save countless lives.

Recognizing that penicillin represented the beginning of a new era for Pfizer, its scientists began an intensive quest to find new organisms to fight disease. In 1950, after conducting more than 20 million tests on 135,000 soil samples collected from around the world, they found a substance that proved effective against a wide range of deadly bacteria. Named Terramycin because it came from the earth, this drug was the first pharma- ceutical to be sold under the Pfizer name in the United States. Its success signaled the birth of Pfizer as a full-fledged pharma- ceutical company.

The 1950s were a time of phe- nomenal expansion for Pfizer. Starting with a network of sales agents in a few countries, the company began to establish offices, subsidiaries, and partnerships around the world, and with its expanding portfolio of innovative products, it soon became an in- ternational powerhouse.

In the 1960s and 1970s, Pfizer continued to develop and market new pharmaceuticals. Fostering a reputation for innovation and creativity, the company produced drugs to treat arthritis, diabetes, depression, heart disease, fungal infections, and a wide range of other diseases.

This commitment to innovation continued throughout the 1980s and 1990s. The organization's current portfolio of products is young, with patent protection for many of its major drugs extend- ing well into the 21st century. These products include Norvasc, the world's leading antihyperten- sive; Diflucan, the world's leading prescription antifungal; Zoloft, the number two antidepressant in the world; Zithromax, the most

To accommodate its expanding business, Pfizer opened an of- fice (left) on Maiden Lane in lower Manhattan in 1868. Nearly a century later, this gleaming skyscraper on 42nd Street (right) became the command center of the com- pany's worldwide operations.

DURING WORLD WAR II, PFIZER RESPONDED TO AN APPEAL BY THE U.S. GOVERNMENT TO EXPEDITE THE MANUFACTURE OF PENICILLIN TO TREAT ALLIED SOLDIERS. SUCCESSFUL IN ITS EFFORTS TO MASS-PRODUCE PENICILLIN, PFIZER BECAME THE WORLD'S LARGEST PRODUCER OF THE MIRACLE DRUG. NINETY PERCENT OF THE PENICILLIN THAT WENT ASHORE WITH ALLIED FORCES AT NORMANDY ON D DAY WAS MANUFACTURED BY PFIZER (LEFT).

THE COMPANY'S DISCOVERY PROGRAM LED TO TERRAMYCIN, A BROAD-SPECTRUM ANTIBIOTIC THAT BECAME THE FIRST PHARMACEUTICAL SOLD IN THE UNITED STATES UNDER THE PFIZER BRAND NAME (RIGHT).

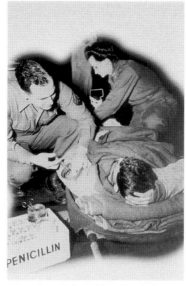

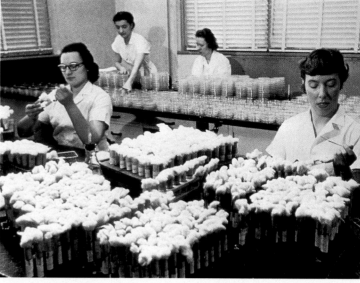

AMONG PFIZER'S BEST KNOWN MEDICINES ARE THE CARDIOVASCULAR NORVASC, THE ANTIDEPRESSANT ZOLOFT, AND THE ANTIBIOTIC ZITHROMAX. VIAGRA, LAUNCHED IN 1998, WAS A BREAKTHROUGH TREATMENT FOR ERECTILE DYSFUNCTION, ESTIMATED TO AFFLICT 100 MILLION MEN—AND THEIR PARTNERS—WORLDWIDE.

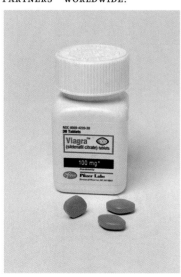

prescribed brand-name antibiotic in the United States; and Viagra, a revolutionary oral treatment for erectile dysfunction. In addition, Pfizer is also a marketer of leading over-the-counter products, including such well-known brands as Visine, BenGay, Cortizone, Unisom, Rid, and Desitin.

Pfizer innovation has not been limited to human health. One of the world's largest animal health companies, Pfizer has taken a leading role in discovering and developing vaccines and medicines that protect and enhance the health of livestock and companion animals. Through its Animal Health Group, Pfizer markets one of the largest-selling and broadest offerings of anti-infectives, anti-inflammatories, vaccines, and other medicines for more than 30 animal species in more than 140 countries. Few of Pfizer's animal health products have generated as much excitement as its new blockbuster, Revolution. This innovative medicine, intro-

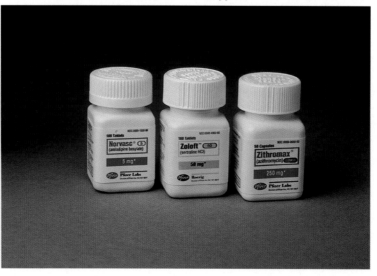

duced in the summer of 1999, protects dogs and cats from heartworms, fleas, and other harmful parasites, with just a spot in front of the shoulder blades once a month.

NEW PRODUCTS, CONTINUED SUCCESS

"The introduction of new and innovative products, as well as the continuing strong performance of established products, has allowed us to outpace the growth rate of the worldwide pharmaceutical market," says Pfizer's President and Chief Operating Officer Henry A. McKinnell, Ph.D., who heads the company's principal operating division, the Pfizer Pharmaceuticals Group. "During the past six years, Pfizer sales on average have grown at well over the rate of the rest of the industry."

At the millennium, Pfizer concluded the most successful decade in its 150-year history. During the 1990s, the decade in which

Steere refocused the company on its core strength—its ability to discover, develop, and market innovative pharmaceuticals—Pfizer launched 11 major new medicines, seven of which are today billion-dollar products. Recognizing the key role the field force plays in the transfer of technology between the company's research laboratories and the practicing physician, Pfizer also increased the size, strength, and quality of its sales forces during the decade, expanding to nearly 18,000 personnel worldwide. For the fourth year in a row, physicians in the United States have cited Pfizer as having the highest quality field sales organization in the country.

A CONTINUING DEDICATION TO RESEARCH

Pfizer's products are the result of its extraordinary commitment to research and development (R&D). Currently, the company has more than 180 research projects in discovery and development. "We're at the forefront in the war against depression, diabetes, cardiovascular diseases, and countless other illnesses. We believe we'll introduce more new medicines for more diseases than anyone else," says Steere. In 1999, Pfizer plowed approximately $2.8 billion into R&D, one of the largest investments by any pharmaceutical company in the world. Simultaneously, the company is continuing to expand its research facilities in Groton, Connecticut; Sandwich, England; and Nagoya, Japan, adding more than 1 million

quare feet to its laboratory re-
earch space, almost doubling its
urrent capacity.

As a result of its strength in
&D, marketing, and sales, Pfizer
as become the partner of choice
or many companies worldwide.
urrently, Pfizer is involved in
wide variety of co-promotion
lliances, research collaborations,
nd licensing agreements with
niversities, institutes, and orga-
izations all around the globe.

IVING BACK TO THE OMMUNITY—GLOBALLY, ATIONALLY, LOCALLY

hroughout its long history, Pfizer
as been committed to helping
thers through a variety of assis-
ance programs. In 1998, the com-
any established a program to
ght trachoma, the world's leading
ause of preventable blindness.
fizer pledged to fight the disease
y providing the antibiotic Zith-
omax to health agencies in Ghana,
Mali, Morocco, Tanzania, and Viet-
am. In addition, because trachoma
s common to overcrowded areas
vith poor water sources, Pfizer is
elping to implement the World
Health Organization's (WHO)
AFE (surgery, antibiotics, face
vashing, and environmental
hange) strategy in these coun-
ries to change the circumstances
hat give rise to this disease.

Pfizer's Sharing the Care pro-
ram, launched in 1993, provides
medicine free of charge to needy,
uninsured patients throughout the
United States. Working through
more than 350 community health
are clinics, Pfizer has to date filled
more than 3 million prescriptions
or more than 1 million patients—

which translates into more than
$180 million in donated medicines.

Pfizer also gives back to the
community on a local level, and
its employees volunteer thousands
of hours annually in their communities. Over the years, the
generosity of Pfizer employees
also has provided many millions
of dollars to United Way—contributions that have been matched
by the company dollar-for-dollar,
and have made Pfizer one of
United Way's top supporters.

THE VALUES THAT DRIVE PFIZER'S SUCCESS

"I believe our outstanding people
and their commitment to our eight
core values have made Pfizer
into the remarkable company
that it is today," says Steere.
"These values—integrity, respect
for people, innovation, performance, leadership, teamwork,
customer focus, and community

service—provide the foundation
for everything we've achieved,
and I am convinced they will help
Pfizer become the world's number
one health care company."

Pfizer's exceptional performance and excellent return to
investors prompted *Fortune*
magazine to name Pfizer one of
the world's most admired companies and the world's most admired
pharmaceutical company in 1997
and 1998. In 1999, *Forbes* magazine named Pfizer Company of the
Year. These honors underscore
the remarkable success Pfizer
has achieved since it began as a
one-product, two-man operation
in Brooklyn a century and a half
ago. The global enterprise that is
Pfizer today is imbued with its
founders' spirit of innovation and
is steadfast in its commitment to
continue to bring to the world
new medicines that will fulfill
unmet medical needs.

PFIZER'S MEDICINES ARE THE
RESULT OF ITS EXTRAORDINARY
COMMITMENT TO RESEARCH AND
DEVELOPMENT. DURING THE 1990S,
PFIZER LAUNCHED 11 MAJOR NEW
PRODUCTS.

THE PFIZER ANIMAL HEALTH
GROUP IS WELL POSITIONED TO
MEET THE MEDICAL NEEDS OF
LIVESTOCK AND COMPANION ANI-
MALS IN INCREASINGLY IMPORTANT
WORLD MARKETS (LEFT).

PFIZER PROVIDES A WIDE RANGE
OF ASSISTANCE TO THOSE IN NEED.
IN 1998, THE COMPANY ESTAB-
LISHED A $150 MILLION PROGRAM
TO FIGHT TRACHOMA, THE WORLD'S
LEADING CAUSE OF PREVENTABLE
BLINDNESS, IN FIVE DEVELOPING
COUNTRIES (RIGHT).

YMCA of Greater New York

AFTER-HOURS VISITORS TO 100 NEW YORK PUBLIC EL-
ementary schools are likely to find quite a surprise: YMCA staff coaching students on how to read
and helping them with their homework. At some public high schools, YMCA
counselors can be found helping students plan for life after high school.

Those going to certain YMCA branches can start a 12-week Personal Fitness program planned by a fitness counselor, or sign up for a class in photography, screen writing, poetry, or acting. The YMCA of Greater New York—the second-oldest YMCA in the nation—has evolved with the times, and today offers something for everyone.

What's in a Name?
The mission of the YMCA has not changed over the years, but the activities that the YMCA uses to accomplish it have grown and expanded, along with the city and the people it serves. And serve it does, with rededicated efforts and innovative programs designed to meet the needs of today's children, teens, adults, parents, and seniors—regardless of their background or beliefs.

"Yes, we're the YMCA, but we're not necessarily young, not necessarily male, not necessarily Christian," says Paula L. Gavin, president of the YMCA of Greater New York. "We're a community service organization, welcoming all people, all ages, all genders,

"Yes, we're the YMCA, but we're not necessarily young, not necessarily male, not necessarily Christian," says Paula L. Gavin, president of the YMCA of Greater New York. "We're a community service organization, welcoming all people, all ages, all genders, all races, all ethnic groups, and all religious affiliations."

all races, all ethnic groups, and all religious affiliations.

"Our mission is the same today as when we were founded in 1852: spirit, mind, and body. Long before the idea of private health clubs ever came about, the idea was, and is, that to be a well-integrated person, you need to have your spirit, your mind, and your body in tune. That's what we are dedicated to, and that has never been altered throughout our entire history."

Responding to the Changing City
As the Industrial Revolution took hold in the mid-1800s, young men flocked to New York. As these men moved from rural areas to the city, the need for safe places for them to congregate also grew. The YMCA of Greater New York was established in 1852, and formed in 1853 by a special act of the New York State legislature to help these young men make the most out of their endeavor.

In those days, the YMCA was an all-male Christian organization that focused on education. It specialized in classes designed to help young men learn a productive trade—one of the earliest courses taught by the YMCA was the first carriage repair course ever created, and later, an auto mechanics course was introduced. Physical fitness has always been promoted at the organization. Volleyball, basketball, and boxing were all invented at the YMCA. Guest rooms for young men were also part of many YMCA buildings.

About the time of World War II, the YMCA began to open up to women as well as men. With the increasing number of two-

reer families, the need for
ild care became prominent.
he organization responded in a
g way, becoming the largest
ild care provider in the private
ctor, offering nursery schools
d after-school programs.

HE VIRTUAL Y

oday, the YMCA offers a wide
nge of contemporary programs
ecifically designed to meet the
eds of the people of New York.
ne of the most significant is the
rtual Y, an after-school literacy-
sed program for elementary
hool students that is brought
rectly to school buildings in
ew York City. This program
cludes reading activities, values
ucation, and recreation.

The elementary school program
aimed at providing a quality
ter-school environment for
hoolchildren in underserved
eas. The organization partners
ith elementary schools in all
ve boroughs. YMCA staff
o out to provide reading-
hancement activities, home-
ork help, recreational activities,
d values education. Funded by
tside sponsors, the Virtual Y
day is assisting more than 8,000
ildren in 100 schools. Some 130
onsors from the private sector
nd the program.

In October 1997, U.S. Secre-
ry of Education Richard Riley
aveled to New York City to visit
e Virtual Y and said, "The Vir-
al Y is really a model of the kind
partnership among business,
e community, and the schools
at we need in every city and
wn in America."

The teen program has an edu-
tional/college/career emphasis,
aching students valuable lead-
ship skills and business tools,
ch as how to write a résumé
d how to handle an interview.
the Youth Entrepreneurship
rogram, teens have opened
ores in three YMCAs. The
outh Skills program emphasizes
e skills that lead directly to
bs, such as computers and
stomer service.

HE LARGEST YMCA IN
HE WORLD

addition to its new programs,
e YMCA's facilities have been

largely transformed, offering
community classes and fitness
programs that bring men and
women together in a positive atmosphere of learning and personal growth, where they can
participate in sports and fitness
programs and develop hobbies
and work-related skills. With 19
branches in all five boroughs, the
New York YMCA is the largest in
the world. A healthy and productive mix of staff and volunteers—
about 3,800 of each—provide
services to more than 150,000
youths and 225,000 adults.

A volunteer- and staff-led
organization since it began, the
YMCA is a perfect example of

the synergy between private and
public efforts to improve the conditions of the communities they
serve. Through fund-raising,
government support, and fees,
the YMCA provides access to
programs to everyone who wishes
to join, regardless of his or her
ability to pay.

"Today's YMCA retains the
commitment of a century and a
half of service to New York," says
Gavin. "Every program is dedicated to imparting education and
values that enhance quality of
life. Respect, responsibility, hon-
esty, and character: these infuse
all YMCA programs. That is our
legacy; that is our future."

TEENS IN THE YMCA'S YOUTH
ENTREPRENEURSHIP PROGRAM
MARCH IN THE LABOR DAY PARADE
WITH GOVENOR GEORGE PATAKI.

ONE OF THE MOST SIGNIFICANT
PROGRAMS THE YMCA OFFERS IS
THE *Virtual Y*, AN AFTER-SCHOOL
LITERACY-BASED PROGRAM FOR
ELEMENTARY SCHOOL STUDENTS
THAT IS BROUGHT DIRECTLY TO
SCHOOL BUILDINGS IN NEW YORK
CITY. THIS PROGRAM INCLUDES
READING ACTIVITIES, VALUES EDU-
CATION, AND RECREATION.

U.S. TRUST
CORPORATION

ONE HUNDRED AND FIFTY YEARS AGO, THE NATION WAS on the threshold of a tremendous surge of expansion and growth. Pioneers were not only the hardy families traveling in covered wagons to carve homesteads out of the American frontier. Pioneers, then as now, were risk takers, entrepreneurs, and

visionaries. Their efforts in business, industry, government, and finance laid the foundation for what would become an unprecedented time of productivity and wealth creation in the United States.

The accumulation of this wealth, in turn, created the need for entities to manage these assets productively and prudently. In 1853, a group of financial pioneers in New York City raised $1 million to create an innovative financial institution—the United States Trust Company of New York. Established to serve as manager, executor, and trustee of personal and corporate funds, the company's earliest clients were the

people who built the nation— railroad barons, merchants, shipbuilders, and industrialists.

Now known as the U.S. Trust Corporation, the firm has developed a reputation for superior performance, unparalleled service, and a commitment to enduring client relationships. Its breadth and depth of resources and expertise make it uniquely qualified to meet the special wealth management needs of affluent Americans.

AN IDEA AHEAD OF ITS TIME
Today, U.S. Trust is the nation's oldest trust company and is as much a pioneer as the people it has served. At first, the idea of a

trust institution was met with some skepticism. In the middle of the 19th century, most Americans of means held their assets in local real estate or business ventures. Cash holdings were not abundant, and there was little opportunity to invest in stocks because so few businesses were publicly held.

During its first 50 years, the company prospered with a thriving banking business via commercial and personal loans, the purchase of mortgages, and other investments. Clearly, U.S. Trust was ahead of its time—the trust company section of the American Banking Association was not even established until 1897.

But by the turn of the century, the rapid industrialization of America had changed the way wealth was created, invested, and managed, making trust services necessary. In addition, the wealth of the country's first industrialists was now being transferred to a new generation, and the ability to preserve this financial legacy was increasingly important.

One of the biggest changes facing trust services at that time was the dramatic shift in ownership structure. Prior to industrialization, wealth was accumulated where owners could manage it themselves, such as family-owned businesses and local real estate investment opportunities. With the securitization of an increasing number of huge enterprises, such as manufacturing plants, foundries, and refineries, clients began to shift assets to stocks and bonds.

This securitization trend accelerated in the 20th century, resulting in increased opportunities for investment. As individuals accumulated capital, they were able to diversify their holdings and become part-owners of many enterprises. Ownership took on new meaning, and wealthy investors needed to rely on

PICTURED HERE ARE H. MARSHALL SCHWARZ, U.S. TRUST CORPORATION'S CHAIRMAN AND CHIEF EXECUTIVE OFFICER (RIGHT), AND JEFFREY S. MAURER, PRESIDENT AND CHIEF OPERATING OFFICER.

U.S. Trust to provide expert advice and to help them manage and administer far-flung investments.

During the 1980s and 1990s, a period of renewed wealth creation for many Americans, U.S. Trust expanded its national presence, as well as its product line, to meet the needs of clients throughout the United States. In addition to its New York headquarters, U.S. Trust today has offices in most of the nation's major wealth centers.

HIGHLY REGARDED

U.S. Trust is now recognized as not only the nation's oldest independent trust and investment management company, but also one of the most highly regarded. With a strategic combination of investment management, financial planning, private banking, and fiduciary services, the firm offers a comprehensive approach to wealth management that is unrivaled. These varied disciplines can be integrated and coordinated to meet all of a client's financial needs or utilized on a stand-alone basis.

U.S. Trust's approach begins with a proven, tax-intelligent investment process. It offers numerous investment options, including domestic and international equities, taxable and tax-exempt fixed-income, and alternative

investments. Over the years, the firm has compiled an enviable long-term record of investment performance, often outperforming the major indices in both equity and fixed-income investing on both a pre-tax and after-tax basis.

Many families served by the company have seen their assets grow with U.S. Trust for generations. Others are corporate executives and entrepreneurs still building their own families' wealth. The key to U.S. Trust's longevity and the success of its client relationships is the firm's heritage of performance, integrity, and quality. U.S. Trust works hard to understand the needs

and concerns of each client and his or her family. The firm is focused on relationships, not transactions, offering a seamless continuity of service and management from one generation to the next.

A wide range of professional skills is required to successfully manage wealth, from structuring customized, tax-intelligent portfolios, to sophisticated financial planning, to innovative strategies for transferring wealth to succeeding generations or to charitable foundations. At every level, U.S. Trust employs experienced, knowledgeable professionals whose expertise is matched only by their commitment to helping the firm's clients realize their goals through creative, innovative, and often cutting-edge solutions.

"Our mission—serving affluent individuals and their families as their principal financial advisor to enable them to preserve and enhance their wealth—is as relevant today as it was when we were founded in 1853," says H. Marshall Schwarz, chairman and chief executive officer. "With the breadth and depth of our professional expertise and our ability to build relationships that endure for generations, U.S. Trust epitomizes the concept of wealth management."

CIBC WORLD MARKETS

THE CANADIAN IMPERIAL BANK OF COMMERCE (CIBC) has been a respected part of New York's financia[l] community since 1872. But it created a frenzy on the floor of the New York Stock Exchange in 1997 when its spokesperson, the legendary Wayne Gretzky, rang the opening bell. He was celebrating

the firm's listing on the oldest, most venerable stock exchange in the country.

"It was a great day for everyone," according to A.L. Flood, then CIBC chairman and CEO. This echoed the full-page ad that ran that day featuring a photo of Gretzky on the stock exchange floor and the message "Another Great Canadian Arrives in New York." What the ad couldn't show was the exchange traders breaking tradition, mobbing the great hockey player for his autograph. This unique moment reflects the impact that CIBC has had, not only in New York, but also in American financial circles over the past 100 years.

A HISTORY OF FINANCIAL STRENGTH

As Canada's largest bank, CIBC ranks among the top 10 in North America. Its first agency branch opened in New York in 1872 to provide financial services to American companies involved in worldwide export/import trade of agricultural products, lumber, cotton, machinery, and natural resources. This branch became a major link for the bank's international business, creating the cornerstone for the firm that would emerge some 100 years later. CIBC Chairman and CEO John S. Hunkin says, "There was never any question that the United States and New York, in particular, would play an important part in CIBC's strategic development."

CIBC's acquisition in 1988 of Canada's premier brokerage firm, Wood Gundy, marked an important first step in the firm's U.S. growth. Renamed CIBC Wood Gundy, the firm helped American investors participate in the issues of Canadian governments and corporations, and ac-

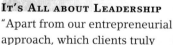
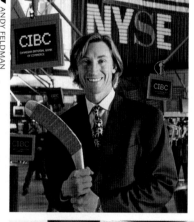

tively participated in major U.S. and Canadian bond syndicates. The globalization of financial markets continued to fuel CIBC['] U.S. expansion. "As our Canadia[n] clients began to look to the U.S. capital markets for funding," say[s] Hunkin, "we started to add the products, services, and people that would help our clients achieve their financial goals."

As part of its continuing expansion of capabilities and prod[-] ucts, CIBC Wood Gundy acquire[d] the Argosy High Yield Group, a New York-based financing boutique. This purchase was followe[d] in 1997, by the acquisition of Oppenheimer & Co., Inc., one of the last privately owned, full-service U.S. securities firms. Oppenheimer contributed important expertise in a number of industry sectors, including technology, gaming and hospitality, and health care.

The acquisition of Oppenheimer added more than 1,200 institutional clients, 160,000 retai[l] clients, and $32 billion in client assets. It also provided CIBC the critical full line of investment banking, asset management, brokerage, and sales and trading ser[-] vices, as well as highly ranked equity research analysts.

IT'S ALL ABOUT LEADERSHIP
"Apart from our entrepreneurial approach, which clients truly

ANDY FELDMAN

ANDY FELDMAN

lue, we made the right invest-
ents in industry expertise so
at we can offer clients not only
e sales, trading, and research
pport, but the dedicated indus-
y analysis that points us—and
r clients—to good ideas that
ill make money," says Hunkin.

At the time of the acquisition
Oppenheimer & Co., Inc.,
e U.S. firm was named CIBC
ppenheimer. It employed nearly
500 people in New York, com-
ning the perfect mix of equity
d fixed-income products, com-
eting the company's strategic
owth objectives. In 1999, CIBC
cided to bring all its global
vestment banking units under
single name, creating CIBC
orld Markets.

Today, CIBC World Markets
as offices in New York and around
e world. It provides a complete
nge of wholesale banking prod-
cts and services to corporations,
stitutions, and governments.
he CIBC Oppenheimer name is
ill used for the firm's private
ient business in the United States.
IBC Oppenheimer offers mutual
nd products and advisory and
ancial planning services for
gh-net-worth individuals.
hroughout its steady growth,
IBC World Markets has continued
focus on the defining feature
at sets the firm apart from the
ompetition—the entrepreneurial,
t-the-job-done approach to
elping its clients succeed.

IVING SOMETHING BACK
IBC World Markets recognizes
e tremendous success it has
njoyed as part of the New York

landscape, and the firm has been
very active in creating programs
to show its appreciation. For its
annual Miracle Day, the company
donates all the trading fees and
commissions raised on the first
Tuesday in December to children's
charities. Since the program first
started in 1984, CIBC World Markets has raised some $23 million
for more than 250 children's
charities worldwide. The company also teamed up with the

New York Rangers to create the
CIBC World Markets/New York
Rangers Children's Charities
Program, which donates more
than $150,000 each year to six
local charities.

CIBC World Markets takes
pride in the part it has played
during the last 125 years in New
York's development, and plans
to continue its role in the city's
economic and community life
for many years to come.

CLOCKWISE FROM TOP LEFT:
A RARE QUIET MOMENT ON THE
TRADING ROOM FLOOR

AN IMPROMPTU MEETING IN THE
LOBBY OF THE MIDTOWN BUILDING

ACTIVITY AT THE WORLD FINAN-
CIAL CENTER LOBBY, WHERE
EMPLOYEES CAN ENTER FROM
SEVERAL LEVELS

New York
Mercantile Exchange

A MAJOR FINANCIAL PRESENCE IN THE CITY, THE New York Mercantile Exchange offers theatrics withou the Broadway stars. Traders wearing brightly patterned jackets gesture wildly and shout to get the best possible prices o everyday items, including gasoline, heating oil, gold, and silver. The New

York Mercantile Exchange is the largest physical commodities exchange in the world, trading products worth billions of dollars each day. The exchange hit a major milestone in 1998 with an annual volume record of 95,018,685 contracts—a 13 percent increase over the record in 1997.

PREPARING FOR THE FUTURE

Established in 1872 as the Butter and Cheese Exchange of New York, it eventually embraced other commodities and became known as the New York Mercantile Exchange in 1882. In 1978, it was the first to introduce energy trading.

The exchange has had many homes over the years; in 1997, it moved to its current location in the World Financial Center in Battery Park City. The current headquarters provides the technology that traders need to keep track of transactions, including a fleet of telephones and computers expected to keep the exchange ticking for at least 25 years into the future.

In 1994, New York Mercantile Exchange merged with the Commodity Exchange (COMEX), the state's second largest, to become the world's largest physical com-

IN 1994, NEW YORK MERCANTILE EXCHANGE MERGED WITH THE COMMODITY EXCHANGE (COMEX), THE STATE'S SECOND LARGEST, TO BECOME THE WORLD'S LARGEST PHYSICAL COMMODITY FUTURES EXCHANGE (TOP).

THE NEW YORK MERCANTILE EXCHANGE IS THE LARGEST PHYSICAL COMMODITIES EXCHANGE IN THE WORLD, TRADING PRODUCTS WORTH BILLIONS OF DOLLARS EACH DAY (BOTTOM).

modity futures exchange. Trading takes place through the NYMEX Division, on which crude oil, heating oil, gasoline, natural gas, electricity, propane, platinum, and palladium are traded; and the COMEX Division, on which gold, silver, copper, aluminum, and the FTSE Eurotop 100 stock index are traded.

As global trading and technology expanded in the 1990s, NYMEX ACCESS was launched to provide overnight electronic trading, expanding operations to more than 22 hours a day. The organization anticipates that after-hours electronic trading will continue to grow, so it is developing an upgraded system for installation before the new year begins.

The exchange continues to introduce new products to drive the anticipated increase in trading volume. The fastest-growing sector is energy, and additional electricity contracts were introduced in 1998 and 1999, reflecting nationwide market deregulation. A pioneering coal futures contract is in the works, and the exchange has announced plans to offer a cash-settled, Middle East sour crude oil contract as well. Metals trading volume has expanded with the introduction of North American aluminum futures and options contracts in 1999, which is expected to generate additional activity.

WELCOMING THE COMMUNITY

Futures and options markets are designed to enable commercial entities to hedge their price risk ultimately cushioning consumer from the shock of price volatility i oil, natural gas, and gold market: In addition, a public marketplac provides price discovery, establishing a price reference that is publically used by thousands of businesses worldwide. These mechanisms benefit users of products made with these commodities, including everything from plastic to film to gasoline.

The exchange contributes more than $1.3 million annually to charity through the New York Mercantile Exchange Charitable Foundation. It supports medical, educational, and children's and social services groups mostly in and around New York City.

The New York Mercantile Ex change welcomes visitors to see firsthand how the world's commodities trading is done. Galleries overlooking each trading floo and an interactive museum dem onstrating how trading works, with artifacts that illustrate the ex-change's history, are open from 9 a.m. to 5 p.m. each business day, free of charge. To catc all the action, however, the best time to visit is between 10 a.m. and 2 p.m.

UR LADY OF MERCY (OLM) HEALTHCARE SYSTEM traces its roots back to 1888, when five Sisters of Misericorde founded a shelter for unwed mothers known as the New York Mother's Home. Within five years of its founding, the center had added general hospital care to its services, and was renamed

Misericordia Hospital. In 1959, after 70 years on East 86th Street, the center moved to East 233rd Street in the Bronx, and became a fully accredited, not-for-profit, voluntary hospital.

Today, under the auspices of the Archdiocese of New York, the system has grown into a complex of facilities throughout the Bronx and Westchester County. In 1969, the hospital added 122 beds to its original 210 beds, and in 1983, the system completed a modernization program that brought the facility to an inpatient capacity of 433 beds. In the following year, the board of trustees changed the name to Our Lady of Mercy Medical Center, following the wishes of the late Terence Cardinal Cooke.

In 1989, the center acquired the 183-bed Pelham Bay General Hospital. Our Lady of Mercy initiated a multimillion-dollar renovation of this facility, including enlargements of the emergency department, new operating and recovery rooms, a new ambulatory surgery site, intensive care unit (cardiac, medical, and surgical), renovation of nursing stations and patient rooms, and equipment replacement.

Our Lady of Mercy opened the Medical Village in Pelham Bay in the early 1990s, providing a broad range of physician specialties in one location. The center sponsors additional Medical Village sites in Co-Op City, Bronx River, High Bridge, Yonkers, and Carmel.

A merger with the 184-bed Saint Agnes Hospital in White Plains gave the OLM system 769 beds. Saint Agnes provides a full range of medical and surgical services, including outpatient and same day surgery for adults and children. Its rehabilitation center provides specialized care to more than 2,000 disabled children each year.

In addition, Our Lady of Mercy Medical Center was granted uni-versity hospital status by New York Medical College in 1996. Residency programs include medicine, surgery, pediatrics, and obstetrics/gynecology. Graduate and continuing medical education is offered to OLM physicians. Recently, the 233rd Street facility was renamed the John Cardinal O'Connor Campus.

A HOSPITAL THAT CARES
Throughout the Bronx and Westchester, the OLM system cares for the medical needs of the people it serves, as well as their social and spiritual needs. It is an active member of the Catholic Health Care Network (CHCN), a 31-member group of Catholic hospitals and nursing homes with more than 9,000

beds. OLM is sponsored by the New York Archdiocese to ensure a Catholic health care ministry in a rapidly changing market. It provides a seamless system of inpatient, outpatient, and home care for an estimated 2.5 million patients a year.

Throughout more than 100 years of service to New Yorkers, Our Lady of Mercy has served with a dedication that reflects its philosophy and mission: to provide quality health care with a deep commitment to human dignity and human rights.

CLOCKWISE FROM TOP LEFT: ALICIA ROMANO, M.D., IS CHIEF OF PEDIATRICS AT OUR LADY OF MERCY'S ROY RODGERS AND DALE EVANS CHILDREN'S CENTER.

ELAINE HEALY, M.D., IS THE DIRECTOR OF GERIATRICS AT SAINT AGNES HOSPITAL, WHICH IS A PART OF OUR LADY OF MERCY HEALTHCARE SYSTEM.

THE NEWLY RENOVATED SAINT AGNES HOSPITAL IS LOCATED IN WHITE PLAINS.

LADENBURG THALMANN & CO. INC.

LADENBURG THALMANN & CO. INC. ENTERS THE MILLEN-nium as a full-service investment banking and brokerage firm, embracing the future while never losing sight of its rich heritage. ▲ Ernst Thalmann, a well-known and widely respected American investment banker, joined with Adolph Ladenburg, a descendant of an established German banking family, to form Ladenburg Thalmann in 1876. By the time the firm joined the New York Stock Exchange in 1879, it quickly achieved a reputation on both sides of the Atlantic as one of the most influential private merchant banking firms. Consequently, Ladenburg Thalmann served as an important international arbitrageur—and a major financial intermediary—between America and Great Britain and the European continent.

A DYNAMIC FIRM

Throughout the early 20th century, Ladenburg Thalmann played an important role in the financing and growth of American industry. Acting as investors, financial advisors, and often as corporate directors, the firm's partners focused their efforts on identifying, counseling, and raising capital for emerging industries, including railroads, utilities, manufacturers, and retailers.

Building upon its solid foundation of traditional merchant banking, Ladenburg Thalmann maintained strong ties to both European financial centers and the emerging American markets. The company's depth and breadth of expertise made it one of the few Wall Street firms to prosper during the Great Depression, placing Ladenburg Thalmann among the most powerful investment banks in the world.

INTO THE NEW MILLENNIUM

Today, Ladenburg Thalmann is entering the new millennium as a full-service investment banking and brokerage firm that meets the varying investment needs of corporate, institutional, and individual clients. The firm is a member of the New York Stock Exchange, Securities Investor Protection Corporation, and all other principal exchanges, and is headquartered in New York with branch offices in Florida and Ohio.

Throughout its history—and still true today—Ladenburg Thalmann has cultivated a high level of performance. Its professionals continuously search for new ways to render value-added service to clients. This has marked the firm's character with a focused and innovative orientation, and consistent performance has validated this philosophy throughout the company's many years of business. Ladenburg Thalmann's traditions translate into practical operating principles today by focusing on developing long-term client relationships and providing clients with direct and ongoing

WITH ITS HEADQUARTERS IN NEW YORK CITY, LADENBURG THALMANN & CO. INC. WAS ESTABLISHED IN 1876.

cess to the firm's most experienced professionals.

AN ORGANIZATION OF SERVICE

Ladenburg Thalmann has proven expertise in a wide range of corporate finance services, including public underwritings, financial advisory, mergers and acquisitions, restructurings and workouts, valuations, and recapitalizations, as well as private placements.

Ladenburg Thalmann's investment research is one of the core strengths that sets the company apart from its competition. Utilizing fundamental, technical, and quantative research methods, Ladenburg's analysts conduct in-depth analyses in order to identify unique investment opportunities. An industry-specific focus further provides the firm's analysts with an edge in identifying dominant trends, interpreting the competitive landscape, and forecasting future developments within their markets.

Ladenburg Thalmann offers a vast array of financial instruments, which helps meet the needs of both its retail and institutional clients. The company has skilled traders that handle an extensive range of financial instruments, and the firm also serves as an active market maker for a multitude of over-the-counter securities. The firm's trading professionals work in a creative and responsive fashion while consistently managing risk effectively.

Above all, the firm is committed to placing its clients' interests first. "Ladenburg Thalmann's first priority and overriding mission is to achieve outstanding results for our clients," says Ladenburg Thalmann's Chairman and Chief Executive Officer Victor M. Rivas. "The firm is uniquely structured to achieve this goal. All areas at the firm are managed by seasoned professionals with experience in a number of disciplines. These individuals share diverse responsibilities: Each is allowed to cross over traditional organizational lines. The value of this efficient organizational structure is clear-cut: Critical decisions are made quickly and decisively, speeding up implementation and enabling clients to capture important opportunities."

IN THE NEW YORK FINANCIAL DISTRICT IN 1901, ACCORDING TO LEGEND, MAVERICK TRADERS STOOD ON THE CURB IN FRONT OF LADENBURG THALMANN'S OFFICES, CRANING THEIR NECKS TO SEE SIGNALS FROM THE COMPANY'S BROKERS. THESE OFFICES WERE DESCRIBED AS BEING "AMONG THE MOST COMMODIOUS BANKING ROOMS IN THE COUNTRY."

MEMORIAL SLOAN-KETTERING CANCER CENTER

DR. KATHLEEN W. SCOTTO, OF MEMORIAL SLOAN-KETTERING CANCER CENTER'S MOLECULAR PHARMACOLOGY AND THERAPEUTICS PROGRAM, IS INVESTIGATING A GROUP OF ENZYMES THAT INTERACT WITH OTHER FACTORS TO TURN GENES ON AND OFF WITHIN CELLS.

THE LOBBY OF THE ROCKEFELLER OUTPATIENT PAVILION WELCOMES VISITORS.

I N 1884, TWO REMARKABLE EVENTS TOOK PLACE IN NEW York City, each one representing a symbol of hope to people looking for help: The Statue of Liberty was unveiled and the New York Cancer Hospital opened, the progenitor of the respected Memorial Sloan-Kettering Cancer Center. ⬛ The world's old-

est and largest private institution devoted to the prevention, treatment, and cure of cancer through patient care, research, and education, Memorial Sloan-Kettering has consistently set the standard of care for people with cancer. Since its founding, it has pioneered countless discoveries in basic science and clinical research that have led to standard-setting innovations in all areas of cancer diagnosis and treatment, including surgery, medical oncology, radiation oncology, pathology, radiology, and anesthesiology.

A tradition of attracting the foremost caregivers and the most respected researchers in the world makes Memorial Sloan-Kettering Cancer Center capable of developing and delivering the most effective treatments available in the care of cancer. It is the close collaboration between these physicians and scientists that gives the organization its unique strength, assuring that new research findings are appropriately and rapidly transferred from the laboratory directly to improving patient care.

But it is the focus on the patient as an individual that makes Memorial Sloan-Kettering truly remarkable. Patients receive care that is uniquely and specifically designed for them. At Memorial Sloan-Kettering, patients are people first.

BREAKTHROUGH CANCER CARE
Memorial Sloan-Kettering has long been known as a leading center for cancer surgery, having developed many of the methods commonly used to treat cancer today. The organization's professionals continue to refine these techniques to improve care, preserve function, and restore appearance. They have developed new chemotherapy drugs, and pioneered ways to make them safer and more effective. The center uses the most advanced

techniques to target radiotherapy precisely to tumor sites.

The hospital was the first center to establish a psychiatry service to help cancer patients and their families and friends cope with the illness. It was also the first to create a service focused

on alleviating cancer pain, as well as a genetic counseling service to help people at increased risk understand and deal with that risk.

There is increasing evidence that the specialized focus of an institution such as Memorial Sloan-Kettering benefits patients.

In a 1998 study published in the *Journal of the American Medical Association*, researchers from Memorial Sloan-Kettering Cancer Center found that mortality rates were 40 to 80 percent lower in hospitals that had the most experience performing a particular surgical procedure.

"Surgical management of a patient with cancer is learned and refined by practice and experience," says Dr. Murray Brennan, chairman of the department of surgery at Memorial Sloan-Kettering and coauthor of the paper. "The more experience the surgeon has in doing a specific procedure and managing patients with a specific cancer, the better the patient's chances that he or she will have a better outcome after the operation."

TEAM TREATMENT

A key advantage for patients at Memorial Sloan-Kettering is its interdisciplinary approach to cancer care. The hospital's disease management approach features teams of experts in many areas and modalities of treatment, with different teams focusing on a particular cancer. Each team has developed standards of care for its site of disease, arranged into treatment pathways for every type and stage of cancer, and reflecting the latest thinking and most advanced technology. The person who seeks help is treated by as many different specialists as needed for various aspects of his or her disease—although there is always one primary doctor who coordinates the patient's care.

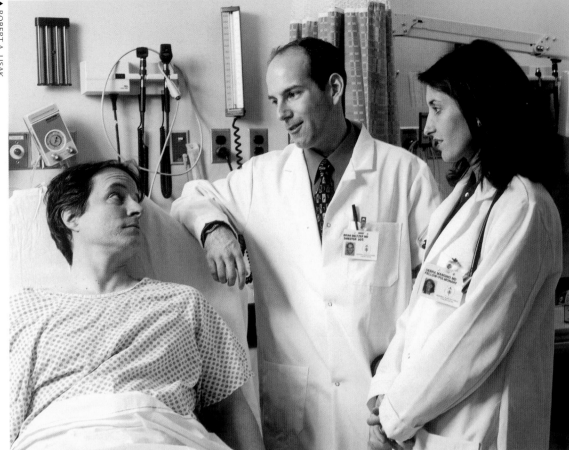

"Today, very few cancers are treated with a single modality such as surgery, chemotherapy, or radiation therapy," says Dr. William J. Hoskins, deputy physician in chief. "Instead, most cancers require combinations of therapy or multidisciplinary treatment. The disease management program centers on the needs of a patient with a particular kind of cancer. This has formalized and strengthened the multidisciplinary care that has long been a tradition at Memorial Sloan-Kettering."

Memorial Sloan-Kettering has 16 disease management teams, each specializing in one or more related diseases. Each team includes surgical, medical, and radiation oncologists, radiologists, pathologists, oncology nurses, and other health professionals as appropriate. These teams treat various aspects of a patient's disease. A 17th team solely provides screening and counseling for early detection and prevention of cancer in the general population.

In addition, the hospital has developed a sophisticated disease management system to evaluate and refine its therapies and provide the best care. This system is a powerful, state-of-the-art technological tool that supports the teams. This unique computer software system brings together data about a single patient from many sources and puts the comprehensive information where it's needed—at the fingertips of the person caring for a patient.

"Our disease management program allows us to care for our patients with the highest level of cancer treatment that can possibly be given," says Dr. David W. Golde, physician in chief, "to constantly improve and to find ways to make that treatment available on a global basis."

DR. BRIAN A. MELTZER, DIRECTOR OF THE URGENT CARE CENTER, SHARES HIS KNOWLEDGE AND VISION WITH CLINICAL FELLOW DR. DEBRA A. MANJINO.

PICTURED HERE IS THE RECEPTION AREA/WAITING ROOM FOR PATIENTS AT THE ROCKEFELLER OUTPATIENT PAVILION.

1889 INTERNATIONAL FLAVORS & FRAGRANCES, INC.

1890 PRICEWATERHOUSECOOPERS

1895 KEYSPAN ENERGY

1896 PARSONS SCHOOL OF DESIGN

1898 BRISTOL-MYERS SQUIBB

1903 LAZARE KAPLAN INTERNATIONAL INC.

1904 WILLIS

1909 CONDÉ NAST PUBLICATIONS

1911 MAIMONIDES MEDICAL CENTER

1913 EXECUTIVE HEALTH GROUP

1918 BENETAR BERNSTEIN SCHAIR & STEIN

1921 BERENSON & COMPANY LLP

1923 AMALGAMATED BANK OF NEW YORK

1923 IBJ WHITEHALL FINANCIAL GROUP

1923 YOUNG & RUBICAM INC.

INTERNATIONAL FLAVORS & FRAGRANCES, INC.

IN THE FIRMAMENT OF THE GLAMOROUS AND COMPETI-
tive New York fragrance industry—and beyond—
International Flavors & Fragrances, Inc. (IFF) is
a fixed star. The name behind many of the best-selling fragrances and flavored
foods around the world, this low-profile, high-impact global company has roots

INTERNATIONAL FLAVORS & FRAGRANCES' (IFF) WORLD HEADQUARTERS ON WEST 57TH STREET IN NEW YORK CITY, NOW ELEGANTLY RENOVATED, WAS ONCE HOME TO A GENERAL MOTORS WAREHOUSE (TOP).

IFF'S FLAVOR TECHNOLOGISTS HAVE A KEEN UNDERSTANDING OF THE COMPLEXITIES INVOLVED IN CREATING FOOD FLAVORS TO SATISFY CONSUMERS' TASTES BOTH LOCALLY AND GLOBALLY (BOTTOM).

in the flavor and fragrance business that go back to 1889. IFF became worldwide in 1959 with the merger of U.S.-based van Ameringen & Haebler, Inc. and European-based Polak & Schwartz. The company went public in 1961, and is one of the few corporations on the New York Stock Exchange that has increased its dividend annually for 38 consecutive years.

IFF is the leading creator and manufacturer of flavors and fragrances used in a wide variety of consumer products. It has retained its industry leadership by exploring the mystery of the senses, while creating commercially successful products for its customers.

Headquartered in an elegantly renovated former warehouse on West 57th Street in New York City, IFF owns and operates sales offices, manufacturing facilities, and creative laboratories in more than 35 countries, employing more than 4,600 people worldwide. With approximately 70 percent of its sales outside the United States, IFF recorded worldwide sales of $1.4 billion in 1998. Fragrance accounted for 58 percent of the company's worldwide sales, and flavors for 42 percent.

A FOUNDATION OF RESEARCH AND DEVELOPMENT

Historically, IFF has prided itself on having the world's largest research and development effort devoted exclusively to the senses of smell and taste. Nearly $100 million is spent annually on investigating how taste and smell translate into value-added products that increase market share.

IFF has been a pioneer in the invention of new and valuable aroma chemical molecules which have transformed the fragrance industry. Patented in the mid-1980s, IFF's Living Flower™ technology, which captures the aroma of a flower at its peak, changed forever the way fragrances are created. IFF researchers expanded the process to include Living Flavor™, capturing at their peak the authentic taste of fruits, vegetables, herbs, and spices.

Nearly 70 master perfumers in 10 creative centers worldwide search the globe for new sources of raw materials for fragrance. One recent expedition into the Amazon rain forest resulted in Neblina, an Yves Rocher holistic perfume that debuted in Paris in June 1999. Based on the Fragrance-of-Life™ Program, IFF scientists have developed a spectrum of scents other than flowers, such as sea breeze and crisp mountain air. IFF perfumers are already incorporating these into commercial fragrances.

Not content with just earthly exploration, IFF researchers sent the miniature rose plant Overnight Scentsation into space in 1998 on NASA's Space Shuttle Discovery with astronaut John Glenn to study the effects of microgravity on fragrance. A flower was chemically sampled with IFF's Solid Phase Micro-Extraction™ (SPME) technique, inserting a fiber needle into the living bloom to collect odorous molecules. IFF's scientists found that the fragrance of the miniature rose changed when it was grown in microgravity. The company predicts that the future of both fragrances and flavors will be enhanced by such research.

IFF's state-of-the-art greenhouse in New Jersey provides

three distinct environments—temperate, desert, and rain forest—where researchers use the Living Flower and other technologies to cultivate, analyze, and reproduce the flavors and aromas of rare plants and fruits from around the world.

Fine Fragrance Nonpareil

Soaps, detergents, and household products claim the majority of IFF's fragrance sales with a 43 percent share; fine fragrances and personal care products comprise 34 percent; and specialty fragrance ingredients make up 23 percent.

In recent years, the company has increased its global market share of the competitive fragrance industry to 17 percent, continuing in its role as the leading fragrance supplier in the world. In 1998, seven of the top 10 best-selling women's prestige fragrances were created by IFF, according to an independent market survey by NPD BeautyTrends. The Magnificent Seven included newer introductions such as Clinique's happy along with classics like Calvin Klein's Eternity and Estée Lauder's Beautiful. "The hallmark of IFF's fine fragrances is that they are truly creative and provide our customers with long-lived market franchises," remarks IFF Chairman and President Eugene P. Grisanti.

The company recognizes the global personal care market as a huge future growth area in many developing countries. One of its goals is to develop these markets over the next several years. IFF also provides high-quality specialty fragrance ingredients to customers and competitors alike; some of these ingredients are used exclusively by IFF.

Think Globally, Taste Locally

In an ethnically driven world market for flavors, IFF has kept ahead of its competition by adhering to the motto Think Globally, Taste Locally. With a worldwide network of flavorists and food technologists, the company is able to provide customers with products distinct to locations, ethnic preferences, and climatic variations anywhere in the world.

IFF flavors are sold to makers of dairy, meat, and other processed foods; beverages; snacks and savory foods; confectionery; sweet and baked goods; pharmaceutical and oral care products; and animal foods. About 55 percent of its flavors are used in beverages, dairy products, and baked goods, and 45 percent in savory and other applications. Much like creating a successful new perfume for a customer, IFF researchers seek out consumers' needs to come up with consumer-designed flavors that truly synergize with brand identity.

Corporate Citizenship

In 1968, with the Monell Foundation, IFF helped to establish the Monell Chemical Senses Center, which performs basic and applied research on taste and smell. Since 1981, IFF has supported the Olfactory Research Fund, of which it is a founding member. The fund's unique mission is to explore human response to odors in order to enhance the quality of life.

IFF employees and the IFF Foundation support a wide variety of charitable organizations—from the arts and sciences to such community-based organizations as hospitals and social service agencies—through monetary

contributions and volunteer work in the metropolitan New York area and around the world.

Looking Ahead

Setting its sights on the future, IFF is poised to retain its global position as the world's leading supplier of fragrances and flavors, while preparing for the challenges of the next millennium. An ever present goal for the company's fragrance business is its expansion in the world fragrance market. IFF's flavor business, going foward, must continue to offer innovative, tasteful solutions to a diverse and dynamic global marketplace driven by high consumer demand for convenience foods, multiethnic cuisines, and health foods.

At IFF's state-of-the-art greenhouse in New Jersey, researchers cultivate, analyze, and reproduce fragrances and flavors with flowers and plants from around the world (top).

Using IFF's proprietary Solid Phase Micro-Extraction™ technology, a perfumer captures a rare orchid's unique aroma in the Venezuelan rain forest (bottom).

PricewaterhouseCoopers

WHEN ONE OF THE WORLD'S MOST RESPECTED professional services firms launches its first branding campaign, it is not surprising that it showcases some of its most important, complex, and exciting projects. What is surprising is that the campaign's focus is not on the firm itself,

but on the people who work for the firm.

This is the central theme that drives PricewaterhouseCoopers' strategic branding campaign. "The principle underlying this theme is that our people, and the talented individuals we seek to join us, must use their knowledge and experience to make a difference," says James J. Schiro, CEO. "The ads embody our brand story by portraying our people sharing knowledge with clients to help solve challenging problems in the worlds in which we work together."

The brand strategy began on the first day of the dramatic July 1998 merger that created PricewaterhouseCoopers. Building on the legacy of two venerable firms—Price Waterhouse and Coopers & Lybrand—PricewaterhouseCoopers embarked on a mission to demonstrate that its people, processes, and ability to understand its clients' and the market's needs will help shape the future of business, and of the world.

"Our people's knowledge and their enthusiasm in providing the best service to the world-class businesses that constitute our clients are enabling us to become the visionary firm we aspire to be," says Nicholas G. Moore, chairman. "The front-edge thinking that is embodied in our people, our ability to leverage that reasoning for all of our employees around the world, and our success in using it to create value for clients will be what defines this new organization in the days and years ahead."

An Orientation for Service

PricewaterhouseCoopers, the world's largest professional services organization, helps its clients build value, manage risk, and improve performance. Drawing on the talents of more than 150,000 people in more than 150 countries, the firm provides a full range of business advisory services to leading global, national, and local companies and public institutions. These services include audit, accounting, and tax advice; management, information technology,

THE CENTRAL THEME OF PRICEWATERHOUSECOOPERS' STRATEGIC BRANDING CAMPAIGN IS ITS PEOPLE, NOT THE WORLD-RENOWNED COMPANY FOR WHICH THEY WORK. "THE PRINCIPLE UNDERLYING THIS THEME IS THAT OUR PEOPLE, AND THE TALENTED INDIVIDUALS WE SEEK TO JOIN US, MUST USE THEIR KNOWLEDGE AND EXPERIENCE TO MAKE A DIFFERENCE," SAYS JAMES J. SCHIRO, CEO. "THE ADS EMBODY OUR BRAND STORY BY PORTRAYING OUR PEOPLE SHARING KNOWLEDGE WITH CLIENTS TO HELP SOLVE CHALLENGING PROBLEMS IN THE WORLDS IN WHICH WE WORK TOGETHER." PICTURED HERE ARE STEVE E. MORGAN, ASSOCIATE (TOP); GRACE CHOPARD, PARTNER, AND HER MOTHER (BOTTOM); AND MICHAEL FLAHARTY, PARTNER (OPPOSITE).

and human resource consulting; financial advisory services, including mergers and acquisitions, business recovery, project finance, and litigation support; business process outsourcing services; and legal advice through a global network of affiliated law firms.

POWERFUL PROGRAMS IN NEW YORK

PricewaterhouseCoopers is proud of its extensive involvement in various community, cultural, and charitable organizations. Partners and staff in the New York metropolitan region, for example, are involved in many local programs, such as Everybody Wins and Streetwise Partners. Everybody Wins is a literacy and mentoring program; its volunteers read to public school children once a week during lunch. Streetwise Partners, a program held in conjunction with the Partnership for the Homeless, is another initiative in which the firm offers one-on-one

training to individuals between the ages of 18 and 60 who are currently on welfare. The training focuses on improving computer, math, grammar, and interviewing skills.

PricewaterhouseCoopers is also committed to the city of New York as a whole. Through its involvement with the New York City Partnership, PricewaterhouseCoopers works with the city's civic leaders and other businesses to help secure New York's position as the business capital of the world. This program promotes public and private action to make New York's school system the finest in the world; to build and rehabilitate the transportation, housing, and other infrastructure necessary to sustain New York's business preeminence; and to foster job creation and entrepreneurial activity while working to remove barriers to business growth.

"Our firm's commitment to New York is demonstrated by

the commitment of our people," says Frank Brown, managing partner of the New York office. "We are lucky to have the opportunity to donate our resources, and I am proud of the time and talent our partners and staff devote to making New York a better place."

IN SUPPORT OF ITS PEOPLE

Internally, the firm has many initiatives and programs that help staff balance work commitments and their personal lives. Dubbed WorkLife Effectiveness, the efforts in the New York practice include initiatives such as flexible work schedules, emergency child care (when regular child care arrangements are not available), and paid paternal leave. The New York office offers a program called Parenting Circles, a forum facilitated by child psychologists that addresses the issues of raising children while maintaining a career. The New York office also offers the WorkLife Seminar Series, a continuing monthly lunchtime series that addresses a variety of issues to help employees improve their business skills and balance their personal lives.

Given the firm's commitment to its people, it comes as no surprise that PricewaterhouseCoopers was placed on the 1999 Top 100 Companies list published by *Working Mother* magazine. The magazine cited the experience of one PricewaterhouseCoopers accountant who assumed she would be "mommy-tracked" after having her second child. Instead, she was tapped into a new mentoring program—and a year later made partner. Even more impressive is the fact that this partner still works part-time.

This is the reality of the firm's commitment to the well-being of its people, and is indicative of the firm's aim to become the employer of choice. To the new PricewaterhouseCoopers, success is not simply a result of corporate strategies and business practices, no matter how exceptional they are. To this unusual organization, true success comes from its people.

KeySpan Energy

KeySpan is the parent company of Brooklyn Union, the nation's fourth-largest natural gas utility, serving more than 1.6 million customers in New York City and Long Island. The company owns and operates more than 6,000 megawatts of electric power generation on Long Island and in New York City, and provides management of the electric transmission and distribution systems and customer services to the Long Island Power Authority's 1.1 million customers. Other KeySpan Energy companies market energy and provide energy facility design, construction, financing and management, appliance service, and energy equipment installation and repair. Through its subsidiaries and investments, KeySpan Energy has additional interests in natural gas exploration, production, processing, and storage. It has investments in a pipeline distribution system in Northern Ireland.

The organization is dedicated to providing excellent customer service at competitive costs to its customers, and it has a strong commitment to the communities it serves, from Staten Island to Montauk and beyond. As part of this commitment, its various companies seek to establish a legacy of environmental excellence throughout the Northeast, and have supported an intense program of economic development and community support that has received widespread attention through the years.

Historical Changes

KeySpan Energy was formed on May 28, 1998, in a merger of KeySpan Energy Corporation and certain businesses of the Long Island Lighting Company. But a look at the history that ultimately created one of the largest energy companies in the nation makes it clear why KeySpan Energy has had such a significant impact on the communities it serves.

The organization can trace its roots back to the early 19th century, when Brooklyn had only about 4,500 people. It was a place where civic-minded citizens worked hard to create the improvements that would in turn shape one of the fastest-growing places in America. After creating a bank and fire insurance company, Joseph Sprague and Alden Spooner applied to the state legislature to incorporate the Brooklyn Gas Light Company—only the fourth gas company chartered in the entire nation.

The firm illuminated the streets of Brooklyn with gas that it manufactured from coal, a radical technology for its day. During this time, the competition became fierce throughout Brooklyn and Queens, and gashouse gangs literally fought on the streets for territory. Eventually, seven different companies came together in 1895 to create Brooklyn Union, which was tough and smart enough to meet the needs of its communities for more than 10 decades as one

KEYSPAN ENERGY HAS A 64 PERCENT INTEREST IN THE HOUSTON EXPLORATION COMPANY, WHICH HAS A GAS WELL IN THE GULF OF MEXICO (TOP).

KEYSPAN ENERGY IS THE LARGEST INVESTOR-OWNED ELECTRIC GENERATION COMPANY IN NEW YORK STATE. ITS RAVENSWOOD PLANT IN QUEENS GENERATES APPROXIMATELY ONE-QUARTER OF THE CITY'S ELECTRICITY NEEDS ON THE HOTTEST DAYS OF SUMMER (BOTTOM).

f the leading gas distribution companies in the nation.

The original board of directors, which included William Rockefeller of the Standard Oil Company, named Civil War General James Jourdan as the first president. On the heels of that brutally competitive era, and with no regulation of the industry as yet, Jourdan had the daunting task of bringing all the separate factions together. He then had to develop an expanded residential and commercial market for manufactured gas—first from coal and then oil—while aggressively competing with the coal dealers who dominated energy at that time.

Through the years, the company continued to grow, dealing with the increasing competition from electricity, but managing to remain dominant with expansions in pipeline capacity, storage, technology, and the development of some significant gas supply projects over the years. The most dramatic project was the first transcontinental pipeline from the southwestern United States, carrying natural gas to the homes and businesses of Brooklyn, Queens, and Staten Island. This project created an extraordinary need for the company to change every single appliance utilizing gas in its 187-square-mile service area to accommodate the almost doubled Btus provided by natural gas, compared to the old manufactured product.

The 1950s also saw a real effort to educate the consumer on the advantages of gas. The organization was involved in home economics education in high schools, teaching girls how to cook with gas stoves, and it had demonstrations in its Brooklyn lobby to help housewives become comfortable with gas cooking.

THE GREATEST CHANGE

Today, deregulation is driving major change in the way KeySpan produces and delivers energy in North America. Natural gas deregulation began in the 1980s, followed recently by the gradual deregulation of the electric industry. The firm had a head start, helping the Public Service Commission to move more aggressively than most states to bring full customer choice to energy use. KeySpan will now be competing not just with other fuels, like oil, but with unregulated marketers as service providers. But deregulation—while deeply impacting many energy companies—is seen as an opportunity at KeySpan Energy. Just as the company throve in the highly competitive era at the beginning

ROBERT B. CATELL IS KEYSPAN'S CHAIRMAN AND CEO.

KEYSPAN ENERGY'S HEADQUARTERS (CENTER FOREGROUND), SYMBOLIZES THE RENEWAL OF DOWNTOWN BROOKLYN AND THE VITAL ROLE THAT THE COMPANY PLAYS IN THE ECONOMIC DEVELOPMENT OF NEW YORK CITY.

As a community-oriented company, KeySpan Energy participates in events such as the Row for a Cure to raise funds to find a cure for breast cancer.

KeySpan employees participate in Employee Appreciation Day at Shea Stadium in Queens. Teamwork at all levels of the company has resulted in excellent customer-satisfaction ratings (left).

A KeySpan control operator at Northport Power Station, one of five major generating plants operated by the company on Long Island (right)

of its history, it is doing it again —adapting to the changes in the business environment, utilizing the rich perspective of its history, spotting new ways to provide more energy to more customers, focusing on the customers, and proactively developing new, aggressive services to meet customer needs. KeySpan is now able to apply its considerable expertise to create a new kind of energy company, positioning itself to become a diverse, customer-focused, superregional energy company headquartered in New York. The KeySpan family of companies now includes natural gas distribution, electric system management, electric generation, unregulated energy services, exploration, production, transportation, and a full range of customer services.

"In achieving our vision of becoming a premier energy company, we believe value creation is paramount," says Robert B. Catell, chairman and CEO. "KeySpan's strategies work together to build our customer base, to provide the resources to supply the increased demand resulting from that larger base, and to take advantage of unique growth opportunities that add value for our customers and shareholders."

An Impressive Array of Services

KeySpan is an energy company that is growing its business in new and exciting ways, and taking advantage of significant opportunities for growth in a competitive environment for both natural gas and electricity.

The organization is truly a multifaceted energy company with more than $7.9 billion in assets, dedicated to serving growing markets in the Northeast

and pursuing energy-related investments in North American and international markets. It engages in several lines of business, from wellhead to burner tip, including natural gas distribution, pipeline transportation, electric generation, electric transmission and distribution services, oil and gas exploration and production, energy-related services, and energy related investments.

KeySpan Energy's core business is gas distribution, conducted by two subsidiaries—Brooklyn Union and Brooklyn Union of Long Island—which distribute gas to 1.6 million customers. The company is also a major and growing generator of electricity. It owns and operates 6,000 megawatts of generation in five large generating plants and 42 smaller facilities in Nassau and Suffolk counties on Long Island, and its recently purchased major facility

n Queens. Under contractual arrangements, KeySpan provides power, electric transmission and distribution services, billing, and other customer services for the approximately 1 million electric customers of the Long Island Power Authority. Other KeySpan subsidiaries are involved in pipelines, gas exploration, production and storage, wholesale and retail gas and electric marketing, appliance service, and large energy-system ownership, installation, and management. The organization also invests and participates in the development of pipelines and other energy projects, both domestically and internationally.

QUALITY OF SERVICE, QUALITY OF LIFE

KeySpan works to improve the quality of life in every aspect of its operations and endeavors in the communities it serves. The firm's vigorous area-development programs have helped to create affordable housing and revive neighborhoods and business districts throughout its territory.

"We see ourselves as an integral part of the community," says Catell. "As a premier energy company, KeySpan wants to identify opportunities to make meaningful contributions to enhance the well-being of the neighborhoods in which we do business."

KeySpan's Cinderella Program has been in place since the 1960s, providing grants for facade and landscape improvements to residential structures and retail stores on commercial strips in downtown areas. This preserves and promotes communities in the

Greater New York City area. The program began with the rehabilitation of Victorian-era brownstone buildings in Brooklyn that had once been among New York's finest. Today, Cinderella is the only corporate program in the New York metropolitan area that awards grants to individuals and community groups to renovate the facades of residential and commercial storefront buildings. These grants are often used with state and city programs to leverage private funds for development.

The company has recently established the KeySpan Foundation, which it endowed with $20 million to award grants to not-for-profit charitable organizations dedicated to education, environmental preservation, the arts, community development, and health and human services. In one of its programs, it joined forces with General Colin Powell to marshal support for business-education partnerships in New York, providing a grant to Junior Achievement New York to further its work in teaching young people to understand business and economics, and the value of education for succeeding in life.

Through partnerships with civic organizations and educators, KeySpan helps the disadvantaged and generates jobs. And it is extending many programs already in place in New York City to Long Island to demonstrate the firm's commitment to the community.

Recently, KeySpan employees and the KeySpan Foundation contributed more than $1.1 million to the United Way, making the company one of the top five

contributors in all of New York City. The company's culture encourages community involvement, and its employees have long supported philanthropic causes, such as serving as mentors to city school children, and bringing meals to the homebound and elderly.

As an organization so thoroughly committed to the welfare of the communities it serves, KeySpan has had a successful history and is ready to face all the challenges of the future. "As we continue to build the KeySpan Energy brand in the new millennium, we are confident that KeySpan Energy is ready to face the challenges of the changing energy marketplace," says Catell. "We know change is constant—but, with an excellent management team, a clear vision, outstanding technological expertise, and dedicated employees, we believe we can be successful."

CLOCKWISE FROM TOP LEFT: KEYSPAN ENERGY IS BUILDING ON A TRADITION OF A CUSTOMER SERVICE FIRST ESTABLISHED BY ITS PRINCIPAL SUBSIDIARY, BROOKLYN UNION, MORE THAN 100 YEARS AGO.

THE GROWING USE OF NATURAL-GAS-POWERED VEHICLES IS HELPING NEW YORK CITY AND LONG ISLAND TO IMPROVE THE QUALITY OF THEIR AIR.

KEYSPAN IS ON THE CUTTING EDGE OF TECHNOLOGY TO PROVIDE THE BEST POSSIBLE SERVICE TO ITS CUSTOMERS.

KEYSPAN'S EMPLOYEES HAVE A NOTEWORTHY RECORD OF COMMUNITY SERVICE. THEY DEVOTE TIME TO COMMUNITY ORGANIZATIONS AND DELIVER MEALS TO THE ELDERLY AND INFIRM THROUGH MEALS ON HEELS.

PARSONS SCHOOL OF DESIGN

ARSONS SCHOOL OF DESIGN IS TODAY A GLOBAL EDUCATION center for art and design. It strives toward its original mission of offering a superior education with the same vigor and dedication that accompanied its founding more than a century ago. In 1896, William Merritt Chase founded the Chase School

primarily as a painting atelier. Later, Frank Alvah Parsons led the school to recognize the role of good design in fulfilling the demands of the Industrial Revolution. In 1907, the Chase School became the New York School of Fine and Applied Arts, and in 1941, it was renamed the Parsons School of Design in honor of its prophetic faculty member, Frank Alvah Parsons. The school's early aim—to educate in an age of ever changing technology—set it apart from other design schools of the day. Today, H. Randolph Swearer, the current dean, leads Parsons toward that same goal.

A testament to Parsons' success is a long list of noteworthy and influential graduates. Among them are fashion designers Donna Karan and Isaac Mizrahi, fashion photographer Stephen Meisel, illustrator Peter de Seve, interior designers Albert Hadley and Juan Montoya, graphic designer Paul Rand, painters Jasper Johns and Edward Hopper, and Claire McCardle, the "mother" of ready-to-wear.

In 1970, Parsons became a division of New School University. Known for its forward-looking leaders in the social sciences, the New School offers Parsons stu-

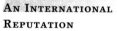

dents its reputation for scholarship in addition to the professional experience of a design school. Students have the opportunity to study a variety of subjects with faculty members and classmates from different cultural backgrounds and varying educational interests.

The school grants a variety of degrees, including a bachelor of fine arts in architectural design, communication design, fashion design, illustration, interior design, photography, and product design; a bachelor of business administration in design marketing; a master of fine arts in painting,

sculpture, and design and technology; a master of architecture; a master of arts in the history of decorative arts; and a master of arts in lighting design.

AN INTERNATIONAL REPUTATION

With an extraordinary curriculum, Parsons has attracted a large and growing student body; enrollment increased by 17 percent between 1994 and 1999. It enrolls 2,400 undergraduate students, 300 graduate students, and 2,000 continuing education students annually, making it one of the largest degree-granting art and design colleges in the nation.

Students come to Parsons from all across the United States and from more than 60 countries—one-third of the student body is comprised of international students. All have come to New York for the unique education that Parsons can provide.

Parsons maintains international design relationships. Many students and faculty members participate in foreign exchange programs with other art and design schools. Global destinations include Parsons Paris; Kanazawa International Design Institute (KIDI) in Japan; the Design School at Altos de Chavon, Dominican Republic; the Samsung Art and

CLOCKWISE FROM TOP:
LOCATED IN NEW YORK, PARSONS SCHOOL OF DESIGN OFFERS VALUABLE PROFESSIONAL OPPORTUNITIES TO ITS STUDENTS, SUCH AS AN INTERNSHIP AT ABC FOR DESIGN MARKETING STUDENT PATRICIA PERDICARO.

INTEGRATING LIBERAL ARTS WITH STUDIO ACTIVITIES, PARSONS PRODUCES ARTISTS WHO GENERATE SMART DESIGN, SUCH AS ASTRID LEWIS.

COMPUTERS USED TO DESIGN PRODUCTS AND BUILD PRECISE MODELS EXEMPLIFY PARSONS' COMMITMENT TO AN EVOLVING CURRICULUM AND FACILITIES TO SET THE PACE OF TECHNOLOGY IN THE DESIGN PROFESSIONS.

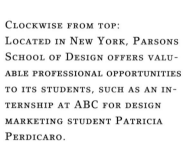

MATTHEW SEPTIMUS

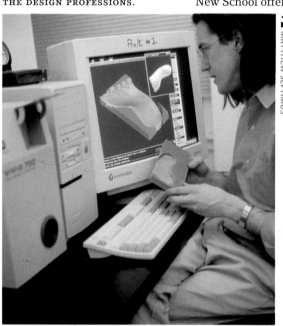

▲ JONATHAN CANNON

Design Institute (SADI) in South Korea; and others.

MANHATTAN STYLE

Located on Manhattan's Fifth Avenue, Parsons is in the heart of historic Greenwich Village. The neighborhood offers students a perfect environment to absorb New York City style, culture, and fashion. The city itself is a center of culture, commerce, and communications, and allows students to strengthen and nurture their imagination. The campus is minutes away from New York's many world-renowned galleries, museums, professional art stores, multimedia corporations, and advertising agencies. In addition, theaters, museums, and concert halls are easily accessible and serve to broaden students' range of influences.

New York offers the best professional opportunities to Parsons students. Industry partnerships with large companies such as MTV, Disney, Sony, Kellogg, Nickelodeon, and IBM help expose students to the real world of designing and its challenges—fixed budgets, deadlines, and professional techniques and materials. By offering such work opportunities, Parsons gives its students an edge toward becoming industry leaders.

By integrating liberal arts with studio activities, the school produces artists who not only generate great designs, but who work to improve situations and create innovations. At Parsons, students are educated to be well versed in all aspects of critical thinking— in other words, to be artists and designers who understand their roles in society.

LOOKING TO THE FUTURE

Moving into the new millennium, Parsons looks ahead to a time of innovation and design excellence. The Center for New Design, which was launched in September 1999, will focus on the need to reinvent design—on how design will affect business and vice versa, and how design can be taught in an atmosphere of change and transition.

With a history that spans more than a century, Parsons could be considered an old school. In reality, it is reestablishing its educational goals to meet the needs of the new era, just as it did at the turn of the last century. Parsons' mission is to shift its curriculum and facilities to serve changes in demographics, economics, culture, technology, and the design profession itself.

THIS STUDENT DEMONSTRATES HER PLANS FOR THE HOTEL SUITE OF THE FUTURE FOR A COMPETITION JUDGED BY BARRY STERNLICHT (SEATED AT LEFT), CEO OF STARWOOD HOTELS AND RESORTS (LEFT).

STUDENTS HAVE THE OPPORTUNITY TO STUDY A VARIETY OF DESIGN SUBJECTS, INCLUDING COMPUTER ANIMATION (RIGHT).

▲ MATTHEW SEPTIMUS

ANDREW ZUMWALT-HATHAWAY (LEFT), AN ARCHITECTURAL DESIGN STUDENT, AND MICHAEL GORDON (RIGHT), A PRODUCT DESIGN STUDENT, ARE SOON TO JOIN THE DISTINGUISHED LIST OF PARSONS GRADUATES. PARSONS IS ONE OF THE LARGEST DEGREE-GRANTING ART AND DESIGN COLLEGES IN THE NATION.

BRISTOL-MYERS SQUIBB

BRISTOL-MYERS SQUIBB—HEADQUARTERED ON PARK Avenue in New York City—is one of the largest companies in the world. It boasts 64 product lines with annual global sales of more than $50 million, including 36 product lines with more than $100 million in annual sales. Its products can be found in virtually every country around the world, and include the highest-quality pharmaceuticals, consumer medicines, beauty and personal care products, nutritionals, and medical devices.

Numbers seldom tell much of a story, even if the numbers are immense. To say a company has more than $18 billion in annual sales certainly speaks to its success, but that doesn't begin to talk about the impact its products have on the millions of people around the world who depend on them every day.

The real story is the young woman in New Jersey whose doctor has prescribed a new and powerful drug, TAXOL® (paclitaxel), that could help her win the fight against breast cancer. Or the five-year-old boy who lost one leg to a rare form of infection, but hopes not to suffer a second amputation thanks to a wound care technology that helped close a devastating injury on his other leg. Or the people of Brazil who see a partner in Bristol-Myers Squibb to help them safeguard a tract of wetlands that is one of the most biologically diverse places on earth.

A MISSION WITH A GLOBAL VISION

"Our mission is to extend and enhance human life," says Charles A. Heimbold, Jr., chairman and chief executive officer of Bristol-Myers Squibb. "That's our purpose on the planet. We are always mindful of that mission and of the values that underlie it every step of the way."

Starting with a dream, a handful of people, and $5,000 in capital, William McLaren Bristol and John Ripley Myers founded their company in upstate New York in 1887 to sell quality medicines directly to doctors. The two partners were always adamant that the company's products were exactly what the catalog said: "Our various preparations contain precisely the articles designated in the formulae, no costly drugs being omitted or replaced in order to meet the competition of irresponsible manufacturers. The utmost care is taken in the selection of the crude drugs, and none but of a known standard of strength are used." By the end of 1889, nine people were on the $32 weekly payroll; not long after that, the company moved to Syracuse, a major railroad center, for better shipping facilities; in May 1898, the firm moved to Brooklyn and took the name Bristol-Myers Company.

In 1858, another man destined to make his mark in business history—Dr. Edward Robinson Squibb—began building the great pharmaceutical company that would bear his name. A perfectionist and idealist at a time when the drugs dispensed by physicians and pharmacists were dangerously imperfect, Squibb dedicated his life—and his new firm—to the production of consistently pure medicines. For many years, numerous Squibb products were manufactured in Brooklyn.

From the beginning, both companies grew steadily, expanding their abilities to improve the health and well-being of people everywhere, and increasing in value to those who invested their money and trust in them. In 1989, Bristol-Myers Company and Squibb Corporation joined forces in what was at that time one of the largest—and what later would be considered one of the most successful—mergers in the industry.

Today, Bristol-Myers Squibb is one of the leading diversified health and personal care companies in the world, with a reputation for growth, innovation, and ex-

OVER ITS LONG HISTORY, BRISTOL-MYERS SQUIBB HAS MARKETED A WIDE RANGE OF WELL-KNOWN CONSUMER BRANDS, FROM SQUIBB'S DENTAL CREAM AND IPANA TOOTHPASTE, TO HERBAL ESSENCES, ENFAMIL, AND EXCEDRIN.

COURTESY OF NYT PICTURES

ellence. Its growth has come from the creation of world-class health, beauty, and personal care product franchises that represent the finest in research, discovery, and development. The company has expanded through strategic alliances, acquisitions, mergers, licensing arrangements, and prudent and productive business collaborations. Some of the well-known names that are now part of the Bristol-Myers Squibb family include Clairol, Mead Johnson, Westwood, ConvaTec, the UPSA Group in France, Matrix Essentials, and Zimmer.

Financially, Bristol-Myers Squibb has proved to be very successful. At the end of 1998, the company's market value exceeded $133 billion, making the organization one of the top 15

publicly traded companies worldwide in terms of market value. Diluted earnings per share grew 14 percent in 1998 to $1.79, and total return to stockholders reached 43 percent. The company has consistently paid dividends since going public almost 70 years ago, and has increased those payments for each of the past 27 years. Its financial strength is also evidenced by the fact that it is one of only eight U.S. industrial companies with a triple-A credit rating from both Moody's and Standard & Poor's.

RESEARCH IS THE FOUNDATION

The heart of any sustained success in the health and personal care products fields is innovation through substantial investment in research and development.

With research funding of more than $1 billion for each of the last eight years, the organization's scientists, technicians, and support staff have helped make Bristol-Myers Squibb a world leader in many areas.

Bristol-Myers Squibb is a global leader in medicines to fight cancer; hip and knee replacements; infant formulas; hair products; and ostomy and modern wound care products. It is also recognized for its strong leadership in therapies for cardiovascular, central nervous system, dermatological, metabolic and infectious diseases, including AIDS; consumer medicines; and other personal care products.

Spearheading the company's research efforts is the Pharmaceutical Research Institute (PRI), with facilities in the United States, Japan, Canada, Europe, and Russia. The PRI scientists are at the forefront in the quest for new drugs to fight cancer; pain; diseases of the cardiovascular, metabolic, and immune systems; infectious and dermatological illnesses; and disorders of the central nervous system. The PRI also has begun to look for better treatment for illnesses of the respiratory and urological systems as well. The company is also involved in numerous collaborations with other biomedical research institutions and biotechnology companies.

THE SPACE SHUTTLE DISCOVERY THAT CARRIED JOHN GLENN FOR NINE DAYS IN THE FALL OF 1998 ALSO CONTAINED PHARMACEUTICAL RESEARCH EXPERIMENTS DESIGNED BY BRISTOL-MYERS SQUIBB SCIENTISTS.

FINDING RELEVANT AND SUSTAINABLE SOLUTIONS FOR THE MANAGEMENT OF HIV/AIDS THROUGH THE COMPANY'S $100 MILLION SECURE THE FUTURE® PROGRAM WILL HELP THE WOMEN AND CHILDREN OF SUB-SAHARAN AFRICA, AS WELL AS OTHER COUNTRIES, TOWARD A MORE PROMISING FUTURE.

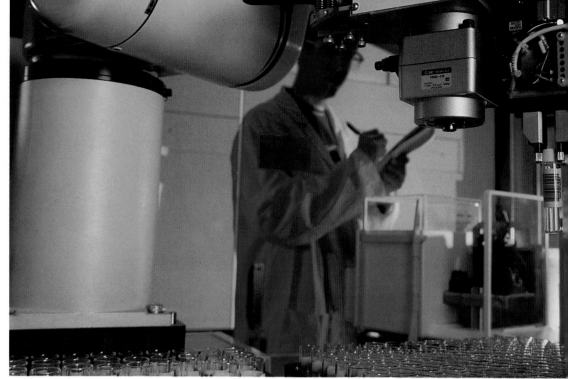

ROBOTS HAVE ELIMINATED PAINS-
TAKING LABOR AT THE LAB BENCH.
HERE, A ROBOTIC ARM AUTOMATI-
CALLY WEIGHS AND DISPENSES DRY
COMPOUNDS FOR STORAGE IN THE
HAYSTACK SYSTEM AT THE PRI IN
WALLINGFORD, CONNECTICUT—
ACCOMPLISHING THE TASK MORE
ACCURATELY AND THOUSANDS OF
TIMES FASTER THAN USING HUMAN
HANDS.

MEAD JOHNSON'S WORLDWIDE
LEADERSHIP IN NUTRITION CAN BE
TRACED BACK NEARLY A CENTURY.
YEARS LATER, THE COMPANY CON-
TINUES TO INCREASE ITS NUMBER
ONE POSITION IN INFANT NUTRITION
AND IS A WORLD LEADER IN CREAT-
ING MAJOR NEW BUSINESSES IN
OTHER CONSUMER NUTRITIONAL
CATEGORIES (BOTTOM LEFT).

IN THE UNITED STATES, BRISTOL-
MYERS SQUIBB WORKS TO ENSURE
THAT EVERY PATIENT WHO NEEDS
PHARMACEUTICAL PRODUCTS HAS
ACCESS TO THEM BY INSTITUTING
PROACTIVE PROGRAMS THAT CAN
BE EASILY AND RAPIDLY ACCESSED
BY PHYSICIANS AND HOSPITALS
(BOTTOM RIGHT).

LEADERSHIP STARTS WITH PEOPLE

About 54,000 talented people
make up the extended Bristol-
Myers Squibb family. These dedicated employees can be found on
nearly every continent on the
globe, working in research, sales,
education, manufacturing, management, and many other areas.
The company's strength derives
from the unique contributions
that each employee brings to the
organization's mission.

"Developing leadership at every level is the top priority of our
company," says Heimbold, "and
to be a successful leader in our
organization, you must be continually creating other leaders.
You exert enormous influence
on an organization through the
people you develop and put into
leadership positions. That
influence is probably greater
than anything you can accomplish as an individual. But there's
no single prototype for the kind
of person who can lead. We all
have different experiences and
perspectives to bring to the table,
and it's that richness that's so
tremendously valuable when
you're operating in a global
marketplace."

The firm's commitment to a
diverse global leadership team is
the driving force behind its ability
to attract and retain the best and
brightest people. Together they
constitute the company's single
greatest asset. To protect that
asset, Bristol-Myers Squibb is
committed not only to maintaining
a diverse workforce, but also to
providing a flexible work environment that accommodates the varied needs of all its employees,
helping them find the right balanc
between their personal and professional lives. A variety of work
life/home life programs are offere
including flexible work arrangements and on-site and backup chil
care centers. And TeamShare, th
Bristol-Myers Squibb employee
stock option program, gives employees at every level an even
greater stake in the company's
future success.

Recently, the depth of the
company's commitment to its
employees was recognized by
two tough critics—*Working
Mother* and *Working Woman*
magazines—which included the
firm on their lists of top employers in the United States.

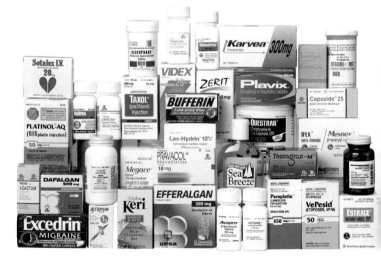

"Everybody should have access to the best medicines that are available," says Heimbold. "If they can't afford those medicines, we work to find ways to get them to them."

In the United States, for example, Bristol-Myers Squibb's Patient Assistance programs provide an opportunity for physician practices and hospitals throughout the country to ensure that indigent patients have access to certain critical medicines. More than 0,000 people received medications valued at more than $35 million without charge through these programs in 1998 alone.

But this is only the start of the company's commitment to public service, a commitment that is explicitly outlined in the Bristol-Myers Squibb Pledge. Among other things, the Pledge commits the company to "conscientious citizenship" and "a helping hand for worthwhile causes," as well as to "the higher standard of moral and ethical behavior."

In sub-Saharan Africa, where HIV/AIDS has devastated societies already overburdened by poverty, the company has committed $100 million over five years to help advance research and provide community support. Called Secure the Future®, this program represents the largest corporate commitment of its kind in the world.

Through its philanthropic giving programs, the Bristol-Myers Squibb Foundation has committed more than $80 million since 1977 in unrestricted funding for biomedical research. This funding has supported five-year grants of up to $500,000 each to more than 180 institutions around the world. In 1998, the Foundation committed more than $25 million to help fund a variety of charitable causes. Among the most significant are educational programs in women's health, science education, and community support programs in central and eastern Europe, China, and the United States. The company— through its Foundation—has also donated more than $30 million in medicines and other products to people in need across the world.

The company has been very active in supporting New York City and its diverse cultural life, including providing money to rebuild a beloved New York synagogue in its neighborhood that was destroyed by fire, and regularly underwriting a variety of arts and cultural programs.

THE NEXT CENTURY

Bristol-Myers Squibb has a wide range of promising medicines ready for launch, pending FDA approval, or recently launched, including Vanlev, a novel breakthrough cardiovascular agent initially for the treatment of hypertension; Orzel, an oral treatment for colorectal cancer; and Tequin, an advanced quinolone antibiotic for a variety of common infections. The firm has entered into an agreement with nine other pharmaceutical companies to work together to gain a better understanding of the biological basis of disease, and thereby work toward developing more and even better treatments than are available today. Other products in the company's rich research pipe-

line include an HIV protease inhibitor, a neuroprotective agent for stroke, and several important anti-cancer compounds, to name a few.

Looking ahead, Heimbold sees great challenges and opportunities for Bristol-Myers Squibb. "Thanks largely to painstaking and costly research, we and others in the pharmaceutical industry have made tremendous advances against diseases like cancer and AIDS," he says.

"But serious challenges remain, like antibiotic-resistant infections and stubborn forms of cancer. I'm optimistic, however, that with increasing levels of investment in R&D—and with the even greater commitment of our 55,000 employees—Bristol-Myers Squibb will continue to blaze new trails in the field of medicine, and fulfill the company's mission to extend and enhance human life, making a difference for all time," says Heimbold.

GENOMICS HAS THE POTENTIAL TO REVOLUTIONIZE HOW BRISTOL-MYERS SQUIBB DOES PHARMACEUTICAL RESEARCH AND DEVELOPMENT. THE COMPANY HAS ESTABLISHED ITSELF AS AN INDUSTRY LEADER IN THIS FAST-GROWING FIELD, WHICH FOCUSES ON HOW THE BODY'S 100,000 GENES WORK IN CONCERT (LEFT).

COMPANY SCIENTISTS USE GENETICALLY ENGINEERED YEAST TO MORE ACCURATELY PINPOINT THEIR DRUG DEVELOPMENT EFFORTS (RIGHT).

LAZARE KAPLAN INTERNATIONAL INC.

ICHELANGELO TOOK A PIECE OF MARBLE, AND BY CUTting and polishing away all that didn't belong, allowed the perfection of the *David* to emerge. That's exactly the process Lazare Kaplan International Inc. goes through to create diamonds that sparkle with dazzling fire—diamonds that merit being called "ideal cut" Lazare Diamonds®.

It takes a phenomenal level of expertise to take a rough diamond and transform it into a cut jewel. Emerging from the earth as translucent pebbles, rough diamonds bear little resemblance to the finished product. Only through careful cutting and polishing does a diamond acquire the coveted characteristics of sparkle, fire, and brilliance.

As Lazare Kaplan once said, "The diamond is the gem that can render the most brilliance—sapphires and rubies are beautiful for their color, but with the diamond, the reflection is its beauty and that is why the cut is so important."

In 1919, a cousin of Kaplan's developed a mathematical formula for cutting diamonds to precise angles and proportions to gain the optimum reflection and refraction of light. Lazare Kaplan adapted that ideal cut theory in that same year, and was the first to cut a diamond to ideal proportions. Lazare Kaplan (the company named for its founder) is still today devoted to the art of cutting the most beautiful diamonds in the world.

Because more of the rough stone must be cut away to achieve such perfection, the ideal cut is costlier to produce than other diamonds. Additionally, the manufacturing process demands a much higher level of skill on the part of the diamond cutter. So rigorous and demanding is the process that only 1 percent of the world's diamonds are ideal cut. Ideal cut Lazare Diamonds quickly became the standard of excellence in diamond craftsmanship. Today, Lazare Kaplan is the oldest and largest manufacturer of these diamonds in the world.

A REPUTATION FOR EXCELLENCE

Founded in 1903, Lazare Kaplan has built a reputation for strict quality control in all aspects of production and grading. Integrity, professionalism, and skilled craftsmanship established the company as the premier manufacturer and marketer of diamonds in the United States, and one of the most respected in the world.

In 1984, majority control of Lazare Kaplan was acquired by Maurice and Leon Tempelsman, and in recent years—despite fierce competition in the U.S. market— the company has experienced tremendous sales growth, a testament to its continuing commitment to quality. The only publicly traded diamond company, Lazare Kaplan is listed on the American Stock Exchange under the symbol LKI, and had sales of more than $260 million in its fiscal year 1999.

"Three factors have contributed to our recent growth," says Leon Tempelsman, Lazare Kaplan's vice chairman and president. "As we have increased our sources and supply of diamonds, we've also broadened our distribution to include more overseas markets. These changes in operations, along with our continued commit-ment to maintain the highest standards in quality control for diamond cutting, have positioned Lazare Kaplan for growth well into the next century."

Lazare Kaplan diamonds are available through a network of more than 1,500 upscale retail jewelers in the United States, Canada, Europe, and the Far East. The stones are sold both as loose unmounted diamonds, individually identified and weighed, and as beautifully finished jewelry.

Asking for Lazare Kaplan diamonds by name assures retail jewelers that they are getting stones of the highest quality. Because every diamond is cut to ideal proportions, absolute consistency is assured, and the strict tolerances that govern color and clarity grading of the stones are a further assurance of integrity.

BRAND IDENTITY

Traditionally, diamonds have been sold as a commodity. Brilliance, sparkle, and fire were the concerns of only the unusual few with an education in diamond-cutting aesthetics. Most buying decisions were based on size and price.

But Lazare Kaplan's philosophy is that diamonds represent something unique and precious, and that the finest diamonds are a symbol of the absolute best that nature and man can create together. The company believes that a knowledgeable consumer will understand and appreciate the value of its stones—both real and intrinsic—and that a good education will also alleviate much of the uncertainty in buying a diamond.

Toward this end, Lazare Kaplan does two things: First, the firm educates consumers through an extensive worldwide communications program designed to show people what comprises the best diamonds. Second, Lazare Kaplan identifies

LAZARE KAPLAN INTERNATIONAL INC. HAS CREATED A UNIQUE, LIMITED-EDITION DIAMOND THAT HERALDS THE NEW MILLENNIUM. AS VALUABLE, LIMITED-EDITION WORKS OF ART, LD 2000 MILLENNIUM LAZARE DIAMONDS ARE NUMBERED AND RESPECTIVELY INSCRIBED IN A SPECIAL SERIES.

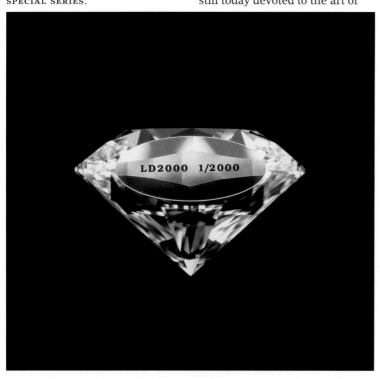

LD2000 1/2000

ach ideal cut diamond it creates s a Lazare Diamond.

Simply, Lazare Kaplan brands ts diamonds. Using its patented aser inscription technique, the ompany inscribes the Lazare Kaplan logo and an individual dentification number on the circumference of each ideal cut diamond over 1/5 carat. Invisible to the naked eye, the inscription an be seen with a jeweler's magnifying loupe. This brand ignature serves as a proof of authenticity and ownership, providing greater security not only n case of loss or theft, but also when the stone is cleaned or reset. But, most important, the inscripion serves as positive proof of authenticity and ownership.

To further brand identity, Lazare Kaplan launched a vigorous advertising campaign. The My Lazare Diamond™ national ads differ from conventional jewelry advertising, showing a floating diamond glowing vibrantly where an actual ring or earring would be. Through a first-person voice, the ads create a reason for the consumer to ask for a Lazare Diamond. Lazare Kaplan's marketing director, Marcee Feinberg, says, "When buying an engagement ring, many women and men focus on the mounting or gold component. In reality, 80 to 90 percent of the cost in buying a diamond ring goes into the diamond. That's what we are emphasizing; that's why we believe the focus should be on selecting the best and most beautiful diamond."

NEW FOR THE MILLENNIUM
Lazare Kaplan has also created a unique, limited-edition diamond that heralds the new millennium. As valuable, limited-edition works of art, LD 2000 Millennium Lazare Diamonds are numbered and respectively inscribed in a special series. Adding to the excitement of this once-in-a-lifetime opportunity, Lazare has announced the LD 2001—a 2.00-carat, flawless Lazare Diamond, valued in excess of $30,000—which will become the prize possession of a lucky millennium sweepstakes winner.

"Our diamonds set the standard in our industry, and so do our communications programs," says Tempelsman. "Making more people aware that the Lazare Kaplan name is the symbol of quality and integrity in diamonds is essential to our continued growth in the decades to come."

EAR ADMIRAL GRACE HOPPER ONCE SAID, "A SHIP IN port is safe, but that is not what ships are built for." In other words, no one ever discovered anything sitting in the same, safe place. It is in exploring the unknown where all discovery, growth, and meaningful success come from. No business that

hopes to grow, succeed, or lead can afford to shrink from the untried and the unfamiliar.

The key to succeeding in new ventures is to effectively imagine the kinds of risks that will be found, in order to prepare for them. This is risk management, determining what it takes to be reasonably prepared to face the unknown. That means not being burdened with over-preparation, not spending too much for things that are extremely unlikely. And certainly not being underprepared or unprotected against probable contingencies.

Willis is a leader in insurance brokerage that specializes in the extremely sophisticated and demanding field of risk management consulting. The company offers comprehensive insurance and risk management services to help its clients master the challenges of an ever changing world. Whether assessing loss expo-

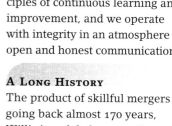

sures, recommending risk control measures, negotiating insurance, designing risk financing plans, or facilitating claims settlements, Willis professionals work as partners with their clients to integrate risk management practices within the client's broader business goals.

"We focus all our attention on listening to and understanding our clients' needs," says John J. Kelly, chairman and CEO of Willis Risk Solutions. "We act as a fiercely competitive team of accountable, empowered individuals, committed to the principles of continuous learning and improvement, and we operate with integrity in an atmosphere of open and honest communication.

A LONG HISTORY

The product of skillful mergers going back almost 170 years, Willis is a global corporation with a respected presence in world insurance markets, a rich heritage of service, and the vitality of a young and growing firm.

Willis Faber & Dumas originated in London in the early 1800s as one of the first Lloyd's brokerage firms. In New York, R.A. Corroon & Co. was established in 1904, which became Corroon & Black in 1966, and by 1989, had grown to be the fifth-largest insurance brokerage in America. In 1990, its merger with Willis Faber & Dumas created the Willis Corroon Group, and after a major investment by Kohlberg, Kravis Roberts & Co., a leading private equity investment firm, Willis once again became a private company—the largest privately

"WE FOCUS ALL OUR ATTENTION ON LISTENING TO AND UNDERSTANDING OUR CLIENTS' NEEDS," SAYS JOHN J. KELLY, CHAIRMAN AND CEO OF WILLIS RISK SOLUTIONS.

COO OF WILLIS NEW YORK JAMES MURPHY (LEFT) AND PRESIDENT AND CEO OF WILLIS NEW YORK GARRETT A. MATHIESON HELP MAKE THE NEW YORK CITY OFFICE THE FLAGSHIP OF THE ORGANIZATION'S NORTHEAST REGION.

WILLIS RISK SOLUTIONS' RISK
MANAGEMENT TEAM OPERATES
WITH INTEGRITY IN AN ATMO-
SPHERE OF OPEN AND HONEST
COMMUNICATION.

eld insurance broker in the
orld.

Today, Willis has more than
50 offices in key international
ommercial centers, and more
an 9,400 employees linked by
he latest electronic mail and
atabase technology. The firm
erves a diverse client base, with
iterests and assets located
round the world. In 1998, rev-
nues were $1.1 billion and pre-
iium volume was $14 billion.

The New York City office is
he flagship of the organization's
ortheast Region, with offices in
ew York, Massachusetts,
onnecticut, New Jersey, New
Iampshire, and Pennsylvania.
he region's 550 employees pro-
ide full-service support for an
rray of clients who represent
he full range of private and pub-
c enterprise, including real estate,
ospitality, financial institutions,
onstruction, chemical/pharma-
eutical, consumer products, and
nedia.

JEW YORK SERVICE

Villis' New York office is orga-
ized into permanent groups of
ccount executives, brokers, and
dministrative staff who work
losely to manage a client's busi-
ess. Each client is assigned its
wn team, comprised of the pro-

fessionals in each field required
to manage its unique account.
The account executive is personally responsible to the client for
the team's efforts and directs
both the strategy and the work.

Each year, the account team
and the client's managers conduct
a stewardship review. There,
they sit down with the client, assess the past year, and develop a
plan for the coming year that
specifies goals and completion
dates, outlines activities, and reinforces the relationship. This
plan is reviewed in quarterly
meetings and summarized in an
annual stewardship presentation.

Willis tailors each and every
service and program to address
its clients' individual needs, and
assesses the results to refine
future efforts. The compliment
Willis most values is when a client
singles the firm out as a key ingredient for its success.

In order to enhance this dedication, Willis has recently under-
gone a significant and far-reaching
program of change during its
transformation to a private company. This has served to refocus
the firm's attention and energies
to an even greater level of client
service. Part of this change has
included a knowledge management initiative that will enable
the firm to retrieve the vast store
of information and knowledge
accumulated over the company's
long history, and apply it in every
situation where it can assist in
providing a client solution.

"We believe in providing the
broadest possible risk management service that will include a
solution to a problem, rather than
just pure advice," says Willis New
York CEO Garrett A. Mathieson.

This kind of client service has
distinguished Willis for nearly two
centuries, and ensures its continued success in the increasingly
important field of risk management
for many years to come.

EXECUTIVE VICE PRESIDENT
OF WILLIS NEW YORK RICHARD
A. LOUGHLIN (LEFT) AND SENIOR
VICE PRESIDENT AND DIRECTOR OF
WILLIS RISK SOLUTIONS ROBERT
F. WALKER MAKE WILLIS A LEADER
IN INSURANCE BROKERAGE.

CONDÉ NAST PUBLICATIONS

THE MAGAZINE PUBLISHING INDUSTRY UNDERWENT A MAJOR transformation in 1909 when a 36-year-old innovator named Condé Nast came to New York and took over the publication of an ailing magazine named *Vogue*. Nast sharpened *Vogue's* general interest editorial to a specific audience: fashion-conscious women.

With that now legendary purchase, Nast established the concept of specialized publications. Using *Vogue* as a starting point, he began publishing magazines directed at specific groups with common interests. A revolutionary idea then, it has become a major force in magazine publishing and the cornerstone of Condé Nast Publications, a high-profile media company whose leadership is evident throughout its 17-title collection.

FROM TOP:

ACQUIRED BY CONDÉ NAST PUBLICATIONS IN 1993, *ARCHITECTURAL DIGEST* IS DISTINGUISHED AS THE WORLD'S MOST RESPECTED MAGAZINE OF FINE INTERIOR DESIGN.

FIRST PUBLISHED IN 1892, *VOGUE* HAS EVOLVED OVER MORE THAN 100 YEARS INTO THE WORLD'S PREEMINENT AUTHORITY ON FASHION.

***WIRED* WAS ACQUIRED IN 1998 AND IS DEDICATED TO PROGRESSIVE TECHNOLOGY AND THE DIGITAL WORLD.**

EARLY ACQUISITIONS

First published in 1892, *Vogue* has evolved over the last century into the world's preeminent fashion authority. Condé Nast's flagship publication, *Vogue* influences new directions in fashion and beauty, and provides a unique perspective on contemporary culture. In 1911, Nast acquired an interest in an architectural journal called *House & Garden*. By 1915, he had taken over the magazine, transforming it into an exploration of interior design as a statement of personal style. In 1993, the magazine (then titled *HG*) ceased publication, but was relaunched in September 1996.

Since its birth in 1914, *Vanity Fair* has defied both imitation and categorization. A chronicle of the arts, politics, and popular culture, *Vanity Fair* merged with *Vogue* in 1936, but reemerged on its own in 1983 with topflight

journalism and photography. And in 1916, Condé Nast introduced an edition of *Vogue* in Britain—the first international edition of any magazine. Today, Condé Nast publishes 45 magazines outside of the United States, including 12 international editions of *Vogue*. Foreign operations include publishing subsidiaries in the United Kingdom, France, Italy, Germany, Spain, Portugal, Australia, and Russia, as well as partnerships with other publishers in Japan, Taiwan, Korea, Greece, Brazil, and Spanish-speaking Latin American countries.

The last magazine Nast personally introduced to his empire was *Glamour*, in 1939. It offered practical options on style and beauty to an audience of working women. Continuous growth at *Glamour* has made it one of the largest-selling fashion, beauty, and lifestyle magazines for young women today.

THE NEWHOUSE YEARS

In 1959, S.I. Newhouse Sr., a Staten Island newspaper publisher, purchased controlling interest in Condé Nast Publications. The same year, the company acquired both *Bride's* and *Mademoiselle*.

Today, the company is overseen by S.I. Newhouse Jr., who set off the largest period of growth

in the company's history with the founding of *Self* in 1979. The magazine targeted a growing audience of health- and fitness-conscious women, and today, celebrates personal health, happiness, and total well-being. A pioneer in the new media arena, *Self* was the first magazine to communicate with readers via telephone hot lines, fax, E-mail, and the World Wide Web. *Gentlemen's Quarterly*, or *GQ*, was purchased from Esquire Inc. in 1979, as well. Under the auspices of Condé Nast, the magazine has become the premier men's magazine in America.

In 1983, Condé Nast acquired *Gourmet*, the celebrated magazine of Good Living, dedicated to the passionate pursuit of dining out, entertaining at home, and travel. *Condé Nast Traveler*, with its Truth in Travel founding philosophy, made its debut in 1987. It is unique among travel magazines in that it mandates that journalists pay their own way and travel anonymously to ensure objective reporting.

Details was acquired in 1988 and repositioned in 1990 as a young men's contemporary lifestyle magazine appealing to the diverse interests of sophisticated Generation X trendsetters. Launched in March 1991, *Allure* is distinguished as the first and only magazine devoted entirely

beauty. No other magazine brings such a high standard of journalism and innovation to this subject.

Architectural Digest and *Bon Appétit* were purchased in 1993 from Knapp Communications Corporation. Founded in 1920, *Architectural Digest* has evolved into the world's most respected magazine of fine interior design, providing a first look at the homes of leaders in entertainment, business, literature, and the arts. *Bon Appétit* was introduced in 1955 and has grown through a succession of owners into America's Food and Entertaining Magazine.

In 1997, the company launched *Condé Nast Sports for Women*, renamed *Women's Sports & Fitness* in 1998, after Condé Nast acquired the same title from Sports & Fitness Publishing. The magazine celebrates the physical life, covering topics relevant to active women: sports, fitness, health, gear, nutrition, beauty, style, and travel. Condé Nast's latest acquisitions include *Wired*, the title dedicated to progressive technology and the digital world, purchased from Wired Ventures in 1998, and *The New Yorker*, the award-winning weekly magazine with distinctive coverage of literature, the arts, business, and politics. The latter was integrated into Condé Nast in 1999 from Condé Nast's parent company, Advance Publications.

NEW FORMATS, NEW MARKETS
In 1995, the company launched CondéNet, a subsidiary for the development of lifestyle-oriented sites on the World Wide Web.

Properties include Epicurious Food, the comprehensive culinary source; Concierge.com, a full-service travel and booking destination; Swoon, the dating and relationships site aimed at 20-something men and women; and Phys., the health and nutrition resource. Each of the CondéNet sites features content from a number of Condé Nast magazines.

Condé Nast is building on its success and moving forward with continued growth with the reloca-

tion of the company's headquarters to Times Square. The new Condé Nast Building at Times Square is the city's first skyscraper to adopt environmentally conscious codes and incorporate them into virtually every aspect of planning and design. It will be the new benchmark from which all 21st-century metropolitan construction standards will be measured, much the same way that Condé Nast magazines have set the standard in their respective fields.

STUART WATSON

MICHAEL O'NEIL

MICHAEL ROBERTS

PATRIK ANDERSON

EXECUTIVE HEALTH GROUP

SUCCESSFUL CORPORATIONS HAVE LEARNED TO CULTIvate their resources and protect their assets. Typically, this includes tangibles such as equipment, materials, and property. However, the most important resource is often the most disregarded—the human resource. Companies who insist on regular maintenance programs protecting computers and other capital assets will leave the protection of their key human resources to chance.

IT STARTS WITH EARLY DETECTION

Executive Health Group (EHG) has been working with large and small corporations for more than 85 years, helping to protect these key human assets. In 1913, health care was quite different. Equipment to view the heart, look into the brain, or analyze the blood was nonexistent. Diagnostic equipment was extremely limited, as was the understanding of disease and treatment medications. It wasn't possible to predict disease, it was uncommon to diagnose it, and a cure was hit or miss. People called the doctor when they were very sick.

Founded in 1913 as Life Extension Institute, EHG was the first U.S. organization devoted to administering physical examinations for the early detection of disease. This was quite a proactive approach and signaled a dramatic change in health care practice—the attempt to keep people healthy, rather than curing those who were already sick.

William Howard Taft was the first chairman of EHG between his tenure as president of the United States and chief justice of the Supreme Court. In the years that followed, the organization instituted many important firsts. It published the *Manual of Procedure in Physical Examination* in 1925, and later, leaflets and articles on the early detection of disease, the benefits of exercise, and the dangers of alcohol, tobacco, obesity, and stress. It conducted a study that found regular physical examinations resulted in improved health and reduced mortality.

Major corporations, such as General Motors, recognized the value of early detection and prevention in reducing health benefit costs, and sought the organization's unique expertise. The institute also developed health care tools such as an executive miniworkout and the health hazard appraisal, forerunners of many contemporary practices.

In 1995, the Life Extension Institute changed its name to

Executive Health Group and moved into new headquarters in Rockefeller Center. New EHG centers were opened in Stamford in 1997 and in Houston in 1999. Facilities are planned for Chicago, Atlanta, and San Francisco in 2000.

A HEALTHY DETECTION RATE

Today, EHG is a leader in the early detection of life-threatening conditions such as heart disease and cancer—illnesses that can strike suddenly at any corporation's most valuable people. The organization performs more than 20,000 EHG Premier physical exams annually, totaling approximately 3 million to date.

Through these exams, the company has discovered that more than 15 percent of employees have significant health abnormalities. Left untreated, these abnormalities could lead to serious illness or disability. A less thorough physical might miss these early warning signs.

For more than 80 years, EHG has offered programs that effectively deal with the early detection of illness and other crucial health-related issues. It has enabled clients to benefit from lowered health care costs, saving a leading international technology company more than $1 million.

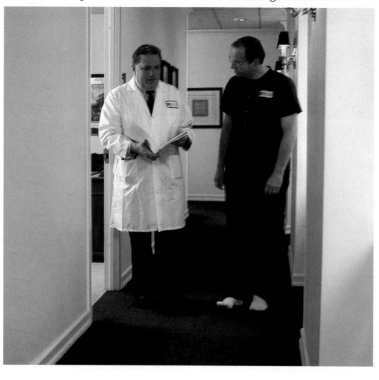

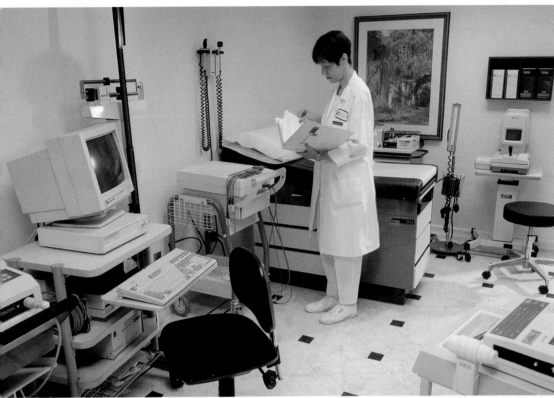

Executive Health Group is not ruled by managed care. It is guided by medical needs—and by the desire to do what is medically right for the patient. As a result, EHG patients always get the comprehensive testing and attention they need, instead of the abbreviated managed care version of an exam. EHG examinations are conducted in a relaxed setting that has been professionally designed for relaxation and comfort. In addition, EHG surveys all of its patients to ensure that everyone is receiving the highest quality care and service.

Proactive Medical Care

Making health care more proactive, EHG has set the industry standard. It provides consistent, high-quality care through state-of-the-art facilities and a network of physicians and health care professionals. Among the board-certified physicians are internists, cardiologists, gastroenterologists, and radiologists, who are all expert diagnosticians. EHG's preventive medical practice is comprehensive, utilizing the latest technologies—such as ThinPrep Pap smears and ultrasound bone scans.

EHG also knows how to treat the executives in its care, providing personalized, private, convenient, high-quality care. Examinations

and testing are done under one roof, with the efficiencies and amenities appreciated by busy professionals.

In addition, EHG is redefining the doctor-patient relationship via information services related to medicine. A new service, which will be available in 2000, utilizes Internet technology to offer a personal medical consultant's expertise to clients. Patients will be able to follow up with their physicians on any question related to an examination, and will have 24-hour, secure Internet access to medical records and Travel Medicine E-Consultations, invaluable for executives on the move. This service will also offer a personalized periodic newsletter to clients regarding medical information and advances related to their individual health interests.

"Over the last century, we are proud to have become the premier provider of comprehensive executive physical examinations," says William Flatley, president and CEO. "We offer an array of services designed to provide the highest level of health care by board-certified physicians, using state-of-the-art technology in the most comfortable and convenient settings. Our mission is to continue to improve our programs and to extend the lives entrusted to our care."

EHG utilizes state-of-the-art technology in comfortable settings.

BENETAR BERNSTEIN SCHAIR & STEIN

EFUSING TO YIELD TO THE SIMPLISTIC NOTION THAT bigger is better, many of today's corporate and business leaders turn to Benetar Bernstein Schair & Stein, a highly focused, boutique labor, employment, and benefits law firm, for expert assistance and representation on workplace issues. Why do so many successful businesses seek out the Benetar firm?

A SPECIAL NICHE

Ask the Benetar firm's clients, as well as their adversaries, their competitors, and the governmental entities and agencies before whom the firm appears, and they will tell you that the answer lies both in the special niche this quality firm has long occupied and in its unusual approach to the practice of law. It is a niche well earned for a firm whose history and tradition span a period of more than 75 years.

The Benetar firm's success begins with its philosophy and standards. The firm seeks lawyers who have a passion for the specific areas of law in which the firm practices, who strive for and care about excellence, and who understand the importance of integrity in the practice of law. As Partner Michael Bernstein says, "Integrity is a key element in the successful results we attain for our clients. The traditional values once commonly associated with the profession—ethics, personal service, and a respect for the law—are essential to the practice of law." These old-fashioned but enduring notions—a hallmark of the firm—are reflected in the Benetar firm's relationship with each of its clients and in the universal respect the firm enjoys.

But there is more to this story. The firm's partners have long been recognized by their peers as leaders in their chosen field. They have chaired the major labor and employment law section and/or committees of the national, state, and local bar associations; have served on a number of advisory task forces and as editors of various legal treatises; and are frequently called upon to write and lecture on the leading issues that confront their clients and other practitioners. Beyond that, they are often sought out by the largest law firms—as lawyers' lawyers—to address the labor, employment, and benefits problems of those firms and their clients.

MEETING CLIENTS' NEEDS

The Benetar firm meets the real needs of corporate counsel looking for attorneys who concentrate in a specific area of the law. The firm's expertise is rooted in the pioneering efforts of its founding partner, David Benetar; its involvement in landmark doctrines and decisions in its field; and the ongoing innovative and practical solutions the firm continues to bring to its clients' problems. The Benetar firm recognizes that solutions are not found in any formulaic approach, but in creative thinking tailored to the specific situation, culture, and problem at hand. This approach has continued to attract an impressive client roster, including many of the world's leading firms in international banking and financial services, insurance, law, accounting, engineering, construction, shipping, manufacturing, publishing, communications, transportation, health care, education, entertainment, retailing, technology, and social services.

The Benetar firm also offers its clients quality personal services at rates that are more than competitive. Here, the firm's size and focused practice are important assets. The Benetar firm, unburdened by the fee structures and economics of the large, institutional firms, is positioned to afford its clients a more flexible and sensible approach to servicing their needs. As Partner Stanley Schair says, "We have recognized the need for a more cost-efficient approach to legal services and are able to give our clients real value."

THE FIRM'S PRACTICE

The Benetar firm represents its clients in every forum and aspect of the employment relationship, whether it be in litigation in the courts, before administrative agencies and in arbitration, or in the context of preventive action and strategies, grievance handling, and collective bargaining negotiations. Its practice also involves counseling in all the areas usually associated with the field and, as

BENETAR BERNSTEIN SCHAIR & STEIN'S PRACTICE IS CENTERED IN NEW YORK CITY, BUT IT SERVES CLIENTS NATIONWIDE.

DIGITAL IMAGERY® COPYRIGHT 1999 PHOTODISC, INC.

ell, in mergers, acquisitions, downsizing and other reorganiations, the design of qualified d nonqualified deferred comnsation plans, and executive mpensation.

While the Benetar firm's prace is centered in the Greater New rk metropolitan area, it serces clients nationwide. The firm also the exclusive New York ember of the Labor Attorneys r Business Network, a coast-coast affiliation of indepennt labor and employment law ms, representing management. n essential requirement for embership is a reputation in e firm's state and surrounding gion for the highest quality lel services. The Benetar firm's ients, especially those with

offices in other parts of the country, gain from the strength and services this affiliation offers.

THE COMMUNITY CONNECTION

The firm's clients also appreciate the special role the Benetar firm has played in New York City and across the state. Its partners hold leadership positions or serve on the boards of many educational, charitable, and business organizations, including the Board of the New York City Partnership and Chamber of Commerce, the city's premier business organization. They also serve as appointed members or chairs of government and community advisory boards.

But the firm is most proud of its support of education. Its attorneys have given generously of

their time to the continuing legal education of practitioners who must keep up with the ever changing developments in the law to serve the public effectively. In the area of public education, especially of disadvantaged and at-risk youth, the firm participates in educational programs citywide and statewide. In recognition of its outstanding record in working with public schools, the Benetar firm was awarded the prestigious Reliance Award for Excellence in Education.

Whether it is in the competence and professionalism that the Benetar firm brings to every client's representation or in its attorneys' personal involvement and sense of obligation in giving back to the community, the Benetar firm stands out.

BERENSON & COMPANY LLP

NEARLY 80 YEARS AFTER FIRST OPENING ITS DOORS, the accounting and consulting firm Berenson & Company LLP remains one of the leading member of the New York business community. Built on a tradition of excellence dis tinguished by personal service and professional expertise, Berenson is

a full-service firm that continues to expand the scope and range of those services to reflect the changing needs of its clients and the changing climate of the times.

Berenson & Company LLP remains rooted in the ethical and academic standards established by Moses and Joseph Berenson in 1921. These founding partners were, for more than three decades, two of the most highly regarded professors at New York's City College. The value of their instruc- tion was enriched by the practical knowledge they brought to the classroom, and their academic experience helped provide the company's clients with exemplary professional services, reflected in their total familiarity with the latest accounting standards, procedures, regulations, and requirements.

Today, Berenson's practice goes beyond traditional audit and tax consulting to include such specialized disciplines as finan- cial services, corporate turn- around and recovery services, and human resources services. Berenson's financial services encompass personal financial,

tax, and retirement planning, in addition to wealth management. The firm's clients—whose rev- enues range from start-up to $750 million—represent virtually every type of industrial and commercial enterprise, as well as not-for-profit organizations, individuals, estates, trusts, and, of course, corporate tax clients.

Drawn largely from the North- east and Mid-Atlantic region, Berenson's clients are a diverse array of middle-market private and public companies whose focus includes manufacturing, wholesaling, retailing, recreation, insurance, natural resource ex- ploration and development, im- port/export, construction, real estate, and such service industries as architectural design, graphic arts, law, medicine, printing, travel, and Internet services.

The significance of this client diversity is Berenson's ability to bring broad-based experience to each specific client situation, tai- loring services to clients' individual needs. The firm's role and counsel frequently make the difference between profit and loss, solvency and insolvency, efficiency and

inefficiency, and security and uncertainty. Similarly, Berenson reputation for integrity, indepe dence, and professional services firmly established among attorne and credit grantors, including banks, insurance companies, ar financial institutions throughou the country. Indeed, the company credibility and performance have made many credit grantors cli- ents themselves, as well as a source of client referrals.

COMMITMENT TO FULL AND PERSONAL SERVICE

For Managing Partner Richard Berenson, the company standar is simple and the challenge is clea "What kind of service would we demand if we were clients?" Th answer is manifest in the active supervision of each and every account.

Personal service is the organization's guiding principle It is exemplified by the quality direct communication between the firm and clients, among part ners and professional staff, and within all levels of the company Berenson's close-knit structure fosters free and easy exchange

THE MANAGERS AND PARTNERS OF BERENSON & COMPANY LLP LEAD THE FIRM INTO THE NEW CENTURY.

ideas and opinions. Tax pro-
sionals and auditing staff con-
ntly review the status and
ection of a client's business,
awing on their cumulative
owledge and experience to
ve problems and offer advice
yond the range of conventional
ditors.

"Our goal is not simply to
nder a financial statement, but
o to find ways to make a client's
siness better," says Berenson.
e observe things they can't
cognize."

In addition to traditional
rification and reporting activi-
s, Berenson & Company LLP
ctions in business and financial
visory capacities. To meet cli-
ts' financial requirements, the
m offers a three-dimensional
rspective on their challenges
d opportunities, beginning
th the expertise and experience
its business-oriented accounts. Subjective and objective
rceptions of clients' operations
e then added to the mix.
renson then looks at the future
help establish systems, proce-
res, financial requirements,
d resources that help the firm's
ents achieve their goals.

"At Berenson, the most im-
rtant measure of success is
w well we serve the client, and
w deeply involved we can be
helping to solve problems and
an wisely for the future," says
renson.

EB DEVELOPMENT GROUP
ID INTERNET SERVICES

e business world is changing
d having a presence on the
ternet has become a necessary
ol. The information age demands
e thing: to communicate effec-

tively with those who want products
and services. Berenson's Web
site, located at www.berenson.com,
demonstrates the company's
dedication to the future of business on the Internet.

Berenson's Internet Services
and Web Development Group
bring the technology and potential of the Internet to clients'
business. The Web Development
Group presents specific com-
munciations and marketing strategies, using technical knowledge
and design sensibilites to create
intelligent and successful Web sites.

MANAGEMENT SERVICES

Recognizing that one of the key
elements in maintaining a healthy
bottom line is human resource
issues, Berenson & Company LLP
created the Employee Management
Services Division (EMS). EMS
provides clients with assistance
in achieving optimal staffing and
executive recruitment, utilizing
Berenson's vast network of contacts to search for candidates
ranging from controller level to
chief financial officers. In addition,
EMS works to ensure effective

training, efficient workflow management, and increased employee
motivation and retention.

TURNAROUND AND RECOVERY
SERVICES

Berenson & Company LLP is
highly regarded and recognized
for its expertise in turning around
troubled companies, restoring
them to financial stability, and
positioning them for future growth.
Utilizing its wealth of knowledge
about the complex factors that
contribute to a company's dis-
tressed financial circumstances,
Berenson develops and assists
in implementing a strategic plan
that rebuilds value, trust, and
confidence by providing realistic,
viable solutions to companies in
crisis.

"We have built a practice and
earned a reputation for integrity,
quality, and excellence undimin-
ished in eight decades in New
York," says Berenson. "That tradition and our enthusiasm for serving our clients now move into the
next century. Quality service,
quality relationships, quality of
life—that's our bottom line."

BERENSON PROUDLY SERVES MANY
INDUSTRIES, INCLUDING (CLOCKWISE
FROM TOP LEFT) NOT-FOR-PROFIT
ORGANIZATIONS, COUNTRY CLUBS/
RECREATIONAL FACILITIES, FASH-
ION ACCESSORIES AND APPAREL,
AND OUTDOOR ADVERTISING.

AMALGAMATED
BANK OF NEW YORK

"AT AMALGAMATED BANK OF NEW YORK, WE NEVER LOSE SIGHT OF OUR HERITAGE, AND WE NEVER FORGET THAT OUR CHARTER IS TO PROVIDE AFFORDABLE AND CONVENIENT BANKING SERVICES TO ALL WORKING MEN AND WOMEN," STATES GABRIEL P. CAPRIO, CEO AND PRESIDENT (TOP).

IN 1923, THE LEADERS OF THE AMALGAMATED CLOTHING WORKERS OF AMERICA (ACWA) UNION —A GROWING FORCE IN THE CITY'S GARMENT INDUSTRY—RECOGNIZED THE NEED TO MAKE AFFORDABLE BANKING SERVICES AVAILABLE TO WORKING MEN AND WOMEN, WHO, UNTIL THEN, DID NOT QUALIFY FOR MOST BANKING SERVICES. AND SO THEY ESTABLISHED AMALGAMATED BANK OF NEW YORK (BOTTOM).

I N THE 1920S, THE BANKS IN NEW YORK CATERED ALMOST exclusively to businesses and wealthy individuals Typically, these banks required tangible collatera in order to approve any type of loan. They also charged fees for their check ing accounts. Requirements like these placed most banking services out of

the reach of working-class people.

In 1923, the leaders of the Amalgamated Clothing Workers of America (ACWA) union—a growing force in the city's garment industry—recognized the need to make affordable banking services available to working men and women, who, until then, did not qualify for most banking services. And so they established Amalgamated Bank of New York.

FORGING A NEW PATH
With the opening of Amalgamated Bank, for the first time a steady job replaced tangible collateral as the basis for lending. The bank provided unsecured loans for individuals who could prove steady employment. Amalgamated Bank also offered loans to workers who needed to acquire housing. These services were available not only to members of the ACWA, but to all working men and women.

By making loans available to the average working person, and by introducing other services such as free checking with no minimum balance, Amalgamated Bank quickly established itself as America's Labor Bank. Through-

out the years, while maintaining sound financial parameters, the bank has continued to pioneer additional ways of providing financial assistance to working people. One such innovative pro gram is the Striker Loan Suppor Program, which makes funds avai able for striking workers, whethe they bank at Amalgamated Bank or not.

Today, Amalgamated Bank is owned by UNITE (Union of Needletrades, Industrial and Textile Employees). This union is the result of the combination of the Amalgamated Clothing and Textile Workers Union (successo to ACWA) and the International Ladies' Garment Workers Union

MAINTAINING A PROUD HERITAGE
Gabriel P. Caprio, CEO and pres ident, believes there is a respon sibility that goes along with bein, America's Labor Bank. "At Amal gamated Bank, we never lose sight of our heritage, and we never forget that our charter is to provide affordable and conve nient banking services to all working men and women. While other banks have instituted fees for all kinds of services—from writing a check to using an ATM– we still persist in offering free checking with no minimum bal ance, as well as free use of our own ATMs. Even when we have to charge a fee for a service, we at tempt to keep it as low as possible, says Caprio.

In recent years, the bank has established additional ways of working on behalf of America's labor force, including the devel opment of the Trust & Investmen Services Division. This division provides active and passive fixed income and equity investment management services for Taft-Hartley plans, as well as other pension funds.

Caprio puts this division's work into a historical perspec-

ve: "During the Second World War, workers' wages were frozen. The laws, however, did allow for the establishment of pension and health funds on behalf of these workers. After the war, these pension funds expanded and many unions established their own trusts as a benefit for their members. Initially, when the bank started its Trust & Investment Services Division, it concentrated in fixed assets, such as short- and intermediate-term bonds. By the early 1990s, however, the division had expanded its investment capabilities to include longer-term bonds and stock investments. Today, total trust assets amount to $14.6 billion with $4.9 billion in assets under management."

ACTIVATING CHANGE

In addition to managing the bank's LongView Group of Funds with the long-term objective of equity growth, Amalgamated Bank also uses its financial leverage in an effort to effect changes in corporate governance policies and social issues through the use of its proxy power. Following clearly defined guidelines, the LongView Funds attempt to participate in the decision-making process of the corporations in

which they are invested. The bank encourages corporate governance modifications that have a positive effect on the corporations' employees and stakeholders, as well as the environment. Amalgamated believes these actions will ultimately increase long-term shareholder value, as well as improve conditions for workers.

Another unique program that has meant a lot to the working men and women of New York is the Amalgamated Bank Housing Loan Program. This program evolved from the bank's strong

support of low- and middle-income multifamily housing.

Most of these housing developments were built in New York between 1927 and 1972. As these developments grow older, many are in need of major renovations, capital improvements, or improvements mandated by new laws and regulations. Since a large segment of these government-assisted projects cannot take advantage of traditional refinancing options, Amalgamated Bank created the Housing Loan Program. This program enables economically viable government-assisted developments to obtain low-cost unsecured loans, with a government agency acting as a third party to the agreement.

Whether it is managing pension funds, helping maintain low- and middle-income housing, or providing low-cost mortgages, personal loans, and banking services for individuals, Amalgamated Bank, with its six branches in New York, has been a major part of the city for more than 75 years. And now with a new branch in Washington, D.C., and a trust company in Los Angeles, Amalgamated Bank is looking for new opportunities to help working men and women everywhere.

IBJ Whitehall Financial Group

I'S RARE TO FIND A FINANCIAL INSTITUTION THAT combines the advantages of size, resources, and stability without the disadvantage of a bureaucracy. Equally rare is a financial institution with the ability to meet the diverse and extensive needs of its corporate and individual clients, and the

ability to respond and approve actions quickly.

IBJ Whitehall Financial Group is that type of organization. For 76 years, it has helped its clients meet their financial objectives. Small-business owners, individuals, and midsized corporations across the United States all look to IBJ Whitehall Financial Group for their financial needs.

The organization earned its reputation for excellence by consistently delivering creative products and quality service in a quick and efficient manner. In addition, IBJ Whitehall is known for the intense focus it brings to its business. "We're a strong institution known for providing outstanding personal service, with a reputation for our expertise, our flexibility, and our responsiveness," says Dennis G. Buchert, president and CEO.

A Distinguished History

The company has a rich history that has helped create its remarkable track record. Established in the early 1800s in London, J.

Henry Schroder & Company provided trade financing to important international merchants. In 1923, sensing that the center of international finance was moving from Europe to the United States, the organization established the J. Henry Schroder Banking Corporation in New York City as its U.S. base. Six years later, the

Schroder Trust Company was formed, and it quickly developed a reputation for serving middle-market clients and wealthy individuals with high-quality financial products and services. In 1978, these two entities merged to form the J. Henry Schroder Bank & Trust Company. Then, in the mid-1980s, The Industrial Bank of Japan, Limited, purchased a majority interest, creating IBJ Schroder Bank & Trust Company. Early in 1999, the company purchased the remaining shares held by Schroders PLC, changing its name to IBJ Whitehall Financial Group.

Responding to Client Needs

Over the years, as clients' needs have changed, IBJ Whitehall has responded by developing a variety of products and services for both individual and institutional clients. As clients have become more financially sophisticated, for example, they have demanded more investment options. IBJ Whitehall's Asset Management Group has significantly expanded what it offers both through the development of a market-neutral investment product and through selective acquisitions. These ex-

MEMBERS OF IBJ WHITEHALL FINANCIAL GROUP'S SENIOR MANAGEMENT TEAM CONTINUE TO FOCUS ON PROVIDING OUTSTANDING FLEXIBILITY AND RESPONSIVENESS TO CLIENT NEEDS (TOP).

IBJ WHITEHALL'S RELATIONSHIP TEAMS RESPOND QUICKLY AND PROVIDE READY ACCESS TO ALL OF THE BANK'S RESOURCES (BOTTOM).

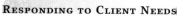

nsions help its clients address eir evolving financial goals.

Similarly, IBJ Whitehall's Corporate Finance Group has its finger n the pulse of the market. When e media and communications dustry exploded with new products, technologies, and companies, e Corporate Finance Group set p a special unit dedicated exclusively to meeting the special nding and financing needs of at dynamic and growing field.

IBJ Whitehall's highly skilled rofessionals thoroughly understand each client's business, financial needs, and short- and ng-term goals. The company's elationship and deal teams are ncouraged to be flexible and eative, to respond quickly, and complete transactions. And the anagement structure is deliberately flat, allowing the organization communicate quickly and to ct decisively. Senior managers e always available to clients, roviding ready access to all of BJ Whitehall's resources.

NTELLIGENT FOCUS
BJ Whitehall does not try to be l things to all people. Instead, it pports its client base by focusng on the U.S. domestic middle arket, offering a variety of customized products and services, cluding cash flow finance, asset-riented finance, cash management services, and custom lending r high-net-worth individuals.

IBJ Whitehall's Corporate Finance Group has also developed strong market franchise through s commitment to the private quity community. Structured nance services provide customized financing for leveraged uyouts, management buyouts, everaged buildups, recapitaliza-ons, and other growth opportu-ities. This focus on the financing eeds of the middle market allows he company to have a consistent trategy. IBJ Whitehall's experi-nce in leveraged finance allows t to structure highly complicated inancings and to execute trans-ctions quickly and efficiently.

IBJ Whitehall's Asset Manage-ment Group offers investment management, such as institutional nd private client investment man-gement services, and quantita-

tive equity management products, as well as private client services, such as custom lending, personal trust, and estate planning.

REACHING OUT TO THE COMMUNITY
Along with a strong focus on what it does best, IBJ Whitehall has always been committed to supporting New York City. This commitment is manifested in many ways. For example, IBJ Whitehall Financial Group has an active Community Reinvestment Act program in New York City. Through a balanced program combining loans to not-for-profit organizations, targeted corporate grants, and technical assistance, the firm effectively deploys financial aid and technical resources to promote neighborhood revitalization, provide job-skills training, and improve public education. IBJ Whitehall employees are also evidence of the company's involvement with the community. On any given day, from the Bronx to Brooklyn, IBJ Whitehall employees can be found mentoring high school students, serving on the boards of not-for-profit organizations, or building homes for the needy.

CONSISTENT SERVICE THROUGH THE DECADES
"Today, our reputation continues to be well deserved," says Buchert. "Our people concentrate on making decisions, completing the transaction. We get the job done. Above all, we conduct our business with a level of integrity that cannot be compromised. We seek excellence in everything we do. We're honest, straightforward, and candid, and we keep our word."

IBJ WHITEHALL HAS EARNED ITS REPUTATION FOR EXCELLENCE BY CONSISTENTLY DELIVERING CREATIVE PRODUCTS AND QUALITY SERVICE IN A QUICK AND EFFICIENT MANNER.

YOUNG & RUBICAM INC.

A S RAPIDLY ADVANCING TECHNOLOGY CONTINUES TO change the way we communicate and make decisions, the role of companies charged with spreading the word is becoming increasingly challenging. Meet Young & Rubicam Inc., a world leader in integrated marketing. For 76 years, Young & Rubicam

has helped clients achieve superior results for their brands by communicating the right message to the right consumer.

A global giant, Young & Rubicam is a marketing and communications network with services in advertising, database management, customer relationship marketing, perception management, health care communications, branding identity, and design. Around the world, it is a company known for its remarkable ability

to stay ahead of the curve, and, in the words of its founder, "resist the usual."

A GREAT START

Young & Rubicam (Y&R) began in 1923 when two men decided to form their own advertising agency with $5,000 and no clients. John Orr Young was the account side, and Ray Rubicam, the writer. They wanted to create a new kind of agency in which writers, artists, media experts, and account man-

agers would share both power and profit.

Not long after it opened, the company won a piece of business from Postum Cereal Co., a small cereal company looking to diversify into other grocery products. Postum acquired several companies, including Jell-O, Minute Tapioca, Log Cabin Syrup, Maxwell House Coffee, and Birds Eye. Ultimately, the company became the food conglomerate General Foods Corp. Y&R found itself in on the ground floor of one of the world's great packaged goods companies, with a constant and growing need to reassure a mass consumer market through advertising.

By 1930, Y&R had 250 employees and about $10 million in billings. Clients included Borden, the Budd Company, Columbia Phonographs, International Silver, Johnson & Johnson, Quaker State, Rolls-Royce, Spalding, and, of course, General Foods. Much of the company's success came from its ability to communicate effectively with its clients' audiences. That came, in part, from Y&R's innovative approach.

"Advertising's first job was to intrigue people into reading something," says Bill Colihan, a copywriter with Y&R in 1936. Rubicam called it resisting the usual. It also came from a thorough understanding of the audiences, the markets, and the competition from research. In 1932, Y&R recruited Dr. George Gallup from Northwestern University to set up a copy department with market research at its core. He made the field a practical reality, interviewing people around the country, digging out real data, and using it to create ads that gave consumers meaningful reasons to buy products represented by Y&R.

By the mid-1930s, every advertiser was heading toward radio. In those days, however, radio was not about creating ads on existing programs, it was about

creating programs to support advertising. Y&R formed a production department and developed some of radio's most successful programs of that time: *The Jack Benny Program*, *The Fred Allen Show*, *Kate Smith Hour*, *Abbott & Costello*, *The Aldrich Family*, *Ozzie and Harriet*, *Inner Sanctum*, and *Arthur Godfrey*.

When television came on the scene, Y&R was equally involved in its early triumphs, including *The Bob Hope Show*, *Captain Video*, *December Bride*, *The Twilight Zone*, *Playhouse 90*, *Goodyear Playhouse*, and *Alfred Hitchcock Presents*.

THE WHOLE EGG

The most significant developments within Y&R began in the 1970s, when the agency committed itself to a broader vision. As marketing continued to evolve, and clients' communications needs became more and more complex, Y&R was ready with an innovative service concept called the "whole egg." Introduced by past Chairman

Ed Ney, it has played a crucial role for the agency in terms of client retention and winning new business. This remarkable concept is simply a means to become a client's best partner, serving all its communications requirements.

To offer true integration of all communications disciplines, Y&R added companies that were considered the best in their various fields—leading companies in public relations and perception management, direct marketing and sales promotion, and identity and design consultancy services, as well as health care communications.

Today, Y&R has six global networks: Y&R Advertising, Wunderman Cato Johnson, Burson-Marsteller, Landor Associates, Sudler & Hennessy, and Cohn & Wolfe. When Y&R's clients need assistance, the organization has the ability to act as a single, unified global network, informed by a holistic view of a brand's needs and a deep-seated belief in the brand.

At the heart of Y&R's approach to communications development is "brand intimacy." In the agency's philosophy, a brand is a differentiating promise that links a product to its customer. The brand assures the customer of consistent quality plus superior value—for which the customer is willing to give loyalty and pay a price that brings a reasonable return to the brand. The ultimate challenge is keeping the relationships between consumer and brand fresh and vital. Brand intimacy means having the people and the tools to get to the heart of a brand and make it stronger.

Y&R has developed a proprietary tool called the BrandAsset® Valuator (BAV) research model, one of the most extensive research programs on branding ever done. To date, more than 90,000 consumers across 30 countries have been interviewed. Information on more than 13,000 brands has been collected, providing up to 50 different scales

(FROM LEFT) ED VICK, CHAIRMAN; PETER A. GEORGESCU, CHAIRMAN EMERITUS; AND TOM BELL, PRESIDENT AND CEO COMPRISE YOUNG & RUBICAM'S MANAGEMENT TEAM.

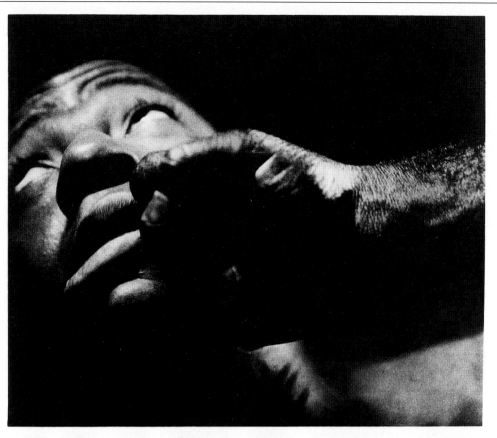

IMPACT

ACCORDING TO WEBSTER: The single instantaneous striking of a body in motion against another body.

ACCORDING TO YOUNG & RUBICAM: That quality in an advertisement which strikes suddenly against the reader's indifference and enlivens his mind to receive a sales message.

YOUNG & RUBICAM, INC. *ADVERTISING*

New York   Chicago   Detroit   San Francisco   Hollywood   Montreal   Toronto   Mexico City   London

This advertisement appeared in June, 1951

Y&R's FIRST CORPORATE CAMPAIGN SOUGHT TO TURN READERS' INDIFFERENCE INTO AN OPEN-MINDEDNESS TO ADVERTISING MESSAGES.

and dimensions of consumer perception. This proprietary data is the source of Y&R's brand-building models, providing insights into client as well as competitive brands for better management of communications.

THE NEW RULES OF BUSINESS

During the 1990s, companies met their profit obligations by working the supply side—containing costs and downsizing to drive productivity. As the returns from this reengineering begin to diminish, manufacturers are once again looking at the demand side of the equation. In plain English, businesses need to boost sales.

"Opportunities and ideas to drive incremental growth are drying up," says Tom Bell, president and CEO. "We're seeing diminishing returns and, as the 1990s draw to a close, so will the viability of managing the supply side as a strategy to increase profitability. Companies will be forced to focus on the top line to drive consumer demand and volume to achieve sustained profitable growth. Where will they turn for wisdom on the demand side of the equation? To their brands. To their marketing partners."

Every aspect of Young & Rubicam's strategy positions the

company to help clients face the new realities of business and attain the results they need. Y&R' five rules of commercial communications form the keys to success

The first principle is to invest in knowledge. "Much of what you thought you knew about managing and growing brands is about as useful as an old Selectric," Ed Vick, chairman, says. "Our proprietary knowledge base, called Brand-Asset® Valuator, gives us and our clients the edge to win."

Next, each individual consumer must have a richer, more involved interaction with all brands of media. Media companies today are under tremendous strain as fragmentation has undercut their audience base. Young & Rubicam Inc. reaches out to the media, working with them to alter the qualitative experience consumers have with their brands.

The third principle is to assess the role of creativity, which will continue to be key in breaking through an increasingly cluttered environment and in reaching an increasingly sophisticated consumer. Creativity is the ultimate lever with which Y&R continues to turn marketing insight and brand knowledge into business results.

The fourth principle is to use multiple communication pathways If businesses still think solely in 30-second time increments, their success in the marketplace will likely be as short-lived. Traditional TV remains integral to any marketing effort, but a business must have multiple communication pathways to find the most effective route to the consumer: deliver the right message, in the right format, at the right time.

The fifth principle is to value support measurement. In today's world, if you can't measure it, it doesn't exist. A communications agency shouldn't get paid just for showing up; showing up is nowhere near enough in today's competitive market. Incentive-based compensation means risks and commensurate compensation for agency and client alike. The clients of Young & Rubicam Inc. measure the results that they achieve; Y&R is an advocate of incentive-based compensation

Remember when just about any innovation could grow your brand?

Life was easy when demand outstripped supply. Back then, just about any innovation had a chance in the marketplace. Not anymore. These days, if your brand doesn't supply exactly what your customer demands, you can bet your competition will. That's why we've invested over $50 million to create the BrandAsset® Valuator, the largest global database about brands. We've talked to 95,000 consumers about 13,000 brands in 32 countries. Our learning crosses every discipline. From advertising to public relations, direct mail to promotion, from insights to Web sites, it offers a new tool for managing brands. So if you're seeking to develop global communication strategies that are not merely innovative, but actually effective, call Daryl Elliott at 1-212-210-4000 and find out more. Or visit us at www.yr.com. We'll be there. Come rain or come shine.

Young & Rubicam Inc.

such that the company shares in the real-world value it delivers.

A Giant among Giants

Headquartered in New York, Young & Rubicam Inc. and its affiliates operate 339 agencies, covering 73 countries worldwide. As a unified global network, the organization is able to share knowledge, experience, capabilities, and disciplines across all of its offices.

After 75 years as a private company, Y&R entered the public market in May 1998. Since its initial public offering, it has met every one of its financial goals. Revenues grew at double-digit rates, to $1.5 billion. The firm won more than $750 million in new business, including Campbell's, Cadbury Schweppes, and Danone, as well as Ford's new milestone European consoli-

dation. All in all, new business billings for the year totaled $1.1 billion, marking the third consecutive year it topped the $1 billion mark. Recently, Y&R won two more significant global consolidations—Barilla pasta and spirit-maker Jim Beam.

The organization's success is also being recognized in the press. Both of the leading U.S. trade publications awarded Y&R one of their top honors. *Advertising Age* named Y&R its Global Network of the Year—citing its client and integrated brand focus, as well as the quality of its global creative product. *Adweek* named Y&R's New York office as its Eastern Agency of the Year.

"Within our company, we continue to build on our strategy of intense client focus, integrated communications, and unequaled expertise related to brands,"

says Georgescu. "We are fortunate to have a management team that rates at the top in the industry. Ed Vick has been a champion of change within our organization and is an invaluable asset. Tom Bell is both a business strategist and an expert in every area of marketing and communications. And Mike Dolan, vice chairman and CFO, deserves much of the credit for the dramatic improvement in our company's financial performance."

Seventy-six years of success and leadership in advertising can best be expressed not as a tribute to the past, but as a promise for the future, as Y&R continues to transform and lead the industry in the decades to come. "We are approaching what I think will be a golden era for marketing," says Georgescu. And, no doubt, for Y&R as well.

Y&R began in 1923 when John Orr Young and Ray Rubicam wanted to create a new kind of agency in which writers, artists, media experts, and account managers would share both power and profit (left).

This ad, part of a 1999 corporate campaign, highlights Y&R's BrandAsset® Valuator, the largest database of consumer perceptions of brands (right).

Maimonides Medical Center

KNOWN FOR PROVIDING WORLD-CLASS PATIENT CARE, Maimonides Medical Center in Brooklyn offers more than 70 primary care and subspecialty programs. The hospital's 850 physicians are international leaders in their fields, and are supported by leading-edge technology and state-of-the-art equipment

NAMED AFTER RABBI MOSHE BEN MAIMON, THE 12TH-CENTURY PHILOSOPHER WHO ESTABLISHED THE CONCEPT OF MEDICINE AS A NATURAL SCIENCE, MAIMONIDES MEDICAL CENTER IS THE THIRD-LARGEST INDEPENDENT TEACHING HOSPITAL IN THE UNITED STATES.

EVER SINCE IT BEGAN AS A SMALL COMMUNITY HOSPITAL IN 1911, MAIMONIDES MEDICAL CENTER HAS BROKEN NEW GROUND IN MEDICAL PRACTICE AND SCIENCE.

The 705-bed facility is complemented by 32 community-based health care centers.

"We have attracted renowned physicians from the finest academic medical centers in the country to join our well-established and admired medical staff," says Stanley Brezenoff, president and CEO. "Careful consideration was given to recruiting individuals who would guide the development of services to address some of the more pressing health concerns found in Brooklyn, especially those affecting our large population of women, children, and the elderly."

The leadership of these physicians is enabling extraordinary progress to be made in such areas as cardiac and vascular care, obstetrics and gynecology, primary care, neonatology, pediatrics and pediatric surgery, emergency medicine and psychiatry, orthopedic surgery, and gerontology.

Named after Rabbi Moshe ben Maimon, the 12th-century philosopher who established the concept of medicine as a natural science, Maimonides is the third-largest independent teaching hospital in the United States. It trains more than 400 residents each year and routinely contributes to the prog-

ress of medicine through its broad base of clinical and laboratory research.

An integral part of the diverse community it serves, the hospital prides itself on its multilingual staff, and offers medical care in 66 languages. It even has the only glatt kosher hospital kitchen in Greater New York.

MEDICAL HISTORY IN BROOKLYN

Ever since it began as a small community hospital in 1911, Maimonides has broken new ground in medical practice and science. Year after year, its reputation has surged forward, its physicians gaining prominence for contributions to pioneering medical and surgical treatments.

Among these accomplishments are the first successful human heart transplant operation in the country in 1967; the first simple test for candida fungal infections, which would later prove significant in organ transplants and heart valve repair; the development of the first commercial pacemaker and the first intra-aortic balloon pump, both in 1970; in 1981, the first fine needle aspiration for biopsies, which eliminated the need for anesthesia and hospitalization for biopsy; in 1991, the first atherectomy in New York State; and, in 1997, the first videoscopic saphenous vein harvesting in the tristate area.

In 1998, Maimonides was honored for its visionary use of information technology with the prestigious Computerworld Smithsonian Award in Medicine, reflecting the medical center's commitment to applying the latest advances in technology to patient care. Today, the hospital is focusing efforts on expanding its ambulatory services, developing collaborative relationships with local physicians, and caring for an immigrant population.

"Pursuing excellence is an ongoing process," says Brezenoff. "Through concerted effort, we are creating an environment and dedicating resources so that Maimonides can serve the distinct needs of a very diverse population and remain a premier medical center with its roots firmly planted in the community."

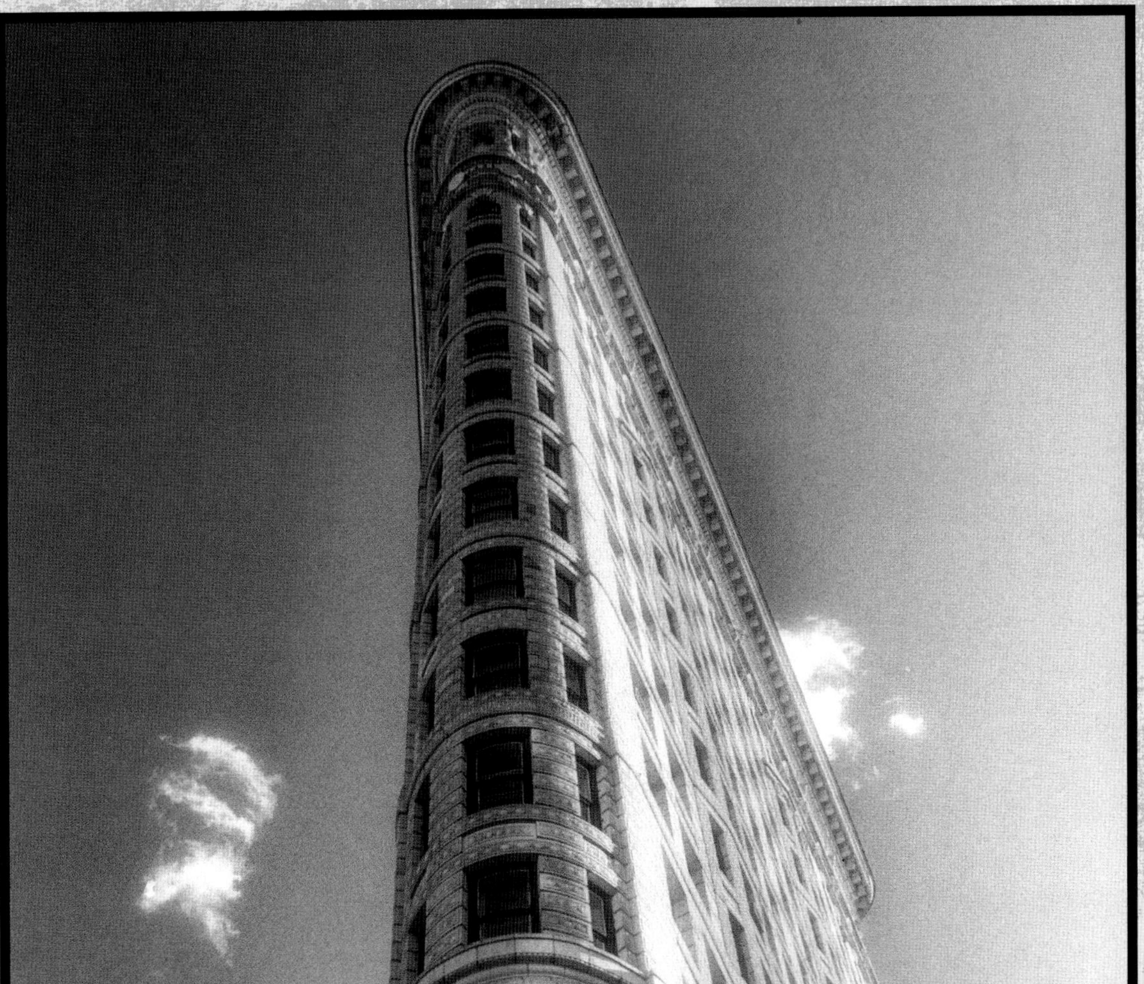

▲ © JONATHAN POSTAL / TOWERY PUBLISHING, INC.

1926 GVA WILLIAMS

1926 INTER-CONTINENTAL HOTELS OF NEW YORK

1927 AMERICAN AIRLINES, INC.

1928 WNBC

1929 D'ARCY MASIUS BENTON & BOWLES

1932 REVLON

1934 EMPIRE BLUE CROSS AND BLUE SHIELD

1935 GIBNEY, ANTHONY & FLAHERTY, LLP

1935 NYC & COMPANY

1944 FASHION INSTITUTE OF TECHNOLOGY

1946 THE DONEGER GROUP

1946 WATSON WYATT WORLDWIDE

1951 LILLIAN VERNON CORPORATION

1955 JACOBI MEDICAL CENTER

1959 THE FOUR SEASONS

GVA Williams

IN TODAY'S INCREASINGLY COMPLICATED AND COMPETITIVE real estate market, the choice of a real estate adviser is a pivotal one. GVA Williams has built a formidable record of success guiding corporate clients and property owners through the intricacies of real estate decisions and transactions. The company combines in-depth research with cutting-edge technology. With more than 70 years of experience, GVA Williams represents its clients by finding the optimal solution for any problem.

BUILDING THE FOUNDATION

Four years after Victor Cohen founded Williams Real Estate & Company in 1926, the Great Depression seized a tight grip on New York's economy and real estate. Financial institutions needed asset managers for foreclosed properties, and Williams became known for its ability to reposition a property by targeting specific types of tenancies and marketing the space through a staff of specialized brokers. One broker, Sydney Roos, became Cohen's partner in 1935. They began to form partnerships with other investors and establish ownership positions in a portfolio of properties.

When real estate strengthened during the economic surge following World War II, Williams helped clients enlarge their portfolios through the creation of investment partnerships. In the 1960s, Jerome M. Cohen and Edwin G. Roos, sons of its owners, joined the firm, while Kenneth and Robert Carmel became the first non-family shareholders. Under their guidance, the company emerged as a significant presence in the growing midtown market, and expanded its base from lofts and showrooms into office space. The firm continued to evolve as its leadership once again passed to a younger generation, President and CEO Michael T. Cohen and Executive Vice President Andrew H. Roos, in the 1980s. Robert L. Freedman joined them as a shareholder in 1984 and was appointed vice chairman in 1987.

Today, GVA Williams has achieved a unique position of recognition and respect in the highly competitive New York corporate real estate market. It is one of the city's few independent full-service firms with substantial firsthand experience as both a landlord and a tenant representative. In addition, its shareholders and employees have an ownership interest in a substantial number of properties. The firm has grown over the decades, and its development of a global presence, as well as its investment in human resources and cutting-edge technology, has elevated GVA Williams to a position of true leadership in an increasingly complex industry.

A FOUNDATION OF SERVICE

GVA Williams provides a full spectrum of real estate services, adapting its service mix and delivery systems to meet the unique needs of each client. The firm offers a combination of intellectual capital, organizational strength,

GVA WILLIAMS' MANAGEMENT COMMITTEE INCLUDES (SEATED, FROM LEFT) VICE CHAIRMAN ROBERT L. FREEDMAN, PRESIDENT AND CEO MICHAEL T. COHEN, EXECUTIVE VICE PRESIDENT ANDREW H. ROOS, (MIDDLE ROW, FROM LEFT) ADAM BACALL, AUDREY NOVOA, STEPHEN SCHOFEL, LEON MANOFF, ROBERT T. TUNIS, ROBERT A. SASS, MICHAEL A. COHEN, MARTIN MEYER, JACK SIEGEL, ALEXANDER JINISHIAN, (BACK ROW, FROM LEFT) ROBERT M. ROMANO, DONALD LUTT, ROBERT BRENNAN, BRIAN GIVEN, BARRY ROSNER, AND FINNBAR J. BONNER.

and technological prowess that focuses on increasing clients' shareholder value. It emphasizes integral processes, accountability, communication, and most important, strategy through vision.

Client relationships often begin with an individual transaction, then evolve into a full, strategic partnership. This is where GVA Williams is able to make its most valuable contribution, namely as an extension of management. Each client is assigned a key account partner, who is responsible for the overall direction of the project team and for utilizing the firm's appropriate competencies on the client's behalf. The key account partner provides single-source accountability during both short-term project work and long-term partnership.

GVA Williams is exceptional among even the most comprehensive real estate services firms in two important respects. The first is that the company has a corporate culture of cooperation, where every client can draw upon the firm's reservoir of manpower and resources, and can enjoy the benefit of its considerable and diversified experience. The second is that GVA Williams invests heavily and continually in its infrastructure. The firm is an industry leader in technology, research, and analytical support.

A Client's Perspective

GVA Williams immerses itself in its clients' concerns to thoroughly understand the unique circumstances of each transaction. The firm believes that a comprehensive real estate management system and a long-range occupancy strategy are essential to support its clients' larger goals and optimize their corporate assets.

GVA Williams has an impressive, 75-year history of enlightened strategic planning and portfolio management. In the office, industrial, and retail sectors, the firm handles long-range planning, acquisitions, dispositions, valuations and appraisals, negotiations, construction, asset and property management, lease administration, auditing and restructuring, and advisory services, including facilities operations and engineering. It studies facility uses for ways to reduce costs, increase productivity, and enhance the quality of the work environment. The firm is always alert for opportunities to capitalize on market conditions to benefit its clients.

Critical to this approach is intelligence—intellectual competence, as well as the ability to gather information. An awareness of market conditions, economic trends, and demographic changes is the key to the success of GVA Williams in the industry. The firm commits a great deal of energy to developing proprietary information, and to maintaining and expanding the leading analytical resources and technological infrastructure.

GVA Williams' international team, comprised of 3,600 professionals in 75 offices, provides local expertise and bridges cultures in more than 23 countries on five continents. Its clients are among the largest corporations in the world, and it prides itself on being one of the New York metropolitan area's most active and respected full-service real estate firms. Led by its third generation of management, GVA Williams is an integrated professional organization dedicated to helping clients meet their rapidly changing real estate requirements as effectively—and strategically—as possible.

GVA WILLIAMS BRINGS VIRTUAL REALITY TOURS OF BUILDINGS TO POTENTIAL TENANTS AND THE BROKERAGE COMMUNITY. THESE TOURS ENABLE POTENTIAL TENANTS TO PREVIEW FLOOR LAYOUTS AND EXTERIOR VIEWS WITHOUT HAVING TO LEAVE THEIR OFFICES.

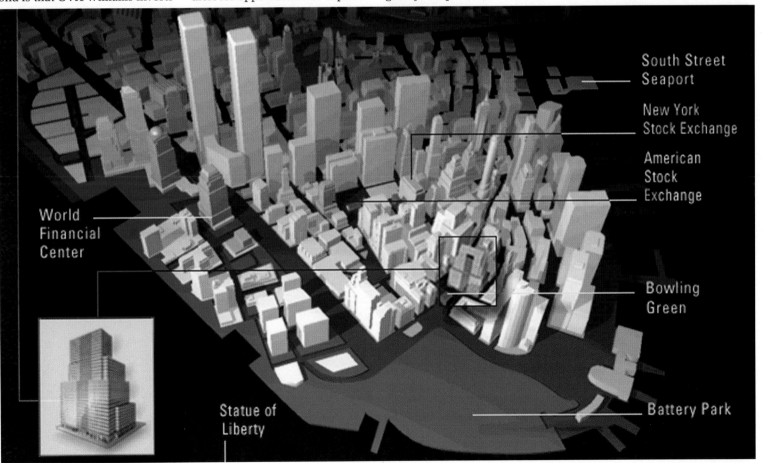

World Financial Center

Statue of Liberty

South Street Seaport

New York Stock Exchange

American Stock Exchange

Bowling Green

Battery Park

INTER-CONTINENTAL HOTELS OF NEW YORK

LEGENDARY FOR DELIVERING EXCEPTIONAL SERVICE IN elegant surroundings, the Hotel Inter-Continental New York has enjoyed a rich history and a level of sophistication that is uniquely New York City. Originally built in 1926 as The Barclay by the Vanderbilt family, the hotel's classic American luxury

reflected the expectations of the city's elite. With nearly 700 guest rooms, the hotel quickly became popular among New York social-register members, movie stars, and prominent political figures.

Over the years, the hotel hired many French chefs to introduce new concepts in fine dining, and created an atmosphere that combined luxury with a dash of the unusual. One signature touch was the latticed brass birdcage, added as a focal point to the lobby in 1945, which contained a number of exotic songbirds.

A NEW BEGINNING

Inter-Continental Hotels, one of the world's leading international luxury hotel chains, acquired The Barclay in 1978. Known for its ability to restore historic properties, Inter-Continental be-

gan a $32 million refurbishment of the property. Restored to its former old-world luxury in early 1982, the hotel was renamed the Hotel Inter-Continental New York. Between 1994 and 1996, the hotel spent an additional $20 million on renovations to the guest rooms and suites, as well as public spaces.

Today, the hotel is undergoing a $50 million refurbishment program, scheduled for completion in 2001. This latest effort will ensure that its luxury accommodations and amenities continue to rank among the city's finest.

MANHATTAN'S SECOND INTER-CONTINENTAL

Recently, the prestigious New York hotel welcomed a second

Inter-Continental property to Manhattan. This hotel, perhaps best known as a Ritz-Carlton, reopened in July 1999 as the Central Park Inter-Continental New York.

"New York is one of the most dynamic and exciting destinations in the world for both business and leisure travelers," says Stephen Brandman, general manager of the Central Park Inter-Continental New York. "Now, with two luxurious Inter-Continental hotels in the city, we are able to offer guests first-class accommodations and service no matter where they prefer to stay."

Long a landmark on Central Park South, the hotel opened in 1929 as the Navarro. Elegantly appointed in traditional European

CLOCKWISE FROM TOP: ORIGINALLY THE BARCLAY, THE HOTEL INTER-CONTINENTAL NEW YORK EXHIBITS OLD-WORLD LUXURY.

VIPS ARE RIGHT AT HOME IN THE REGALLY APPOINTED PRESIDENTIAL SUITE OF THE CENTRAL PARK INTER-CONTINENTAL NEW YORK.

THIS HOTEL, PERHAPS BEST KNOWN AS A RITZ-CARLTON, REOPENED IN JULY 1999 AS THE CENTRAL PARK INTER-CONTINENTAL NEW YORK.

decor, the 25-story property boasts oversized suites, some featuring terraces overlooking the park, with marble floors and working fireplaces. With its exclusive location on Central Park South, the hotel is within walking distance of Fifth Avenue shops, Broadway theaters, and Central Park. It offers spectacular park views from many of its 208 guest rooms and 16 suites.

VIPs from heads of state to celebrities are right at home in the hotel's regally appointed Presidential Suite, complete with a marble foyer, living room with fireplace, four balconies overlooking Central Park, dining room, and master bath with whirlpool.

While the decor may be old-world, the Central Park Inter-Continental New York offers many thoroughly modern, five-star amenities considered requisite by today's sophisticated traveler. Rooms are fully equipped with dual-line telephones, voice mail, and modem hookups. Spacious bathrooms of Italian marble feature telephones, makeup mirrors, scales, terry-cloth robes, and hair dryers.

Guests looking for award-winning dining need only visit the Fantino Grill, the hotel's restaurant, under the direction of Chef de Cuisine Michael Walsh. The 1999 Zagat New York survey described this first-class steak and fish eatery as a "hidden delight," awarding it a 25 out of a possible 30 for both service and decor.

MAKING SERVICE MAGIC

Of course, these two hotels' elegant amenities would be meaningless without another Inter-Continental hallmark: consistent, first-rate service. "That's why each and every guest receives personalized service that is second to none in the city," says Christopher R. Perry, director of marketing. "And in New York, service is crucial."

Inter-Continental defines service as "knowing our guests by name, not by room number," adds Perry. "We take pride in knowing individual guests' preferences, such as room type, food and beverage requests, and much more."

What makes this caliber of service possible? The company's rigorous hiring process, training program, and resources. And Inter-Continental's Service Magic program ensures that staff members understand the company's vision to be the best at all times.

PREEMINENCE THROUGH INNOVATION

Inter-Continental has always been a pioneer in the industry, from the trend-setting VIP treatment of its Six Continents Club guest loyalty program, to the inventive New American Cuisine of the Hotel Inter-Continental New York's renowned Barclay Bar & Grill.

And the innovative programs keep coming. There's Kids in Tow, designed to entertain guests' children with a fun-filled backpack while providing parents

with handy items like electrical outlet covers. And the Just Like Home in-room menu serves up home-style comfort food, from Reuben sandwiches to meatloaf.

New additions include the Meetings Place program, where meeting planners are provided with a pre-keyed cellular phone to gain instant access to the hotel's conference staff, and every meeting room is fully equipped with the latest technology. Guests can also take advantage of the Cyber Assist service, which provides 24-hour, on-site technical assistance to solve all computer and presentation equipment-related problems.

ALL IN THE DETAILS

With two deluxe Inter-Continental hotels now in New York City—an established property located just off Park Avenue at 48th Street, and the new hotel on Central Park South—guests can easily find an Inter-Continental that suits their travel needs. Whichever Manhattan location guests select, they are certain to find the legendary Inter-Continental hallmarks that have made the hotel chain's reputation the world over: a luxurious setting, innovative programs, and attentive, personalized service designed to make their stays as comfortable as possible.

"There are a multitude of choices in New York, and we have a high degree of return guests," says Perry. "When guests leave our hotels, we know they'll be back."

THE PRESIDENTIAL SUITE AT THE HOTEL INTER-CONTINENTAL NEW YORK MIRRORS THE OLD-WORLD CHARM AND MODERN CONVENIENCES OF THIS HISTORIC HOTEL (LEFT).

GUESTS LOOKING FOR AWARD-WINNING DINING NEED ONLY VISIT THE FANTINO GRILL, THE CENTRAL PARK INTER-CONTINENTAL NEW YORK'S RESTAURANT (RIGHT).

AMERICAN AIRLINES, INC.

THE HISTORY OF AMERICAN AIRLINES, INC. IN THE NEW York area goes back more than 70 years, and is filled with enough aviation milestones to fill a history book. The airline traces its New York roots to 1927, when one of its predecessor companies, Colonial Airways, began scheduled service in the area.

Several years later, Colonial and numerous small carriers were folded into what would become American Airways and, in 1934, American Airlines.

One of those early predecessors was called Robertson Aviation, which featured a pilot who quietly went about the job of flying the mail and a few passengers along the way. Not long after that, the pilot—Charles Lindbergh—made a little more noise with his *Spirit of St. Louis* airplane, which he used to make the first solo crossing of the Atlantic.

In the 1930s, American brought the first DC-3 service to New York, moved its headquarters to New York from Chicago, introduced the first flight attendants, and introduced the concept of the Admirals Club at New York's LaGuardia Airport. Incidentally, American was among the first air carriers to serve LaGuardia, and celebrated 60 years of service there in late 1999.

SERVICE AND EXPANSION

Today, American and its regional airline affiliate, American Eagle, provide more than 220 daily departures from New York's LaGuardia and John F. Kennedy (JFK) airports, as well as Newark International Airport. The airline also serves MacArthur (Islip, New York), Stewart International (Newburgh), and Westchester County (White Plains) airports. All are a vital part of the American/American Eagle network that provides nearly 4,000 flights a day to more than 230 airports worldwide.

At New York's JFK Airport, American has continued to bring important new international service and expansion. In the 1970s, American expanded into the Caribbean, and today is the leading carrier in that region. In the 1980s and 1990s, the airline greatly expanded its European presence; that expansion will continue into the new century as well. Also during the 1990s, American expanded its service between New York and Latin America.

American's latest route is its already successful New York-to-Frankfurt flight. In 2000, American will introduce its highly acclaimed international flagship, the Boeing 777 wide-body, on its service from JFK to London's Heathrow Airport.

American Airlines' industry-leading innovations continue to this day. Whether it is the first computerized reservations system (SABRE), the first frequent flyer awards program (AADVANTAGE, still the largest with 36 million members), Admirals Clubs or Executive Centers throughout its worldwide network, award-winning International Flagship Service, electronic tickets or enhanced gate readers that simplify travel and the airport boarding process, the world's most popular airline Web site at www.AA.com, or the hundreds of new, state-of-the-art aircraft joining the fleet, American continues to provide innovations that make a difference to its customers.

COMMITMENT TO NEW YORK

Just as important as its rich history and current success is American's commitment to New York for the future. Nowhere is that more evident than the airline's recent announcement that it will build a new, $1 billion, 59-gate terminal at JFK International Airport. Announced on the 40th anniversary of the first coast-to-coast commercial jet flight—another American first—the new terminal solidifies JFK's position as one of the region's premier international gateways for the new century.

Constructed in four major phases and slated for completion in 2006, the mammoth facility will have nearly 2 million square feet of space, and will be the

largest and most advanced terminal at JFK. Its passenger check-in area will be so enormous that it will dwarf Giants Stadium in comparison. The building's three concourses will be able to accommodate more than 14 million passengers a year.

The new facility will replace American's two existing terminals and will use an adjacent, 42-acre site acquired for expansion several years ago. In addition, more than 1,000 new construction jobs will benefit the New York area during the expansion activity. The phasing of the project will allow American to continue its JFK operations without interruption while the construction work progresses.

"This represents one of the boldest expansion programs in American's history and a long-term commitment to New York and Kennedy Airport as one of our principal international gateways," says Donald J. Carty, American's chairman and CEO. "Kennedy has always been a big part of our airline, even when it was known as Idlewild, and now we're making sure that JFK is a cornerstone of our international operations in the new millennium."

JUST AS IMPORTANT AS ITS RICH HISTORY AND CURRENT SUCCESS IS AMERICAN'S COMMITMENT TO NEW YORK FOR THE FUTURE. NOWHERE IS THAT MORE EVIDENT THAN THE AIRLINE'S RECENT ANNOUNCEMENT THAT IT WILL BUILD A NEW, $1 BILLION, 59-GATE TERMINAL AT JFK INTERNATIONAL AIRPORT.

AMERICAN WAS AMONG THE FIRST AIR CARRIERS TO SERVE LAGUARDIA, AND CELEBRATED 60 YEARS OF SERVICE THERE IN LATE 1999.

WNBC

TELEVISION HISTORY WAS MADE ON JULY 1, 1941, WHEN WNBC—then called WNBT—signed on the air at 1:29 p.m., signaling the beginning of commercial television in the United States. WNBC was not simply the first child of the new technology, but the parent and pioneer of that technology as well.

It was a day of many television firsts. At 2:30 p.m., 4,000 television sets tuned in for the station's first show—a live telecast of a baseball game between the Brooklyn Dodgers and the Philadelphia Phillies from Ebbets Field. Two game shows also premiered that day, *Truth or Consequences* and *Uncle Jim's Question Bee*.

Viewers also witnessed the first commercial sponsor to air on a telecast. A Bulova clock was placed in the lower right-hand corner of the test pattern as an announcer read the time. Bulova paid $4 for the first commercial and $5 for the use of the facilities. America also saw its first televised pair of dish pan hands, courtesy of Irene Hubbard, the original star of the Ivory soap commercials.

WNBC's NUMBER-ONE-RATED 11 P.M. NEWS TEAM FEATURES (CLOCKWISE FROM LEFT) METEOROLOGIST JANICE HUFF, SPORTS ANCHOR LEN BERMAN, ANCHOR CHUCK SCARBOROUGH, AND ANCHOR SUE SIMMONS (TOP).

THE WORLD-FAMOUS NEW YORK CITY MARATHON MADE ITS DEBUT ON WNBC ON NOVEMBER 7, 1999.

CHANGING THE WORLD

The idea for commercial television was first conceived in 1928 and developed in an RCA television lab—named W2XBS—which operated from a transmitter in the Bronx's Van Cortlandt Park. Over the next few years, commercial television would continue to evolve. On January 16, 1930, a television program originating from NBC's Fifth Avenue studios was transmitted onto a six-foot screen for an audience at the Proctor Theater on Third Avenue and 58th Street. Soon after, NBC assumed control of W2XBS from RCA.

A year later, NBC began experimental telecasts from a transmitter located atop the Empire State Building. W2XBS began the industry's first regular schedule of television service on April 30, 1939, when President Franklin Roosevelt opened the New York World's Fair.

It was in these early stages of development that the visionaries at NBC began exploring and demonstrating the medium's vast potential. NBC provided viewers with entertainment from films to variety acts, and broadcast sporting events and news programs, including television's first coverage of the Republican and Democratic political conventions in 1940.

Today, WNBC reflects the talent, tradition, diversity, and vitality of the New York-area neighborhoods it informs, serves, and celebrates. The award-winning *NewsChannel 4* news team—including longtime co-anchors Chuck Scarborough and Sue Simmons, sports anchor Len Berman, meteorologist Janice Huff, anchor Jane Hanson, and newer team members Lynda Baquero and Maurice DuBois—carries on the tradition of excellence for the nation's leading local news organization.

With more than 30 years at WNBC, Senior Political Correspondent Gabe Pressman is the embodiment of that tradition. Pressman, whose career spans five decades in New York, is considered the dean of New York broadcast journalists. He is the recipient of such prestigious journalism honors as the Edward R. Murrow Award, the George Foster Peabody Award, the Olive Award, eight New York Emmys, and the 1996 Governor's Award from the National Academy of Television Arts and Sciences, New York Chapter.

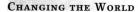

V. SAILER

A TRUE LOCAL TELEVISION STATION

WNBC is the flagship station of the NBC network: a local dynamo in the nation's largest, most influential, and most competitive media market. At the helm of the flagship since 1996 is President and General Manager Dennis Swanson, whose emphasis on increased involvement in the diverse communities and concerns of New York has helped make WNBC the leading revenue-producing station in the nation.

A 40-year veteran of broadcast journalism, Swanson opened doors to many of New York's local communities, spearheading special programs on issues impacting the tri-state area, such as education and race relations. Under his direction, WNBC was the first network affiliate station to broadcast the Puerto Rican, West Indian, Italian, and Irish communities' annual parades. WNBC also joined forces with the Hispanic Federation, Inc. and the Caribbean-American Chamber of Commerce to present a live telecast of the Hurricane Georges Relief Effort '98. In addition, WNBC provided the United Negro College Fund with four hours of commercial-free airtime for its annual telethon.

Even hometown sports rivalries were reconciled when *GameDay New York*, a collaboration between WNBC and NBC sports, debuted in 1998, giving viewers a weekly look at both the Jets and the Giants. WNBC added yet another Big Apple sports tradition to the schedule when it broadcast live coverage of the world-famous 1999 New York City Marathon.

"WNBC is charged with representing diversity in one of the most diverse areas of the country," says Swanson. "We have a long-standing commitment to represent that diversity through our programming and employment efforts, and to serve the needs and address the concerns of our community as a whole."

That commitment was recognized when WNBC was awarded a 1999 Good Egg Award by Advertising New York, which honored the station for its corporate good deeds and commitment to volunteerism. In 1998, WNBC employees attended more than 400 local events and volunteered nearly 3,100 hours to various local organizations.

The station also received its first national Emmy Award for Community Service in 1998 for a 30-minute fire safety special, "How to Survive a Fire," hosted by nationally renowned WNBC and *Today Show* weathercaster Al Roker.

The local station that gave birth to a national network continues to celebrate New York on a national scale as well. In 1996, WNBC expanded its coverage of the annual lighting of the famous Rockefeller Center Christmas Tree to one hour. The following year, the program was syndicated across the country, and in 1998, it was expanded to a two-hour broadcast, with one hour televised live by the NBC network as a prime-time special. The tradition continues in 1999, as viewers across the nation will once again be able to share in this quintessential New York holiday extravaganza that showcases the splendor of the season, the unity of the citizens, and the renaissance of New York City.

NBC/GLOBE PHOTOS

CLOCKWISE FROM TOP: WNBT CAMERAS HIT THE STREETS TO CAPTURE EARLY NEW YORK NEWS.

WNBC'S ANNUAL LIGHTING OF THE FAMOUS ROCKEFELLER CENTER CHRISTMAS TREE SHOWCASES THE TRADITION AND BEAUTY OF THE HOLIDAY SEASON.

WNBC'S ANNUAL COVERAGE OF THE ST. PATRICK'S DAY PARADE IS ONE OF THE MANY COMMUNITY EVENTS TO AIR ON THE STATION.

D'ARCY MASIUS BENTON & BOWLES

'ARCY MASIUS BENTON & BOWLES IS A GLOBAL ADvertising and communications company that has a passion for creating brand leaders around the world. The agency's unique approach to brand leadership goes beyond traditional category benefit ownership to stake a claim in the future of where

the category is headed.

D'Arcy's vision of brand leadership in the digital age is based on optimizing the value of a brand at all key points of contact and connection with the consumer to deliver the full range of marketing communications solutions to clients above, beyond, and through the line. Today's marketplace demands that agencies shift the focus to output versus process, resulting in better ideas faster. D'Arcy's blue-chip client roster includes Procter & Gamble, General Motors, Coca-Cola, M&M Mars, Ernst & Young, and Capital One.

A RICH HERITAGE OF LEADERSHIP

D'Arcy's passion for creating brand leaders is the richest part of its heritage and the touchstone for the future. D'Arcy Advertising opened its doors in St. Louis in 1906, and Coca-Cola, a fizzy brown soda water from Atlanta, was one of its first clients. Over the next 50 years, D'Arcy established the Coke brand as a global monolith that has become one of the most recognizable products in any culture.

Agency founders Bill D'Arcy, Mike Masius, Bill Benton, and Chester Bowles were innovators whose leadership and vision withstood the test of time. D'Arcy

made advertising history with the creation of famous brand icons like Santa Claus for Coke, Mr. Whipple for Charmin, and the original Budweiser Frogs for Anheuser-Busch. Memorable slogans like "Look, Mom, no cavities" for Crest, "Good to the last drop" for Maxwell House, and "Tide's in, dirt's out" for Tide became a part of popular culture, along with recent favorites like "Twix. Two for me. None for you," "Taste the rainbow" for Skittles, and "Do you feel lucky?" for Cadillac Seville.

D'Arcy Masius Benton & Bowles has helped to shape the course of advertising history in many other ways as well: D'Arcy invented the electrotypes that standardized newspaper ads in the 1920s, and created the first outdoor billboards; Benton developed the principle of con-

sumer polling; and Bowles is known to have executed the first-ever testimonial campaign, which remains one of the most effective forms of advertising used today. And Theodore MacManus, founder of D'Arcy's holding company, the MacManus Group, penned one of the most provocative and memorable ads of the century for Cadillac. *The Penalty of Leadership*, an essay that ran only once, repositioned Cadillac as the standard for American luxury cars.

In 1985, two great companies—D'Arcy MacManus Masius Worldwide and Benton & Bowles—each with its own distinguished heritage, joined together to form D'Arcy Masius Benton & Bowles to carry on the proud tradition of innovative brand-building work that has spanned most of the 20th century.

NEW APPROACH TO LEADERSHIP

But true leaders are restless. They look beyond today and past the horizons of tomorrow. D'Arcy's new approach to leadership is all encompassing and seeks new ways of optimizing the value of a brand by utilizing the agency's proprietary strategic processes: Brand Vision and the Leadership Equity Model. This leadership approach results in new ways of targeting consumers, new ways of communicating the brand to all who influence it, and new ways of teaming and working together to achieve category-best advertising for all of the firm's clients. D'Arcy's leadership teams center around the specific needs of individual clients and are led by a triad of global account, creative, and planning directors to drive world-class standards of quality and creativity to businesses everywhere. D'Arcy's leadership creativity results in award-winning, category-best advertising that increases sales and builds brands to leadership status for clients around the globe.

LEADING BY EXAMPLE

D'Arcy's talented team of more than 6,000 individuals in 131 offices in 75 countries is bound together by a passion for creativity and leadership in all of its forms. Ultimately, D'Arcy believes that success hinges on the creativity of its people and that true leader-

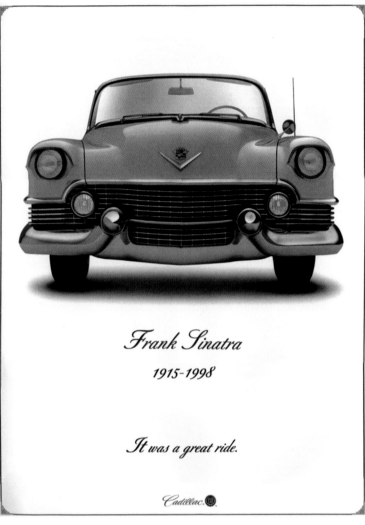

Frank Sinatra

1915-1998

It was a great ride.

Cadillac.

D'ARCY MADE ADVERTISING HISTORY WITH THE CREATION OF FAMOUS BRAND ICONS LIKE SANTA CLAUS FOR COCA-COLA (RIGHT).

FRANK SINATRA WAS MEMORIALIZED IN THIS 1998 CADILLAC TRIBUTE ADVERTISEMENT CREATED BY D'ARCY (LEFT).

ship begins with the individual. The people of D'Arcy are encouraged to be leaders themselves, boldly passionate in their commitment to creating brand leaders for D'Arcy clients around the globe.

In the true spirit of leading by example, D'Arcy Masius Benton & Bowles has done for itself what it asks of clients and has rebranded itself as D'Arcy for the new digital age. Today, D'Arcy stands poised to enter the new millennium as one company, with one vision, as one unified brand strongly committed to creativity, passion, and leadership.

Even the Lone Ranger never rode alone.

Teaming isn't a corporate buzzword. It's a core belief. Which means you can always depend on our 85,000 people who want to ride by your side. Together, we can think and do more. Saddle up.
www.ey.com

CONSULTING · TAX · ASSURANCE

ERNST & YOUNG
FROM THOUGHT TO FINISH.™

D'ARCY'S BOLD GRAPHIC LOOK FOR ERNST & YOUNG MAKES "FROM THOUGHT TO FINISH" STAND OUT IN A CROWD.

REVLON IS ONE OF THE WORLD'S BEST-KNOWN NAMES IN cosmetics and is a leading mass-market cosmetics brand. The company's vision is to provide glamour excitement, and innovation through quality products at affordable prices. To pursue this vision, the company's management team combines the creativity

of a cosmetic and fashion company with the marketing, sales, and operating discipline of a consumer packaged goods company. The company believes that its global brand-name recognition, product quality, and marketing experience have enabled it to create one of the strongest consumer brand franchises in the world, with products sold in approximately 175 countries and territories.

The company's products are marketed under such well-known brand names as Revlon ColorStay, Revlon Age Defying, Almay, and Ultima II. To further strengthen its consumer brand franchises, the company markets each core brand with a distinct and uniform global image, including packaging and advertising, while retaining the flexibility to tailor products to local and regional preferences.

A History of Innovation

Incorporated in 1933, Revlon was founded by nail polish distributors Charles and Joseph Revson, along with nail polish supplier Charles Lachman, who contributed the L in the Revlon name.

The company began its success with opaque and long-lasting enamel sold to beauty salons. The company revolutionized the cosmetic industry by introducing nail enamels matched to lipstick in fashion colors more than 60 years ago. Revlon sold its nail polish through department stores and selected drugstores, focusing on middle-income and affluent customers.

Advertising helped to boost Revlon sales. Its use was a fateful step for the company—never again would cosmetic manufacturers attempt to sell beauty items without it. The company also began labeling nail enamels with evocative names like Fatal Apple and Kissing Pink, which were descriptive while offering the promise of novelty.

In 1940, Revlon introduced a full-color revolutionary advertising campaign stressing the importance of cosmetics as a fashion accessory, and featuring the novel idea of "matching lips and fingertips." Sales more than doubled from the previous year based on the success of Revlon's innovative advertising campaign.

During World War II, Revlon contributed directly to the war effort by manufacturing first-aid kits and dye markers for the navy At war's end, the firm bought the cutlery manufacturer Graef & Schmidt, allowing Revlon to produce its own manicure and pedicure instruments.

Following the war, Revlon was one of America's top five cosmetic houses. To improve its market position, the company introduced biannual nail enamel and lipstick promotions tied to seasonal clothing fashions. Each promotion featured a descriptive color name to tempt the buyer, full-color spreads in fashion magazines, color cards showing the range of colors in the promotion, and display cards reproducing or enlarging consumer ads. Packaging was designed specifically for each line.

Revlon also turned to television sponsorship to boost sales and was one of the first cosmetic companies to fully utilize this new medium. In December 1955, Revlon offered stock to the public, and at the end of the following year, it was listed on the New York Stock Exchange.

In the 1960s, Revlon acquired shoe polish company Knomard, Ty-D-Bol, Evan Picone, U.S. Vitamins & Pharmaceutical Corporation, and a partial interest in Schick. Revlon laid the groundwork for its highly successful international presence in the 1960s, bringing the American look to the rest of the world through advertising featuring U.S. models.

Revlon began the 1970s by acquiring Mitchum Company. Charlie fragrance was introduced in 1973 as the first lifestyle fragrance designed for a young working woman market. Revlon became the first cosmetic company

REVLON'S VISION IN THE NEXT MILLENNIUM IS TO CONTINUE TO CONTRIBUTE TO THE QUALITY OF LIFE FOR WOMEN THROUGHOUT THE WORLD THROUGH GLAMOUR, EXCITEMENT, AND INNOVATION WITH AN UNERRING EYE FOR BEAUTY.

to sign a model/celebrity spokesperson—Lauren Hutton—and became a major sponsor of the Academy Awards.

In 1985, Revlon was acquired by a subsidiary of MacAndrews & Forbes Holdings. In 1996, Revlon acquired Almay, Cindy Crawford signed her first contract as a Revlon spokesperson, and the Most Unforgettable Woman celebrity advertising campaign focused on Revlon's color authority.

In the 1990s, Revlon revolutionized the retail cosmetics industry by moving away from department and specialty stores to reach a greater number of women who preferred the convenience and value of shopping at mass-market retailers. Through innovative product development and marketing, Revlon quickly increased its total market share. As a result, the Revlon brand rose from the number three to the number one brand in mass color cosmetics.

Continuing Innovation

Working collaboratively with marketing, sales, R&D, and operations, Revlon management has continued to identify and evaluate important market potential. ColorStay Lip Color was introduced, creating a whole new category of long-wearing, transfer-resistant lipstick. ColorStay became the number one lipstick in the U.S. mass cosmetic market within 12 weeks. The ColorStay collection was then launched, providing long-wearing technology in foundation, eye colors, eye liners, and lip pencils. Revlon Age Defying foundation for women 35 and over was launched, featuring a proprietary formula that doesn't settle into fine lines and wrinkles. The *Revlon Report* also premiered both in-store and in magazines, offering consumers the latest seasonal makeup and fashion news.

In 1999, Revlon launched a series of highly successful products, including Revlon ColorStay Liquid Lipcolor, ColorStay Compact Makeup, Revlon Moisture-Stay Lipcolor, Revlon EveryLash Mascara, and the Glowtion Skin Brightening franchise, an expansion of the Ultima II line.

Concern for Women's Well-Being

Beyond external beauty, Revlon is concerned about women's lives and well-being, and has dedicated both support and financial resources to critical health causes, including breast and ovarian cancer, skin cancer, fertility, and AIDS. Spearheaded by Chairman Ronald O. Perelman, Revlon has committed extensive resources to the fight against breast and ovarian cancers by supporting the work of dozens of research, education, self-help, and advocacy programs in the United States and Canada. Since 1990, Revlon and the Revlon Foundation have committed more than $25 million to women's health issues.

In 1990, a gift from the Revlon Foundation helped establish the Revlon/UCLA Women's Cancer Research Program, which conducts leading-edge research into new ways of diagnosing and treating breast and ovarian cancer. In addition to prolonging hundreds of lives, the program's most important achievement to date is the discovery research and initial clinical investigations leading to the development of Herceptin®, the FDA-approved first gene-based treatment for any major cancer.

In 1998, Revlon announced a new partnership with the National Council of Negro Women to develop programs that support the wellness of African-American women, including a study of the awareness and understanding of breast cancer issues. The company also continues to support a wide range of other efforts, including the Revlon Run/Walk for Women in New York and Los Angeles.

Revlon's vision in the next millennium is to continue to contribute to the quality of life for women throughout the world through glamour, excitement, and innovation with an unerring eye for beauty.

REVLON REVOLUTIONIZED THE COSMETIC INDUSTRY BY INTRODUCING NAIL ENAMELS MATCHED TO LIPSTICK IN FASHION COLORS MORE THAN 60 YEARS AGO.

SINCE 1990, REVLON AND THE REVLON FOUNDATION HAVE COMMITTED MORE THAN $25 MILLION TO WOMEN'S HEALTH ISSUES.

EMPIRE BLUE CROSS AND BLUE SHIELD

THE LARGEST INSURER IN THE STATE, EMPIRE BLUE Cross and Blue Shield has been a part of New Yorkers' lives for more than 60 years. In recent years, Empire has focused its considerable resources on strengthening its organization as a competitive and innovative leader in health care. The firm has reformed and restructured itself in order to prepare for the challenges and opportunities facing the health care industry ahead, and to ensure that it continues to provide the highest standards of quality and reliability in every aspect of its service and operations.

"We are committed to quality in all of the work that we do," says Michael A. Stocker, M.D., president and CEO of Empire. "The health of our members and the quality of the care they receive are of the utmost importance to everyone at Empire. We strive to provide the very best service to our members, our customers, and the physicians, hospitals, and other providers who belong to our networks."

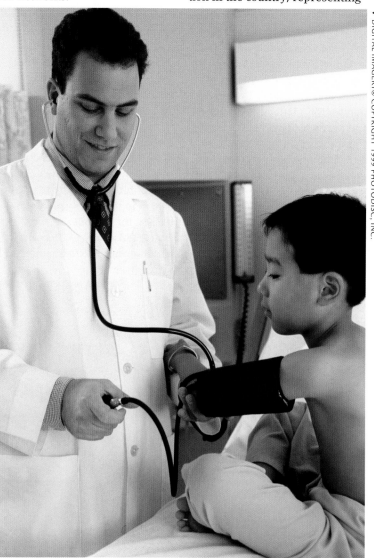

EMPIRE BLUE CROSS AND BLUE SHIELD WILL CONTINUE TO BE AN IMPORTANT PART OF NEW YORKERS' LIVES FOR DECADES TO COME.

HEALTHY CHANGES

It all began in New York in 1921, when a group of New York City hospital representatives, physicians, and business leaders met to consider the organization of a hospital service plan that would both provide a new and broader base of support for hospitals, and help families of average means pay their hospital bills. In 1934, this group incorporated as the Associated Hospital Service (AHS) of New York. Fifty years later, after a number of consolidations and mergers, it became Empire Blue Cross and Blue Shield. Today, Empire is the largest not-for-profit health insurance organization in the country, representing more than 10 percent of Blue Cross and Blue Shield's business nationwide.

There is little resemblance between the care given to the sick in 1934 and what is routinely provided to patients today. A host of breakthroughs in medical science, as well as the development of more sophisticated equipment, new diagnostic methods, and improved treatment modalities, have resulted in better ways of caring for the sick and increased life expectancies. Empire has responded to these changes over the years by taking a leadership role in expanding benefits where needed, and by developing innovative approaches to alternate delivery systems and health care cost containment.

In 1994, Stocker came to Empire to focus the organization's operations to prepare for the changing health care environment. He had already earned national prominence both in the practice of medicine and, as president of CIGNA Health Plan, in the delivery of health care services. As a medical doctor, Stocker is uniquely qualified to lead Empire into the future with a refined and effective philosophy: To establish, maintain, and improve efficient programs for nonprofit health care financing through the private sector, and to act on behalf of government at all levels in the administration of health care benefits for those protected under government-sponsored programs.

RECENT ACCOMPLISHMENTS

Over his tenure, Stocker has accomplished some extraordinary things within Empire Blue Cross and Blue Shield while implementing his philosophy. "We are in good shape financially," says Stocker. "Empire ended 1997 with a surplus of $378.3 million, up $76.9 million from 1996 and our largest surplus in recent memory. We have achieved significant improvements in customer service and satisfaction, reducing the amount of time we take to answer phones, pay claims, and respond to customer questions. Empire now ranks as one of the top 10 Blue Cross and Blue Shield plans in the United States in terms of customer service satisfaction. We have increased our managed care membership by more than 45 percent during the past year, making Empire one of the fastest-growing managed care companies in the region."

Stocker continues, "Empire now offers the broadest choice of leading hospitals and doctors, as well as new, innovative approaches to health care coverage. In addition, we offer a Medicare health maintenance organization and a workers' compensation program. Empire's plans are further strengthened by our investment in technological advances that help us improve member health. Sophisticated data analysis processes now allow us to track and measure the health care needs of our membership, so that we can help members when they need it. Our information technology allows us to improve customer service and reduce costs, so that we can deliver our services more efficiently."

SELECT SERVICES

Empire distinguishes itself among health insurers by providing individuals and groups of all sizes with an array of exceptional health plans that offer comprehensive benefits and convenient access to excellent networks of health professionals. Empire's managed care portfolio currently features Direct Connection EPO, Direct Connection HMO, BlueChoice HMO, Empire Deluxe PPO, Empire Dental Preferred PPO, BlueChoice Senior Plan, and BlueChoice Workers Compensation.

The organization's indemnity product line contains TraditionPLUS Hospital, Wraparound, CompreCare, Empire Dental TraditionPLUS Medicare Supplement, and Prescription Drug. Plans also offer pharmacy, dental, and vision options.

Currently, Empire serves the health care needs of more than 4.7 million customers in approximately 16,600 accounts. Its major clients include health organizations, financial companies, labor union organizations, corporations, and government groups.

Building on its long history in the health care industry, while evolving to meet the changing needs of managed care, Empire Blue Cross and Blue Shield will continue to be an important part of New Yorkers' lives for decades to come.

EMPIRE'S INFORMATION TECHNOLOGY ALLOWS IT TO IMPROVE CUSTOMER SERVICE AND REDUCE COSTS, SO THAT IT CAN DELIVER SERVICES MORE EFFICIENTLY (TOP).

FOUNDED IN NEW YORK CITY, EMPIRE IS THE LARGEST NOT-FOR-PROFIT HEALTH INSURANCE ORGANIZATION IN THE COUNTRY, REPRESENTING MORE THAN 10 PERCENT OF BLUE CROSS AND BLUE SHIELD'S BUSINESS NATIONWIDE (BOTTOM).

GIBNEY, ANTHONY & FLAHERTY, LLP

WHEN INTERNATIONAL COMPANIES SEEK TO ESTABLISH themselves in the United States, New York is often the city of choice. And while the first thing they are likely to want is the fastest route from the airport to Wall Street or Midtown, the second will almost certainly be a law firm that can help

them navigate U.S. laws and practices. In a perfect world, these companies would find a firm that also knows how to handle a good portion of their business problems, and one that is a respected member of the New York community.

These needs are met by Gibney, Anthony & Flaherty, LLP, the law firm that provides a broad range of expertise to international companies seeking to do business in the United States. Midsize, it is large enough to offer the resources and experience needed to facilitate the transfer and establishment of international business in both New York and the United States. But the firm is small enough to offer what most can't—a sincere personal interest and involvement in the affairs of its clients.

Gibney, Anthony & Flaherty, LLP approaches its clients not simply as their legal counsel, but as partners who look for ways to be of service in helping them establish and develop U.S. operations. The firm prides itself on its ability to solve a client's problems, or to assist in seeking the solution. In a city not particularly known for its warmth, Gibney, Anthony & Flaherty, LLP has chosen to do business in a caring, friendly manner.

This unusual mix of attention and expertise has earned the firm a unique position in New York. It handles some of the most recognized organizations on the New York scene, including Rolex, Louis Vuitton Malletier, L'Oréal, Brunschwig & Fils, and some of the emerging businesses now flourishing in New York City's Silicon Alley, such as the Attik Design. Finally, the firm's roster of clients features arguably the most famous of all New York organizations—the New York Yankees. In a real sense, this makes Gibney, Anthony & Flaherty, LLP integral to the New York scene.

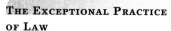

THE EXCEPTIONAL PRACTICE OF LAW

Gibney, Anthony & Flaherty, LLP has offices in New York City, with associated offices in Geneva and London, and a network of local counsel in major cities around the world. For more than 60 years, the firm has counseled clients in every field, from individuals and start-up businesses to multibillion-dollar conglomerates.

Most significantly, its close involvement with client entrepreneurs and executives has given the organization an extensive track record in far-ranging legal and business problems. This has challenged Gibney, Anthony & Flaherty, LLP to develop what has become its distinguishing signature in client service—the company serves first and foremost as a proactive problem solver for its clients. The firm's experienced professionals seek to identify issues before they arise, and strive to be ready with creative and innovative options long before action needs to be taken.

EXTENSIVE SERVICES

Gibney, Anthony & Flaherty, LLP's practice areas include corporate and commercial transactions, taxation, corporate finance, intellectual property and licensing, sports and entertainment, immigration, customs, real estate, litigation and arbitration, not-for-profit organizations, employee benefit plans and ERISA, creditors' rights, domestic relations, wills, estates and trusts, publishing, government relations, labor and employment, and antitrust and unfair competition.

The firm is particularly well known for its representation of major international businesses and sellers of prestige products, and for its work in the anticounterfeiting, corporate acquisition, and executive immigration fields. Its expertise in immigration, labor and employment, tax, and intellectual property makes Gibney, Anthony & Flaherty, LLP the ideal firm for foreign companies entering the U.S. market.

The People behind the Practice

Gibney, Anthony & Flaherty, LLP has assembled a talented group of 40 attorneys from a wide variety of backgrounds and specialties, enabling the company to provide a wide range of services to its international clientele. One of the firm's distinguishing characteristics is the ability of its members to speak a total of 12 different languages fluently, and its people can articulate the most complicated legal issues with complete clarity to their foreign-based clients.

The firm's partners are active and renowned in their fields of endeavor in the New York community. One of the partners is the chairman of the New York State Athletic Commission, and other partners hold chairmanships in a wide variety of organizations, including the New York City Economic Development Corporation. The firm has published a primer, *Starting a Business in the United States*, that is required reading in several U.S. business schools and is found in foreign consular offices throughout the world.

Yet the organization also understands that balance in life is important to a healthy working environment. The people at the firm work hard for their clients, but are also committed to their families and their communities. The organization feels that people who are happy and satisfied on a personal level make much more effective and productive professionals at work.

It's a formula that has been successful for the firm since its founding, and one that ensures that when international organizations want a capable and experienced, yet friendly law firm to deal with the intricacies of U.S. business law, they'll turn to Gibney, Anthony & Flaherty, LLP.

THE FIRM OCCUPIES TWO FLOORS OF THE ROLEX BUILDING, LOCATED ON FIFTH AVENUE AT THE CENTER OF MIDTOWN MANHATTAN.

LOUIS VUITTON MALLETIER PRODUCTS ARE SYNONYMOUS WITH BOTH ELEGANCE AND CREATIVITY. THE FIRM IS PLEASED TO REPRESENT LOUIS VUITTON MALLETIER AND ITS U.S. AFFILIATES.

NYC & COMPANY

"THE CITY IS BACK, TIMES SQUARE IS BACK, BROADWAY is back, fashion is back, and business is back, with new industries locating here for the first time," say Tim Zagat, chairman of NYC & Company. "Our image impacts all of the city's industries, tourism, and business development." Until recently, no organi-

zation had been designed to market all of New York City as a place to live, visit, and build a business. This had been the case even though business decisions, as well as travel and convention decisions, are driven in significant ways by image. That's why the New York Convention & Visitors Bureau decided it would be both effective and advantageous to expand its efforts to include business development. Renamed NYC & Company in 1999, the organization is dedicated to the premise that New York City should be the destination of choice for everyone in the world, whether they are looking for an exciting vacation or a resource-rich environment for a new business.

NYC & COMPANY IS DEDICATED TO THE PREMISE THAT NEW YORK CITY SHOULD BE THE DESTINATION OF CHOICE FOR EVERYONE IN THE WORLD, WHETHER THEY ARE LOOKING FOR AN EXCITING VACATION OR A RESOURCE-RICH ENVIRONMENT FOR A NEW BUSINESS.

PROMOTING NYC FOR BUSINESS AND PLEASURE

NYC & Company promotes more than 63,000 hotel rooms, 18,000 dining spots, 550 museums and galleries, 300 theaters and nightclubs, and countless retail establishments—not to mention the city's $1.4 billion convention, exhibition, and meeting industry.

New York City is enjoying record-breaking visitor levels— more than 33 million visitors annually, spending in excess of

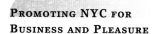

$14 billion, with a total economic impact of $20 billion. The city's market share, which was previously on the decline, has recovered. Tourism is responsible, directly and indirectly, for creating some 244,000 New York City jobs. With a highly effective series of marketing programs and campaigns, these figures indicate that NYC & Company has been quite successful in its efforts.

UTILIZING THE CITY'S POSITIVE IMAGE

The city's image worldwide is at an all-time high. Crime levels are at 30-year lows. New York City is now ranked the safest large city in America. The streets are cleaner, the parks are welcoming, and there are more jobs. Culturally, economically, and socially, the city is riding the crest of good times.

While continuing its efforts in personal and business-related tourism, the new NYC & Company also facilitates visits for foreign businesses considering relocation or expansion to New York. More proactively, the organization "matchmakes" through an international outreach program that promotes all the advantages, resources, assets, and opportunities available to any company that

would benefit from a New York operation.

"New York is an amazing place. While we are a city of immense diversity, we have strong bonds that unite us in our love of this city and the pride we take in its revitalization and new image," says Zagat. "We learned the hard way that the city's image is directly related to its economic well-being. It is this positive image that helps us sell our city. Yes, it stimulates tourism, but it also stimulates economic development of every kind."

THE FASHION INSTITUTE OF TECHNOLOGY (FIT) IS EVERY-thing that its name implies and more. It is indeed a world-renowned institution of higher education for careers in the fashion industry, with a list of alumni including such designers as Calvin Klein, Norma Kamali, and David Chu of Nautica. But over

its 56-year history, the college has expanded in size and scope, and now offers highly respected programs in a wide range of design and business areas, from interior design to international trade, cosmetics marketing to computer animation, textile development to toy design.

FIT is rooted in industry and the world of work. And though the college is now associated with many industries and professions besides fashion apparel, FIT's commitment to career education is still its hallmark, as well as a source of pride to an institution whose industry connection is an integral part of its history.

A FASHIONABLE START

In the early 1940s, two men—educator and former tailor Mortimer C. Ritter and Max Meyer, a retired cloak and suit manufacturer—decided that New York needed "an MIT [Massachusetts Institute of Technology] for the fashion industries" to ensure vitality in apparel manufacturing. They helped to create the Educational Foundation for the Fashion Industries to promote education in the field. In turn, the Foundation obtained a charter from the New York State Board of Regents, and secured space and equipment from the New York City Board of Education for its newly

created institute, opening in 1944 with 100 students. A few years later, FIT became part of the State University of New York, with the authority to confer the associate in applied science degree.

Over the years, the college continued to broaden in scope, transforming itself from a small, garment-industry trade school into an internationally recognized college with a modern, eight-building campus and a sophisticated curriculum, offering a variety of study-abroad options. Today, it has more than 12,000 students, and offers associate's, bachelor's, and master's degrees in 30 different subject areas.

STYLISH CONNECTIONS

FIT is known for its faculty—a remarkable group of professionals who do much more than teach.

All have industry experience, and many are currently employed in industry or have their own businesses. Their real-world, hands-on approach to education makes the FIT experience especially relevant.

FIT's location in the heart of Manhattan provides a great opportunity for students to participate in the college's extensive internship program. Each year, internships are offered by more than 1,500 corporations, including retailers and designers, radio and television networks, consumer magazines, and most major corporations in New York City. About 40 percent of eligible students parlay their internships into full- or part-time jobs. In addition to internships, FIT offers both contacts and career placement services, leading to an 88 percent placement rate for students who seek such assistance.

This success illustrates FIT's commitment to its mission: to prepare students for their careers. "FIT's mission is to educate students for careers in a world different from the one we know today. This focus reinforces our commitment to produce technically proficient graduates with problem solving and analytic skills," says FIT President Dr. Joyce F. Brown. "They will emerge as creative practitioners and leaders and be able to answer questions we have yet to ask."

CLOCKWISE FROM TOP:
LOCATION, LOCATION, LOCATION:
FIT'S MODERN CAMPUS ON SEVENTH
AVENUE AT 27TH STREET AND
NEW YORK CITY MERGE AS ONE.

AT 10 YEARS OLD, FIT'S TOY DE-SIGN PROGRAM WAS THE FIRST OF ITS KIND, AND PLACES NEARLY 100 PERCENT OF ITS GRADUATES IN JOBS EACH YEAR BY COMBINING THE ANALYTICAL AND CREATIVE WITH A HANDS-ON APPROACH.

STATE-OF-THE-ART COMPUTER FACILITIES PROVIDE STUDENTS THE OPPORTUNITY TO EXPLORE TECHNOLOGY AND ITS INTEGRATION IN DESIGN AND BUSINESS PRACTICES, AS WELL AS TO PREPARE FOR CA-REERS AFTER COLLEGE.

HENRY DONEGER FOUNDED THE DONEGER GROUP.

ABBEY DONEGER IS THE PRESIDENT OF THE DONEGER GROUP.

HERE IS SOMETHING VERY SPECIAL ABOUT WORKING IN New York's apparel industry. Maybe it's walking down the long stretch of Seventh Avenue known as Fashion Avenue, flanked by hundreds of apparel showrooms, and bumping into an internationally recognized designer. Or maybe it's anxiously awaiting the unveiling of the latest designs during Seventh on Sixth, the biannual runway shows held underneath billowing white tents in Bryant Park.

Whatever it is, the business of fashion is an arena in which New York City plays an important and ever changing role. The action is fast paced in the fashion industry, and the players are many. One of the leading players is The Doneger Group.

The Doneger Group's role in the industry is to help its clients achieve greater sales, increase profits, gain market share, and realize their full potential. As the undisputed market leader in fashion merchandising consulting and service-oriented buying, the firm is a dominant force in the fashion industry. Doneger's retail client base ranges from fine specialty and department stores to discount stores and mass merchants worldwide.

A specialized business, The Doneger Group has contributed to the unique advantages that New York has to offer the fashion industry. In a spacious, well-equipped facility, the offices and conference rooms of The Doneger Group contain merchandise samples of key items that identify the most fashion-forward trends in all categories of women's, men's, and children's apparel and accessories, and home furnishings. Providing the highest level of service and quality information to its clients ranks as The Doneger Group's top priority, which defines the firm's position as the industry's leading fashion merchandising consulting firm. The company's mission is to provide clients with the industry's finest network of resources, information, and services to help them succeed in today's retail environment and prepare for the future.

A VISION OF INDUSTRY LEADERSHIP

The Doneger Group had its beginnings in one man's desire to fill a niche in the marketplace. In 1946, in the midst of the postwar boom, Henry Doneger identified the need to assist women's specialty retailers in researching the apparel and accessories markets to better address customer needs. His vision provided the foundation for the industry's leading resident buying office and fashion merchandising consulting firm. Doneger had the foresight to build the meaningful relationships with industry manufacturers that laid the groundwork for servicing his retail clients.

Doneger positioned the company as an integral member of the fashion industry. His business network grew continuously because he believed in people and felt that the success of the company was a direct result of the quality of its employees. Henry Doneger's son and current company president, Abbey Doneger, has followed in his father's footsteps, driving the growth of the business through the expansion of its staff and services.

MERCHANDISING INSIGHT

Doneger market specialists conduct research on a daily basis to identify and recommend the most important items and resources

n all merchandise categories. Then, in both one-on-one consultations and group presentations, Doneger's merchandising team addresses the specific needs of each retail organization. In addition to servicing an impressive list of U.S.-based retailers, the company—coordinating through its HDA International division—consults with retailers from more than 20 countries throughout the world. The eyes of the world are on New York and The Doneger Group through a combination of stateside trend information, sourcing opportunities, and American merchandising ideas, helping international retailers gain a different perspective and new strategies for their businesses.

Through D^3 Doneger Design Direction, the talents and insights of the firm's trend forecasters provide a service for clients that is unmatched in the marketplace. Available to retailers and manufacturers, as well as companies interested in the business of style tracking and trending fashion, is a range of fashion forecast reports and services that only Doneger's consultants can provide. From a major presence at the leading fashion shows around the world to an expert voice on all aspects of retail markets, the D^3 color and

trend forecasting team is in the lead in its ability to guide clients in anticipating the fast-paced world of fashion and retail trends.

Doneger's on-line division utilizes the Internet as an effective communication tool. The company's Web site at www.doneger.com introduces the company and provides an overview of services. Doneger Online offers a range of service options, including up-to-the-minute market information, trend direction, industry news, resources, time-sensitive promotional opportunities, and virtual showrooms where a retailer can shop a specific manufacturer's line, obtain information on the

products, and even place an order, if desired. This and other new media programs currently in development will help to change the very nature of apparel buying and sourcing.

Looking to the future, The Doneger Group is strategically positioned to capitalize on its talented team of retail merchandising specialists, its technology expertise, and its unfaltering vision to provide leadership to clients and the fashion industry. Abbey Doneger is confident that his company's role in the global fashion industry will foster prosperity for its clients and continued success for the company in the decades to come.

THE OFFICES AND CONFERENCE ROOMS OF THE DONEGER GROUP CONTAIN MERCHANDISE SAMPLES OF KEY ITEMS THAT IDENTIFY THE MOST FASHION-FORWARD TRENDS IN ALL CATEGORIES OF WOMEN'S, MEN'S AND CHILDREN'S APPAREL AND ACCESSORIES, AND HOME FURNISHINGS. PROVIDING THE HIGHEST LEVEL OF SERVICE AND QUALITY INFORMATION TO ITS CLIENTS RANKS AS THE DONEGER GROUP'S TOP PRIORITY (TOP LEFT AND RIGHT).

DONEGER ONLINE'S FASHION INFORMATION SYSTEM IS CHANGING THE WAY CLIENTS RESEARCH AND BUY APPAREL (BOTTOM).

Watson Wyatt Worldwide

WHAT HAPPENS WHEN THE MOST RESPECTED BUSINESS newspaper in the country, *The Wall Street Journal*, conducts a survey among its subscribers, asking them to rate consulting firms on the value of services delivered to their clients? If your firm is Watson Wyatt Worldwide, the results are simple,

but impressive: a number one ranking for delivering value to clients. For more than 50 years, Watson Wyatt has sought to distinguish itself from its competitors by attaining higher and higher levels of client satisfaction—and its efforts have clearly paid off.

CONSULTING WITH THE CLIENT IS ESSENTIAL FOR SUCCESS AND CLIENT SATISFACTION. WATSON WYATT'S NEW YORK CITY OFFICE BRINGS VALUE TO CLIENTS LOCALLY AND AROUND THE WORLD, WORKING WITH THE FIRM'S OFFICES IN 90 LOCATIONS.

WATSON WYATT WORLDWIDE'S MARKET-DRIVEN RESEARCH ENSURES THAT ADVICE IS BASED ON FACT, NOT ON CONVENTIONAL WISDOM (BOTTOM LEFT).

HIGHLY TRAINED AND COMMITTED PROFESSIONALS, WATSON WYATT CONSULTANTS ARE, ABOVE ALL, STRATEGIC THINKERS (BOTTOM RIGHT).

A global consulting firm, Watson Wyatt brings together two disciplines—people and financial management—to help clients improve business performance. Watson Wyatt has more than 5,000 associates in 32 countries. They are backed by the best and most current research on people and financial management issues. The firm's associates include consultants, actuaries, attorneys,

physicians, nurses, and other specialists in the areas of human resources, employee benefits, health care, compensation, communications, and technology.

IN THE COMPANY OF EXCELLENCE

Watson Wyatt recognizes that companies today are facing unique issues in the increasingly global market, such as the new social contract between the employer and employee; the impact of the aging workforce; managing change within the organization; attracting and retaining effective employees; supporting strategy with the right technology; implementing effective compensation and benefits strategies; achieving success through people and financial management; and analyzing demographics and helping to align people to handle the imminent workforce structure crisis.

To meet these challenges, Watson Wyatt provides an array of services, each designed to help clients move closer to the ideal of maximizing their human capital and their financial resources in tandem, a complex equation when faced with changing workforce demographics and increasingly demanding and unforgiving financial markets.

The firm offers three key areas of client services. Its Benefits Consulting services address the design, financing, administration, and communication of retirement and group benefits and health care programs to attract, keep, and motivate a client's workforce. Watson Wyatt's Human Capital Group helps a company focus its competitive advantage through the development and implementation of compensation, performance, and other programs that align its workforce with its business strategy. HR Technologies works to achieve improved administration of human resource programs and employee services delivery.

DISTINGUISHING CHARACTER

Historically, many consultants have prided themselves on their role as objective, independent, outside professionals—the rationale being that an independent viewpoint would more objectively bring issues to the attention of management. Watson Wyatt approaches client service differently. The collaborative consulting approach starts with *ClientFirst*™— where consultants work with clients to define needs and expectations, and then measure their performance according to mutually agreed-upon standards. Building on research-based innovation and a deep knowledge of clients' businesses, Watson Wyatt partners with them to provide tailored solutions. The firm prefers to function as a part of the client team so that it gains a uniquely inside point of view on the client's business objectives and its financial and human resources. When Watson Wyatt reviews a client company's policies, it does so fully understanding the internal ramifications. The firm brings its professional perspective to bear on the issue and makes recommendations that integrate human resources issues with business strategies to add shareholder value.

MICHAEL DARTER

Client projects typically have a three-step process. The first is the discovery phase, where the consultants identify and articulate issues and obtain all necessary information. The second is the invention phase, where Watson Wyatt works hand in hand with the client to develop solutions that fit the working environment and prevailing business strategies. Finally, in the delivery phase, Watson Wyatt executes the appropriate solutions from a broad range of possibilities.

Watson Wyatt's creative approach to problem solving has led to an outstanding collection of innovative ideas. For example, one of the top three significant retirement design innovations in the past 20 years—the pension equity plan (PEP)—was invented by the firm in 1993 and has been adopted by many Fortune 100 companies. The firm also developed the first interactive retirement planning system—the prototype of its VISION retirement planning software—for one of the world's largest companies, to encourage employees to share the responsibility for planning for their retirement.

TECHNOLOGICAL LEADERSHIP
Watson Wyatt continues its leadership in technology by developing many intranet applications. The firm developed an employee opinion survey process to support organizational change toward total quality management. Its Electra software program is a unique retirement design tool, allowing clients to quickly analyze and compare the level of benefits provided to an employee under different types of retirement plans.

In addition, Watson Wyatt emphasizes research-based consulting, ensuring a comprehensive working knowledge of all pertinent internal and external issues affecting a client's unique situation. By maintaining a constant watch on changing trends and issues facing business, both locally and globally, Watson Wyatt can better prepare clients for fluctuating circumstances. For example, as early as 1984, Watson Wyatt recognized problems with the solvency of the Social Security system, and published a report on the subject titled *The Sleeping Giant Awakens*.

It is little wonder *Wall Street Journal* survey respondents ranked Watson Wyatt number one in the consulting industry when it comes to delivering value to clients. Since opening its doors in 1946, Watson Wyatt has been earning the ranking every day.

CLOCKWISE FROM TOP: THE COMPANY VALUES ITS OWN PEOPLE, AND WORKS HARD TO RECRUIT, SELECT, AND DEVELOP ASSOCIATES WHO SEE EXCEPTIONAL WORK AS A KEY COMPONENT IN HOW THEY DEFINE THEMSELVES.

WATSON WYATT ENCOURAGES TEAMWORK IN ALL AREAS, FROM CLIENT WORK TO OFFICE-SPONSORED SPORTS TEAMS. THE FIRM ALSO PARTICIPATES IN THE COMMUNITY THROUGH ITS SUPPORT OF CHARITABLE ORGANIZATIONS, INCLUDING THE DOE FUND, FOR WHICH IT IS A CORPORATE SPONSOR.

WATSON WYATT CONSULTANTS MEET CHALLENGES WITH ALL OF THE ENERGY AND RESOURCES REQUIRED TO DEVELOP INNOVATIVE SOLUTIONS.

LILLIAN VERNON CORPORATION

ROM A KITCHEN TABLE IN A SLEEPY SUBURB OF NEW York City to homes and offices across America, Lillian Vernon Corporation has grown from one housewife's dream into one of the leading specialty catalog and on-line retailers in the country. Publicly traded on the American Stock Exchange,

the company has sales in excess of a quarter-billion dollars. Guided by founder and Chief Executive Officer Lillian Vernon, the company continues to define and redefine the size, scope, and direction of the direct marketing industry.

What was once a 16-page, black-and-white catalog of practical personal and household accessories has grown with its audience, incorporating new products and technologies along the way. Today, the company publishes 34 editions of eight specialty catalog titles that feature gift, household, gardening, kitchen, Christmas, and children's products. The catalogs average 96 pages, feature more than 700 products, and have a total circulation exceeding 188 million.

In 1974, Lillian Vernon opened its first outlet store in Mount Vernon. While there are now 15 stores in Delaware, New York, South Carolina, and Virginia, the company still emphasizes the shop-at-home concept it helped pioneer. Its products have been featured on television's QVC shopping network, and its traditional print catalogs are now augmented by the company's state-of-the-art Web site, www. lillianvernon.com. On-line customers can view more than 400 best-selling products, and can order any of the 6,000-plus products featured in the catalogs, using an electronic order blank. The company also has a Business to Business Wholesale Division.

TODAY THE LILLIAN VERNON CORPORATION PUBLISHES 34 EDITIONS OF EIGHT SPECIALTY CATALOG TITLES THAT FEATURE GIFT, HOUSEHOLD, GARDENING, KITCHEN, CHRISTMAS, AND CHILDREN'S PRODUCTS. THE CATALOGS AVERAGE 96 PAGES, FEATURE MORE THAN 700 PRODUCTS, AND HAVE A TOTAL CIRCULATION EXCEEDING 188 MILLION.

GUIDED BY ITS FOUNDER AND CHIEF EXECUTIVE OFFICER, LILLIAN VERNON, THE COMPANY CONTINUES TO DEFINE AND REDEFINE THE SIZE, SCOPE, AND DIRECTION OF THE DIRECT MARKETING INDUSTRY.

IN THE BEGINNING

From its humble beginnings in 1951—when Vernon invested $2,000 of wedding gift money and placed a $495 ad in *Seventeen* magazine—Lillian Vernon Corporation has grown into an industry leader. The company's first products were a leather handbag and belt set, which sold for $5.58. What set the offer apart was that both

the bag and the belt could be personalized with the customer's initials, free of charge. The ad generated $32,000 in orders, and Lillian Vernon Corporation was launched.

Five years later, Lillian Vernon mailed her first catalog to the 125,000 customers who had responded to her ads. That first effort featured an expanded product line that included combs, blazer buttons, collar pins, and cuff links, all offered with personalization free of charge. Today, Lillian Vernon Corporation operates one of the largest in-house, state-of-the-art personalization departments in the country. Monogramming free of charge remains a company hallmark.

THE WOMAN BEHIND THE COMPANY

As a pioneering businesswoman, Vernon has a long-standing commitment to serving other women and her community. An active

member of the Committee of 200, a group of the nation's most influential businesswomen, Vernon was the first female member of the American Business Conference and a member of the Women's Forum. She has received many honors, including the American Red Cross Good Neighbor Award, Big Brothers/Big Sisters National Hero Award, and Ellis Island Medal of Honor. She has also been inducted into the Direct Marketing Association Hall of Fame.

Vernon encourages the careers of women, both on her own staff and in the workplace in general, and has enjoyed being a mentor. "When I started my business 48 years ago, there were only a few female role models in business, and they were limited to businesses aimed at the female market. I hope my success has contributed to the level of respect women in business have earned," says Vernon.

W

HEN THE FOUR SEASONS OPENED, IT SURPRISED THE culinary world. Never before had a restaurant so captured New Yorkers' imagination with seasonal food and sleek design. "Both in decor and in menu, it is spectacular, modern and audacious . . . and it is perhaps the most exciting restaurant to open in New York within the last two decades," wrote the *New York Times* back in 1959, just after the restaurant opened. For five decades, The Four Seasons has been recognized for setting new standards of excellence for food, service, and atmosphere. Today, it is a classic—named Best Restaurant in America by the James Beard Foundation.

A DARING ADVENTURE

The Four Seasons is unlike any other restaurant. Everything, from the ingredients to the furnishings, has been specially created to celebrate design, service, and food. Built by Philip Johnson and Ludwig Mies van der Rohe, two of the 20th century's most influential architects, The Four Seasons spared no expense in creating the first luxurious American restaurant. With an unprecedented budget of $4.5 million, its creators envisioned a space that embodies the philosophy of "less is more."

What they built was Manhattan's only landmarked restaurant. With soaring, 20-foot, floor-to-ceiling windows, the restaurant features shimmering gold chain curtains that ripple up hypnotically, sealing off the outside world. Art by such geniuses as Picasso, Lichtenstein, and Miró fills the space as guests sit beside a bubbling, white marble pool. Many of the furnishings are part of the design collection of New York's Museum of Modern Art, including the Mies van der Rohe Brno chairs, the brandy snifters, and the silver bread baskets.

A LEADER IN THE CULINARY WORLD

While the architecture brings visitors to The Four Seasons, it is the service that locals love. With a warm and caring staff, the restaurant offers a friendly oasis from Manhattan's hectic pace. As the *New York Post* notes,

THE FOUR SEASONS IS UNLIKE ANY OTHER RESTAURANT. EVERYTHING, FROM THE INGREDIENTS TO THE FURNISHINGS, HAS BEEN SPECIALLY CREATED TO CELEBRATE DESIGN, SERVICE, AND FOOD.

"The Four Seasons showcases the best qualities of Manhattan as the millennium approaches. It celebrates prosperity but not pretension. It is at once vast and intimate, cosmopolitan and cozy."

It's not just the setting and service that set The Four Seasons apart from the competition. The restaurant is best known for its philosophy about food. The first restaurant to introduce the idea of changing seasonal menus to America, The Four Seasons was created to celebrate local ingredients at their peak of freshness. The restaurant refused to serve ingredients out of season and, in the process, revolutionized the culinary world.

True to its name, The Four Seasons surveys local farmers and fishermen in search of the season's most delicious ingredients, and brings them to the table in surprising combinations that perfectly reflect the city's many cultural influences.

Whether guests visit for the design, the service, or the food, one thing is certain, the *New York Times* notes: "In the many years that The Four Seasons has been pampering its patrons, it has learned how to send each one out of the door with a sense of having lived, if only for a few hours, the life of the very rich."

WHILE THE ARCHITECTURE BRINGS VISITORS TO THE FOUR SEASONS, IT IS THE SERVICE THAT LOCALS LOVE. WITH A WARM AND CARING STAFF, THE RESTAURANT OFFERS A FRIENDLY OASIS FROM MANHATTAN'S HECTIC PACE.

SUSAN STAVA

JACOBI MEDICAL CENTER

Located in the Bronx, Jacobi Medical Center provides quality health care for some 1.2 million Bronx and New York-area residents, and proudly continues as a place of learning and groundbreaking advances in the field of medicine. ✦ Founded in 1955, Jacobi Hospital Center consisted of two

hospitals: Jacobi Hospital and Van Etten Hospital. Jacobi Hospital was named in honor of Dr. Abraham Jacobi, known as the father of American pediatrics; and Van Etten Hospital was named in honor of Dr. Nathan Bristol Van Etten, a prominent Bronx physician, known for his deep concern for the poor.

With more than 538 beds, Jacobi Medical Center has grown into the largest public hospital in the Bronx. It operates six community-based health centers throughout the Bronx that provide general adult and pediatric examinations and health screenings for a variety of concerns, including high blood pressure, diabetes, breast cancer, and prostate cancer.

Jacobi Medical Center is a member of the New York City Health and Hospital Corporation (NYCH&HC) and partners in the North Bronx Healthcare Network, one of six regional networks established by NYCH&HC. The center employs 3,154 people and offers a complete range of services, such as acute, specialty, general, and psychiatric care.

CARING SERVICE

Patients from all over the tristate area come to Jacobi Medical Center for treatment at the facility's

trauma center—one of only two Level I trauma centers in the Bronx. It serves as the regional trauma center for north Bronx and lower Westchester County, New York, communities with separate, specialized treatment areas for adults, children, and patients in need of emergency psychiatric care.

Fire victims and others suffering from oxygen deprivation, including New York City firefighters, are brought to Jacobi's Hyperbaric Center, which houses the region's only multiperson hyperbaric chamber. Founded in 1983, the Hyperbaric Center continues to treat more than 200 emergency patients each year for smoke in-

halation, carbon monoxide poisoning, and driving injuries. The center also offers a complete array of elective oxygen therapy to combat infection and promote healing.

Burn victims are treated at Jacobi's burn unit, the only burn service in the Bronx and the second largest in New York City. The Burn Center opened in 1963 as the first and only unit of its kind in the area. It has an international reputation for 35 years of pioneering clinical research and teaching early surgical intervention to preserve skin and minimize infection.

Jacobi's Women's Health Center is considered a model primary care program, and includes a new Breast Care Center that provides the full spectrum of women's health needs from adolescence through maturity. The center is acclaimed worldwide for its work with high-risk pregnancies and for its efforts to reduce low birth weight and infant mortality. Thanks to a Level III neonatal intensive care unit with one of the best records in the country, the center delivers 2,200 babies annually, with 40 percent by nationally acclaimed midwifery services.

Jacobi also operates the first hospital-based Pediatric AIDS

CLOCKWISE FROM TOP: AT THE HELM OF JACOBI MEDICAL CENTER'S ADMINISTRATION IS JOSEPH S. ORLANDO, EXECUTIVE DIRECTOR.

JACOBI PROVIDES CARE TO SOME 1.2 MILLION BRONX AND NEW YORK-AREA RESIDENTS. THE CENTER OFFERS A COMPLETE RANGE OF ACUTE, SPECIALTY, GENERAL, AND PSYCHIATRIC SERVICES.

BURN VICTIMS FROM THROUGHOUT GREATER NEW YORK RECEIVE TREATMENT AT JACOBI'S BURN UNIT, THE ONLY BURN SERVICE IN THE BRONX AND THE SECOND LARGEST IN NEW YORK CITY.

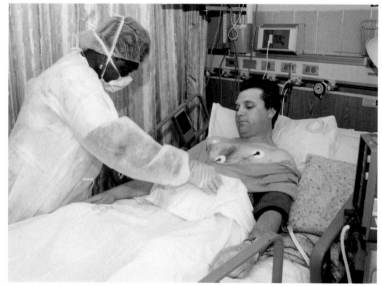

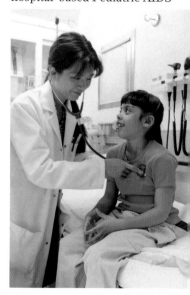

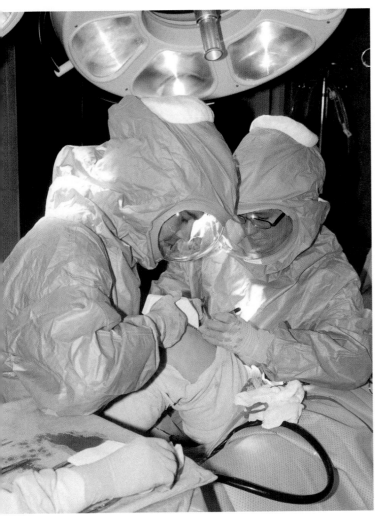

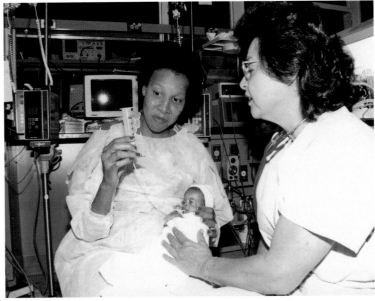

Day Care Program in the country, as well as a state-of-the-art out-patient center for adult AIDS patients. The center provides complete medical and psychological services in a single location, and both programs are designed to keep patients healthy and at home for as long as possible.

A Leader in Research

Treating and caring for patients is only one facet of Jacobi Medical Center; it's also world-renowned for leading the way in medical research. In the 1950s, Jacobi took a proactive stand in treating tuberculosis and produced the first significant breakthrough in Tay-Sachs disease, a disorder inherited among Eastern European Jews. It was also the first municipal hospital center, after Bellevue and Kings County, to implement its own psychiatric units.

Other firsts include separating good cholesterol that protects against atherosclerosis, and performing the world's first coronary bypass operation. Jacobi surgeons were also the first in the United States to use mechanical staple sutures, and the first to use mini-computers to monitor patients' blood circulation and lung function.

Jacobi was also the site of the country's first National Institutes of Health General Research Center for the severely ill and injured, which prompted the introduction of germ-free isolators in the operating room and at bedside to prevent infection. This research led to Jacobi's delivery of the world's first germ-free baby.

Because of its stellar reputation, Jacobi is one of the foremost medical teaching centers in New York, focusing on patient care, research, and education. It sponsors approved residency and fellowship training programs in more than 40 specialties and subspecialties, and is a major academic affiliate and teaching site of the Albert Einstein College of Medicine.

In 1998, Jacobi inaugurated an innovative affiliation agreement with North Central Bronx Hospital to create the Jacobi/ North Central Bronx Physicians' Alliance, which provides first-rate physicians and clinical services at both institutions. This partnership means the alliance's more than 375 physicians have a full-time commitment to the mission, objectives, and success of the network, its patients, and its staff.

Jacobi's dedicated staff continues to attract international attention thanks to ongoing research in emergency trauma and burn care. In the near future, the center plans to expand its ability to treat trauma patients with the creation of an even larger trauma center, an upgrade of the Burn Center, and an expansion of primary care capacities. These expansions and its ongoing mission to provide medical care to the New York area will continue to place Jacobi Medical Center at the forefront of medical treatment and research in New York and around the world.

CLOCKWISE FROM TOP LEFT: SOME OF THE NATION'S FINEST MEDICAL AND PROFESSIONAL PERSONNEL PROVIDE FIRST-RATE PATIENT CARE AT JACOBI MEDICAL CENTER.

BY HELICOPTER OR BY AMBULANCE, PATIENTS FROM THROUGHOUT THE AREA COME TO JACOBI'S TRAUMA CENTER—ONE OF ONLY TWO LEVEL I TRAUMA CENTERS IN THE BRONX.

THE WOMEN'S HEALTH CENTER IS BACKED UP BY A LEVEL III NEONATAL INTENSIVE CARE UNIT WITH ONE OF THE BEST OUTCOME RECORDS IN THE COUNTRY.

1962 Manhattan East Suite Hotels

1965 American Warehousing/American Stevedoring

1968 New York State Metropolitan
Transportation Authority

1968 United Nations Development Corporation (UNDC)

1970 MultiPlan, Inc.

1970 New York City Health and Hospitals Corporation

1971 Structure Tone Inc.

1972 Covenant House

1972 First American Title Insurance Company
of New York

1975 The Trump Organization

1980 Data Industries Ltd.

1981 Bloomberg L.P.

1983 York Hunter

1984 Computer Generated Solutions, Inc.

1987 JLC Environmental Consultants, Inc.

1988 Bristol Plaza

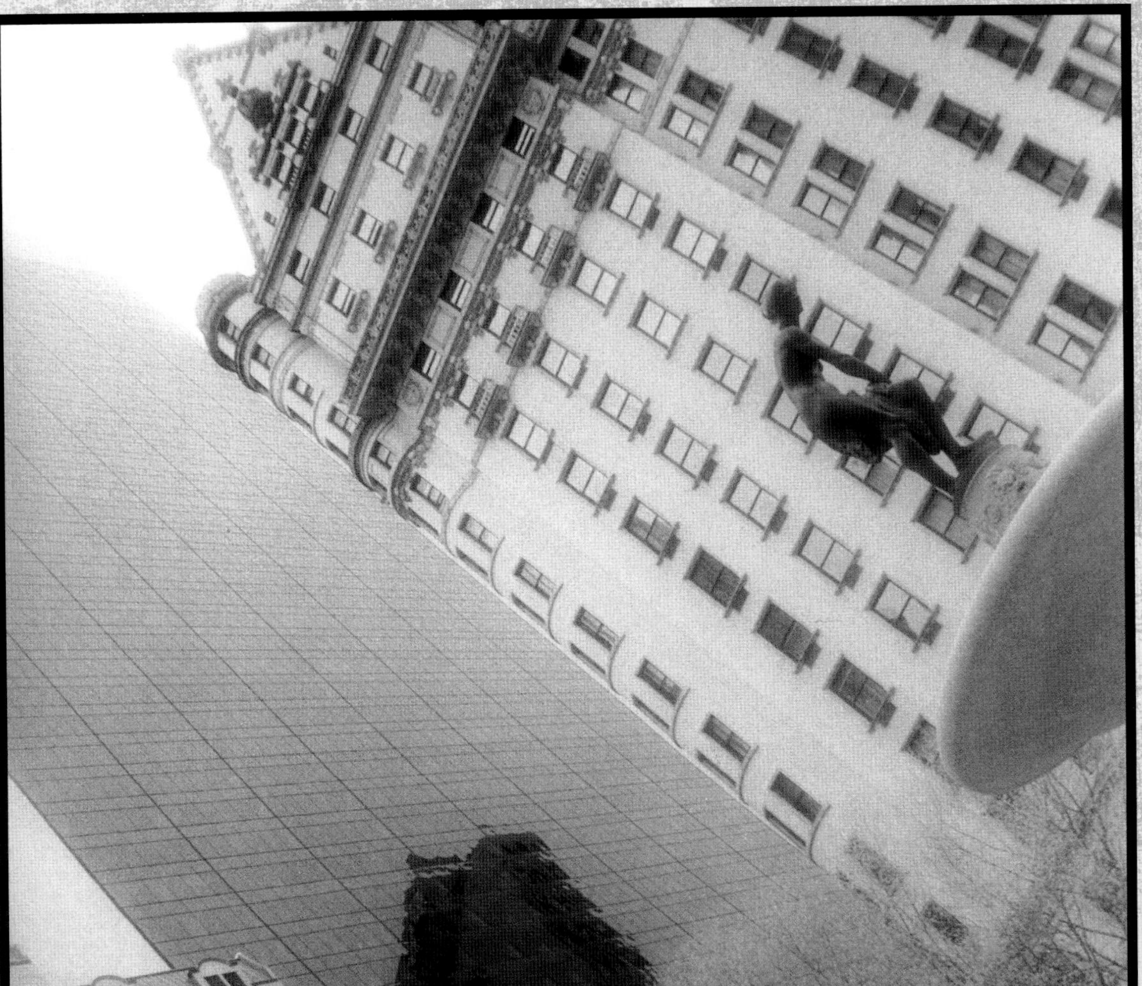

▲ © JONATHAN POSTAL / TOWERY PUBLISHING, INC.

MANHATTAN EAST
SUITE HOTELS

all-suite hotel group.

Today, with 10 properties and more than 2,100 units in New York City, Manhattan East Suite Hotels are a haven for savvy business travelers and corporate travel planners. The hotels count many of the city's major financial and banking firms, as well as other Fortune 500 companies, among their most loyal clients.

HIGH ATOP THE BEEKMAN TOWER HOTEL, THE SPECTACULAR TOP OF THE TOWER OFFERS MAGNIFICENT VIEWS OF THE CITY (LEFT).

THE PARTNERS OF MANHATTAN EAST SUITE HOTELS ARE (FROM LEFT) DANIEL DENIHAN, BROOKE BARRETT, LAURENCE DENIHAN, JOHN FERRARI, PATRICK DENIHAN, AND DONALD DENIHAN (RIGHT).

LOCATION, LOCATION, LOCATION

Founded in 1962 by Benjamin J. Denihan, Manhattan East Suite Hotels started with one property: the 130-unit Lyden Gardens, New York City's first all-suite hotel. Nearly indistinguishable from its brownstone neighbors, the Lyden Gardens sits on a tree-lined stretch of East 64th Street.

From this humble beginning and a firm grasp on the old real estate success axiom—location, location, location—Denihan sought to offer visitors "the New Yorker's New York," and began acquiring, building, and opening hotels in such neighborhoods as Sutton Place and Murray Hill. The hallmarks of each hotel were incomparable value and personalized service.

Manhattan East Suite Hotels offer considerably more living and closet space than standard hotel rooms, along with the convenience of a fully equipped kitchen. Most of the hotels provide fitness centers, restaurants, room service, and meeting facilities. Still, it is the sense of family that truly sets Manhattan East Suite Hotels apart. The owners treat their employees like family and, in turn, the staff treats each and every guest like family.

A VARIETY OF SITES

The Shelburne Murray Hill, situated on a distinguished corner of Lexington Avenue among rows of town houses and historic churches, brings a residential ease and comfort to its guests. From its 272 graciously appointed suites to its rooftop garden, the Shelburne Murray Hill is a favorite home away from home for many regular visitors.

With 523 suites, Southgate Tower in New York's fashion district is not simply the largest hotel in the Manhattan East Suite Hotels family, it is the largest all-suite hotel in New York City. Its Seventh Avenue location makes it convenient to Pennsylvania Station, Madison Square Garden, and the Jacob Javits Convention Center, as well as the famed Broadway theaters, restaurants, and nightspots.

At the Surrey Hotel, impeccable service and style have been the hallmark since 1926. Acquired by the Denihan family in 1971 and transformed into a modern, all-suite property, this Upper East Side hotel is among the most luxurious of the Manhattan East Suite Hotels group. Minutes from Central Park and the world-renowned Madison Avenue galleries and boutiques, the Surrey houses Café Boulud, home of the acclaimed French chef Daniel Boulud.

The Eastgate Tower on East 39th Street bears the distinction of being the first hotel designed and built by the Denihan family. The property is situated in the historic Murray Hill neighbor-

▶ JAY BRADY PHOTOGRAPHY

hood, and is within convenient walking distance of many midtown businesses, restaurants, and shops.

Strategically located on East 34th Street, the 248-suite Dumont Plaza boasts close proximity to Madison Avenue's corporate centers; in fact, it is within walking distance of all that mid-Manhattan has to offer. Since its opening in 1986, Dumont Plaza has become a preferred place to stay, whether for brief business trips or for long-term stays.

The Newest Addition
The newest addition to the Manhattan East Suite Hotels family is The Benjamin, located on East 50th Street at Lexington Avenue. A homage to the company founder, The Benjamin is the company's flagship property and its first four-star Executive Suite Hotel.

The Benjamin retains the design and flair of its original archi-

tect, Emery Roth, who designed the 30-story building in the 1920s as the Hotel Beverly. Roth was famous for creating buildings that resembled Italian Renaissance palazzi, with soaring spires and a grand sense of entry. The Benjamin lobby reflects this aesthetic with its domed ceiling, Venetian mirrors, and grand staircase that leads to The Benjamin Lounge, where guests can relax and enjoy the view from the hotel's arched, Palladian windows.

An ambitious project, The Benjamin was literally rebuilt from the ground up, allowing the designers to retain Roth's elements while creating a 21st-century Executive Suite Hotel. Each of The Benjamin's 209 rooms features conveniently placed appointments and easily accessible communications facilities, ergonomically designed desks and chairs, and an array of furnishings. For a healthy retreat from

the stress of daily business, the Woodstock Spa and Wellness Center and the executive fitness center are available to guests. For dining, visitors can choose around-the-clock room service or treat themselves to the latest incarnation of world-renowned chef Larry Forgione's restaurant, An American Place.

Plans are under way to add to the ever growing family of Manhattan East Suite Hotels, with properties in the Wall Street area and mid-Manhattan's West Side in progress. As the new millennium unfolds, the company may go beyond New York City's borders for the first time. New hotel expansion—possibly in New Jersey and Long Island— will bring a taste of the company's family-style hospitality to others in the region. Manhattan East Suite Hotels plan to make the "New Yorker's New York" available to travelers outside the city.

CLOCKWISW FROM TOP LEFT: THE EASTGATE TOWER ON EAST 39TH STREET BEARS THE DISTINCTION OF BEING THE FIRST HOTEL DESIGNED AND BUILT BY THE DENIHAN FAMILY.

THE BENJAMIN RETAINS THE DESIGN AND FLAIR OF ITS ORIGINAL ARCHITECT, EMERY ROTH, WHO DESIGNED THE 30-STORY BUILDING IN THE 1920S AS THE HOTEL BEVERLY.

THE PLAZA FIFTY OFFERS EVERY SUITE TYPE, INCLUDING PENTHOUSE EXECUTIVE SUITES THAT FEATURE TERRACES WITH SPECTACULAR MIDTOWN VIEWS.

BUILT IN 1928, THE ART DECO BEEKMAN TOWER HOTEL WAS RECENTLY DECLARED A NEW YORK CITY LANDMARK.

AMERICAN STEVEDORING

THE PORT OF NEW YORK AND NEW JERSEY COMPLEX IS one of the busiest ports in the world and requires a great deal of expertise from the companies operating there to ensure cost efficiency for customers. American Stevedoring offers the service, technology, and organization to ensure that every job is handled in a swift and efficient manner, with customer service as its highest priority.

A subsidiary of American Stevedoring, Inc. (ASI), American Stevedoring provides premier service to the shipping industry on both sides of the New York Harbor. With dedicated management and a dynamic labor force, the organization boasts exceptional levels of quality, productivity, and transportation efficiency.

PORT SERVICES

The firm's parent, American Stevedoring, Inc., is a multiservice port operator and transportation service provider with more than $50 million in annual revenues. Founded by Sabato Catucci in 1965 as a small trucking concern servicing the Port of New York, ASI has since grown to be one of the most dynamic stevedoring companies in the region. It is a family-run organization, providing a personal level of service and commitment through its full range of transportation services.

ASI operates two container facilities in the port: the Red Hook Marine Terminal and the Marsh Street Terminal at Port Newark, New Jersey. The marine terminal in Brooklyn is a 110-acre facility with five active container cranes, more than a million square feet of warehouse space, and two major bulk-handling yards.

Today, the Red Hook Container Terminal handles a record 65,000 containers. With a capacity of almost twice that number, Red Hook is poised for even greater growth. Located at the center of the world's largest consumer market, it provides quick access to the crucial markets east of the Hudson River; for cargo headed west, an innovative cross-harbor barge links up with the nation's highway and rail networks. Red Hook is also two hours closer to open water than any other facility in the harbor, further reducing shipper operating costs.

STATE-OF-THE-ART EQUIPMENT

American Stevedoring has invested millions of dollars in state-of-the-art handling and computer equipment. Serviced by four container cranes and more than 2,000 feet of container berths, Red Hook's operation is ideal for emerging carriers who are servicing specialized and niche cargo markets. American Stevedoring also handles a variety of break-bulk and bulk cargo—from coffee and cocoa to paper and steel. Moving more than 450,000 tons of cargo, Red Hook allows delivery directly to local markets. In addition, with more than 340,000 square feet of warehouse space for stripping and stuffing, American Stevedoring provides efficient dockside handling, thereby getting products to market more rapidly.

With world trade expanding at a rapid rate, America Stevedoring has demonstrated the capacity to provide bottom-line savings to meet the growing needs of carriers, shippers, freight forwarders, and logistics planners.

AMERICAN STEVEDORING PROVIDES PREMIER SERVICE TO BOTH SIDES OF THE NEW YORK HARBOR.

T EVERY SHIPPING PORT AND HUB, THERE IS A NEED TO warehouse cargo conveniently and efficiently, particularly when handling sensitive commodities. American Warehousing provides this service in the Port of New York, one of the busiest harbors in the world. Licensed by the New York Coffee, Sugar, and Cocoa Exchange, American Warehouse operates four expansive storage facilities for the coffee and cocoa industries. Recognizing the need for quality storage, American Warehousing has developed a premier operation to service this cargo, providing first-rate service to this sensitive market.

With its extensive experience in the marketing, handling, delivery, and distribution of cocoa and coffee, American Warehousing offers an ideal opportunity to expand this market and give customers a competitive edge. Rail and truck access, a flexible and creative management team, and centralized operations place American Warehousing at the forefront of the coffee and cocoa commodity industry.

PART OF A COMPREHENSIVE ORGANIZATION

American Warehousing is a subsidiary of American Stevedoring, Inc. (ASI), a multiservice port operator and transportation service provider. With more than $50 million in annual revenues, ASI offers port development services, direct stevedoring, and lashing for container, bulk, and neo-bulk products; state-of-the-art warehouse operations; and related truck, chassis, and container support services.

ASI was founded by Sabato Catucci in 1965 as a small trucking concern servicing the Port of New York. From this initial start, ASI has grown to be one of the most dynamic stevedoring companies operating in the region. Today, it remains a family-run organization, providing a personal level of service and commitment throughout its wide range of transportation services.

DEDICATED MANAGEMENT TEAM

To oversee all aspects of the operation, ASI has a skilled and dedicated management team. Working closely with each cus-

tomer, this team is committed to ensuring that each and every job is handled in a swift and efficient manner, with customer service as ASI's highest priority. Recognizing how critical information is to the transportation industry, this team has an integrated computer data system that allows for real-time delivery of information to each customer, speeding the handling and delivery of cargo.

At the center of the largest consumer market in the world, ASI is in an excellent position to provide efficient and innovative services to the transportation industry. With the expansion of world trade, ASI has demonstrated the capacity to provide bottom-line savings to all its customers.

WITH ITS EXTENSIVE EXPERIENCE IN THE MARKETING, HANDLING, DELIVERY, AND DISTRIBUTION OF COCOA AND COFFEE, AMERICAN WAREHOUSING OFFERS AN IDEAL OPPORTUNITY TO EXPAND THIS MARKET AND GIVE CUSTOMERS A COMPETITIVE EDGE.

ALMOST EVERY MAJOR AMERICAN CITY HAS ITS OWN PUBLIC transportation authority. But New York's Metropolitan Transportation Authority (MTA) is truly like no other. Founded in 1968, it is the largest mass transportation company in North America, having subways, buses, railroads, tunnels, and bridges

that move more than 2 billion customers each year—a group that comprises nearly one in every three users of mass transit and two-thirds of all rail riders in the entire country. MTA bridges and tunnels carry upwards of 250 million vehicles per year, and this vast transportation network serves more than 14 million people in a 4,000-square-mile area that fans out from New York City through Long Island, southeastern New York State, and Connecticut.

The MTA goes far beyond subways and buses. The system is comprised of New York City Transit, Long Island Rail Road, Long Island Bus, Metro-North Railroad, and Bridges and Tunnels, and requires nearly 60,000 employees to operate. While nearly 85 percent of the nation's workers need automobiles to get to their jobs, four out of every five rush-hour commuters to New York City's central business district avoid traffic by taking MTA, which has the largest bus fleet in the country and more trains than all the rest of the country's subways and commuter railroads combined.

A REBIRTH OF THE SYSTEM
Since 1982, the MTA has been carrying out America's most extensive transportation rebuilding project. Some $34 billion has been invested between 1982 and 1999 in replacing or overhauling the subway and bus fleets, and the MTA is in the process of replacing the railroad fleets as well. Capital program investments have funded the rebuilding of maintenance shops and many of the 2,000 miles of subway and railroad track, rehabilitation of scores of its 468 subway stations, and conversion of more railroad stations to high-level platforms for faster and safer travel. In addition, the MTA has undertaken restoration of the historic Grand Central Terminal and the Pennsylvania (Penn) Station.

The MTA's most recent technological innovations, MetroCard and E-ZPass, are revolutionizing fare and toll payment systems on subways, buses, bridges, and tunnels. MetroCard automated fare collection has paved the way for free transfers between subways and buses, multiple-ride bonuses, and weekly, monthly, and daily transit passes for the first time in the history of the subway. Additionally, EZPass electronic toll collection has transformed regional highway travel, decreasing traffic congestion, reducing pollution, and speeding the commute of tens of thousands of daily MTA customers. No sooner was MetroCard technology completed than the MTA began providing new fare benefits to its nearly 7 million daily customers. By eliminating two-fare zones on July 4, 1997, the MTA liberated those customers, giving them a new sense of freedom by including free bus-to-subway transfers and saving each of them an average of $750 a year.

THE SPIRIT OF NEW YORK
What makes travel in New York truly different from the rest of

THE METROPOLITAN TRANSPORTATION AUTHORITY (MTA) IS COMPRISED OF FIVE OPERATING AGENCIES—INCLUDING MTA NEW YORK CITY TRANSIT (TOP)—WHICH TOGETHER MOVE 2 BILLION CUSTOMERS EACH YEAR.

THE VERRAZANO-NARROWS BRIDGE (BOTTOM) IS RUN BY MTA BRIDGES AND TUNNELS.

the country is not only the size and the scope of the system, but its character and the place it has in the daily lives of people who live here.

Transportation in New York is a public experience, and the people responsible for its transit system have chosen to make it a shared pleasure. The facilities that form the system are considered public spaces, capable of reflecting the style and spirit of a great city.

"As public transportation became part of the fabric of New York's life, its founders determined the integrity of art, architecture, and industrial design was of vital importance to the great public works they were commissioning," says E. Virgil Conway, MTA chairman. In fact, a part of the original design contract for the first subway just served as a touchstone for all future efforts: "The railroad and its equipment constitute a great public work. All parts of the structure . . . where exposed to public sight, shall therefore be designed, constructed, and maintained with a view to the beauty of their appearance, as well as their efficiency."

Inspired by the City Beautiful movement of the late 19th century, the subway's founders, as well as the architects of Grand Central Terminal and the original Pennsylvania Station, believed that building public works meant building them wonderfully. Every element of art, architecture, and industrial design was intended to show respect for the customer

The MTA system also includes (clockwise from top left) MTA Long Island Bus, MTA Long Island Rail Road, and MTA Metro-North Railroad.

and uplift the experience of travel.

"These visionaries established a sound and admirable model, one that we reaffirm," says Conway. "Good design, inspired architecture, and art that reflects the energy and spirit of New York remain essential to MTA's ongoing capital investment program."

AN ARTISTIC RENEWAL

Unique among public transportation properties is the MTA's remarkable Arts for Transit Program, which demonstrates commitment to the integrity of art and design. As the transportation network has been restored and renewed, the art, architecture, and design of the past have been preserved and protected, while new works have been commissioned among

local artists to enhance the facilities that comprise the system. The old and new coexist, and the timeless unity of form and function is honored.

The MTA has also orchestrated the Music Under New York program, which licensed local entertainers, including musicians, singers, and dancers to perform in public areas of the system. Another program, Poetry in Motion, offers readings of poetry on subways throughout the system.

"The permanent art and entertainment that graces our stations and public spaces adds a sense of comfort and security, and reinforces the identity of individual stations," says Conway. "It brings a vitality to travel that makes the experience inviting, as well as convenient and quick."

UNITED NATIONS DEVELOPMENT CORPORATION (UNDC)

NEW YORK CITY'S CLAIM TO BE CAPITAL OF THE WORLD is based not just on its position as the global center of finance, fashion, and the fine arts, but also on the presence of the worldwide headquarters of the United Nations (UN). And with more than 30,000 jobs and more than $3 billion spent annually in the local economy, the UN and its associated diplomatic community contribute significantly to New York City's economic health. While the Big Apple certainly offers many unique advantages, one crucial element in the UN's continued presence here has undoubtedly been the efforts of United Nations Development Corporation (UNDC), a little-known New York State public benefit corporation.

The UN moved into its headquarters on First Avenue in 1948. In fewer than 20 years, the United Nations organization had grown from an initial membership of 51 nations to a truly worldwide body with 120 member nations and a number of subsidiary agencies, most notably United Nations Children's Fund (UNICEF).

Not surprisingly under the circumstances, the UN's original headquarters complex was no longer adequate to meet the organization's needs. Yet at that time, there were virtually no of-fice buildings in the immediate vicinity into which the UN could expand. Finding conveniently located office space was even more difficult for member nations' missions, and demand for housing in the area far exceeded supply. Even hospitality was a problem: Suitable hotel accommodations in the neighborhood surrounding the United Nations were simply nonexistent, placing a burden not only on visiting dignitaries, but on New York City's efforts to provide essential security. The situation became so troublesome that suggestions were made that the United Nations move its headquarters out of New York altogether.

In 1968, the State of New York and New York City responded to this growing problem by creating UNDC. The corporation's mandate was simple: to help meet the needs of the United Nations community for more office space, hotel accommodations, appropriate housing, and other essential facilities close to UN headquarters. Today, UNDC, working with architect Kevin Roche (a winner of the Pritzker Prize) and his firm, has fulfilled that mandate in splendid fashion, having developed and operated approximately 1.8 million square feet of space in the UN's vicinity. One and Two UN Plaza—striking 40-story green glass towers directly across from United Nations headquarters—contain not only more than 700,000 square feet of office space for UN agencies and missions, but the 427 rooms of the United Nations Plaza Hotel as well. Directly across East 44th Street, Three UN Plaza (UNICEF House) includes not only the worldwide headquarters of United Nations Children's Fund, but also apartments housing UN and mission staff, as well as a handsome, tree-lined public plaza with a striking backdrop of rocks and trickling water. Significantly,

DESIGNED BY KEVIN ROCHE, THE UNITED NATIONS DEVELOPMENT CORPORATION'S PROPERTIES AT ONE AND TWO UN PLAZA, AS WELL AS THE UNICEF HEADQUARTERS, ARE PROMINENT FIXTURES IN THE CITY'S SKYLINE.

all three of these first-class buildings have been planned, financed, constructed, and operated by UNDC at no cost to the taxpayers of New York City and New York State.

RESPONSIVE TO THE COMMUNITY

In the early 1990s, UNICEF, concerned that New York City's tight real estate market would not be able to meet the organization's needs for expanded headquarters space in a cost-effective manner, seriously considered moving its headquarters out of the city and even out of the United States altogether. UNDC responded by purchasing office condominium units in a first-class building on Manhattan's East Side for lease to UNICEF at an affordable rent, thus ensuring the continued presence of the agency's headquarters in New York City. This carefully constructed plan even included tenanted space so that UNICEF could expand gradually without paying for space it didn't yet require. By 1998, however, UNICEF's plans and priorities had changed: It was clear that the agency would not need as much space as originally thought. Again responding to the agency's needs,

UNDC was able to sell those condominium units and thereby eliminate a potentially costly burden for UNICEF.

Similarly, at the time UNDC was created, the private sector had not managed to create any suitable hotel accommodations convenient to UN headquarters. UNDC responded by creating and maintaining the award-winning United Nations Plaza Hotel within its buildings at One and Two UN Plaza. When, after more than 20 years of successful operation, it was clear that the hotel was securely established, UNDC, in cooperation with New York City and the State of New York, determined that it made sense to turn the hotel over to the private sector—and so, in 1997, the hotel was sold to Regal Hotels International in a transaction that resulted in a payment to the City of New York of $85 million.

The development of the UN complex and UNDC's ongoing work in the community have served as a catalyst for the commercial and residential revitalization of the surrounding area, creating housing and employment opportunities for New Yorkers and tax revenues for the city. As the new millennium begins, the

efforts of UNDC have transformed the neighborhood and helped to secure the UN's long-term presence in New York City—all without spending a single taxpayer dollar.

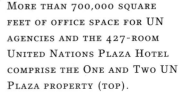

MORE THAN 700,000 SQUARE FEET OF OFFICE SPACE FOR UN AGENCIES AND THE 427-ROOM UNITED NATIONS PLAZA HOTEL COMPRISE THE ONE AND TWO UN PLAZA PROPERTY (TOP).

THE TREE-LINED URBAN PLAZA ADJACENT TO UNICEF HOUSE IS ADORNED WITH A BACKDROP OF ROCKS AND TRICKLING WATER (BOTTOM).

MultiPlan, Inc.

MultiPlan, Inc. is a nationally admired, New York-based managed care company, which over the past decade has grown into a 50-state network of some 2,900 hospitals, 41,000 ancillary facilities, and more than 219,000 practitioners. Local commitment and national strength have made MultiPlan the health plan of choice for hundreds of clients and for the 23 million Americans who enjoy easy access to affordable coverage available from the network's providers.

Long before the rising costs of health care became a popular topic for policy debate, MultiPlan from its beginnings in 1970 was practicing cost containment on behalf of clients. Long before patients' rights became a political issue, MultiPlan was actively engaged in projects designed to preserve and enhance relationships among payers, consumers, and providers. Long before the dawn of the 21st century, MultiPlan had forged a strategy to foster choice, ready access, and reasonable costs as a better solution to festering health care problems. Today, MultiPlan is the largest general-service preferred provider organization (PPO) in the United States.

"Many proponents of managed care are new to the program," says Donald Rubin, MultiPlan chairman and co-CEO. "That's not a criticism. They just finally realized that quality health care had to be more affordable if it was to be more accessible—a principle we've been practicing for 30 years."

Rubin founded MultiPlan following his tenure as a senior executive with a health maintenance organization in New York and his previous role as administrator for a variety of labor-management/ERISA plans. He was one of the first in the field to negotiate fees for hospital charges as a way of helping contain health care costs.

"A number of labor union health and welfare funds had approached us and asked if we would negotiate with hospitals on their behalf to continue providing health care services to their members," recalls Rubin. "At the time, the general reaction we got from hospitals was 'We don't negotiate rates, we set them.' Still, we were able to sit down with them and work out a structure that was agreeable to all. We cooperate with providers without losing sight of our original goal: to provide value to our clients and to meet their needs."

MultiPlan offers enrollees a growing network of carefully selected individual and group health care practitioners that span the spectrum of disciplines, including general practice, internal medicine, pediatrics, cardiology, neurology, oncology, OB-GYN, ophthalmology, psychiatry, psychology, social work, podiatry, and chiropractic services.

MultiPlan's network includes more than 278,000 physicians and other practitioners nationwide, including more than 12,000 in the New York metropolitan area.

Harvey Sigelbaum, who joined MultiPlan in 1996 as president and co-CEO, believes the key to success in the highly competitive health care environment is to bring MultiPlan's experience and credibility to bear in support of both its clients and its provider network. "We plan to stay ahead," Sigelbaum says. "That means we must measure our success by the value we bring to all of our partners."

Both Rubin and Sigelbaum believe America's health care

MultiPlan, Inc. Co-CEO Harvey Sigelbaum leads the growth of the largest general-service preferred provider organization (PPO) in the United States.

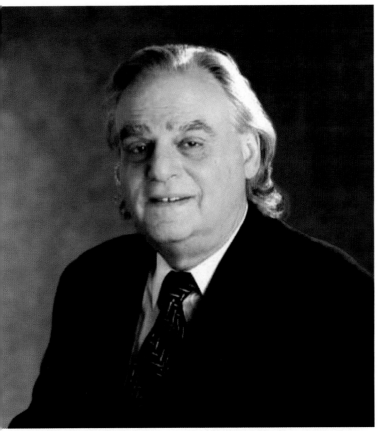

system has been improved by the health care debate during the past several years. Says Sigelbaum: "We see our role today as America's managed care partner—beneficial to our clients as well as to the nation's health care providers and hospitals. The nation's hospitals, MRI units, and freestanding surgery centers, among others, need preferred provider organizations more than they might think."

Rubin adds, "In the very short term, hospitals would be able to charge much more to patients who were not covered by Blue Cross. But then, in the outcry from the payers, patients, and employers that would certainly follow, the government would step in with rigid regulations to ensure that nobody was being overcharged. Simply put, PPOs are valuable to hospitals because we have enough clout to press providers for efficiency and high-quality care without resorting to government pressure. We are proof that the free market really works."

MultiPlan facilities cover all enrollee health care needs, including hospital stays; psychiatric and chemical dependency treatment; physical rehabilitation and ambulatory surgery; home health

care; long-term care; and ancillary care, which involves diagnostic and advanced procedures, organ transplant surgery, and medical air transport.

MultiPlan's nationwide network also makes savings possible when insured patients require treatment outside their usual geographic area. With MultiPlan coverage, enrollees avoid the extra expenses that can be incurred when services outside the network are needed.

MultiPlan's alliance with its network hospitals has created a long list of added values enjoyed by the facilities. A library of critical pathways is available to participating facilities and their medical staffs, sparing them the enormous expense of developing their own clinical pathways. A toy car and Christmas card program finds MultiPlan donating small, battery-powered vehicles and holiday cards for use by children in hospitals and by hospital fund-raisers selling the cards in gift shops. Another program provides grants to rural hospitals to help them upgrade quality.

The company's growth over its first 30 years has been dramatic. Today, the majority of MultiPlan's 300 employees work at its New York City headquarters on Fifth

Avenue. The work environment there is as reflective of the founder as it is of the company. The conference rooms are named after New York museums, such as the Metropolitan, the Museum of Modern Art, the Cloisters, and the Whitney. And the walls showcase an abundant variety of artwork, with the vibrant colors of museum posters and paintings creating an atmosphere of exuberance and enthusiasm that reflects the company's success.

"The future is bright for MultiPlan. We are constantly refining and expanding our scope of services, developing new products, and creating innovative, risk-sharing programs for our clients," says Rubin. "We look forward to a time when universal coverage is a reality. We will continue to provide our clients with the best value and access to the highest-quality medical care available. It was the founding goal of this company, and it has never changed."

DONALD RUBIN IS CHAIRMAN AND CO-CEO OF MULTIPLAN (LEFT).

MULTIPLAN IS COMMITTED TO GIVING BACK TO THE COMMUNITY. A TOY CAR AND CHRISTMAS CARD PROGRAM FINDS MULTIPLAN DONATING SMALL, BATTERY-POWERED VEHICLES AND HOLIDAY CARDS FOR USE BY CHILDREN IN HOSPITALS AND BY HOSPITAL FUND-RAISERS SELLING THE CARDS IN GIFT SHOPS (RIGHT).

I N A CITY KNOWN FOR VARIETY IN HEALTH CARE, IT might seem surprising that one in five New Yorkers receives his or her health care from the New York City Health and Hospitals Corporation (HHC). Founded in 1970, the system today includes 11 hospitals, five long-term care facilities, six diag-

nostic and treatment centers, and an HMO. From locations throughout New York City, HHC delivers a wide variety of services to 1.5 million people.

With annual revenue of $4.1 billion, HHC handles nearly 1 million cases in its emergency rooms each year, as well as some 4.8 million ambulatory care visits, and 1.8 million primary care visits. Approximately 225,000 patients are discharged yearly, and more than 25,000 babies are born in HHC hospitals each year.

In this turbulent time in health care management, it is significant that HHC is financially healthy. Under the leadership of President Luis R. Marcos, M.D., and its board of directors, HHC has operated in the black since 1996—and has a considerable reputation among health care organizations throughout the world. HHC has educational affiliations with Columbia University, New York University, Mount Sinai School of Medicine, and State University of New York Health Science Center at Brooklyn, making HHC the largest medical training facility in New York City.

But what is most remarkable are HCC's exceptional physicians and caregivers who reflect the diversity of its community. HHC likes to say that it speaks the language of its patients.

RESTRUCTURING FOR
THE FUTURE

Ten years ago, it would have been hard to imagine the turnaround that has taken place at HHC. The corporation recognized early on that to achieve success while providing quality health care, it needed to reshape how it delivered its care and handled its business operations.

Consequently, HHC shifted its approach from simply treating diseases to preventing illness, promoting wellness, and finding viable alternatives to hospitalization. The corporation used

NEW YORK CITY HEALTH AND HOSPITALS CORPORATION PROVIDES HIGH-QUALITY, COMPASSIONATE PATIENT CARE TO 1.5 MILLION NEW YORKERS EACH YEAR.

managed care as a vehicle to encourage patients to participate more actively in their own care; to allow more patients to be treated at home; to educate patients to seek ambulatory care, rather than costly emergency room visits; and to encourage the use of primary care facilities. The results are reflected in the substantial reductions both in the number of hospitalizations and in the length of hospital stays.

MEANINGFUL RECOGNITION

Since its founding, HHC's facilities have achieved meaningful recognition. Kings County Hospital Center, for example, was the site of the first open-heart surgery in the state. Its physicians invented the world's first hemodialysis machine, conducted the first studies of HIV infection in women, and produced the first human images using magnetic resonance. Bellevue Hospital Center, America's first public hos-

pital, is a leader in replantation microsurgery, and houses an internationally respected center for brain and spinal cord injuries. Harlem Hospital Center has a state-of-the-art ambulatory care pavilion and a new magnetic resonance imaging unit, and operates a tuberculosis center that is considered a national model. Jacobi Medical Center is known for the first coronary bypass, Elmhurst Hospital Center established the country's first children's health center, and physicians at Sea View Hospital Rehabilitation Center and Home first developed the drug that would cure tuberculosis. And Lincoln Medical and Mental Health Center has a nationally recognized asthma center and operates one of the busiest emergency rooms in the nation, handling 350 visits per day in 1998.

All of these efforts support HHC's mission: "to provide quality health care to all the people of New York City, regardless of the ability to pay."

ALL ACROSS THE FAMED NEW YORK CITY SKYLINE, shoreline, and almost any other part of Manhattan, one name is helping to redefine the cityscape: The Trump Organization. When applied to a project, the name tends to instantly enhance its appeal, raise its profitability, and ensure its success.

The magic behind the company belongs to entrepreneur and multibillionaire Donald J. Trump, New York City's largest real estate developer and the chairman, president, and visionary of The Trump Organization.

Dubbed simply "the Donald" by New Yorkers, Trump uses his celebrity status, reputation for success, and vast knowledge of the real estate world to generate fantastic accomplishments. Ironically, it was the rebounding of his empire following a dramatic setback during the real estate crash of the early 90s—one of the greatest comebacks the financial world has ever seen—that solidified Trump's reputation as a true winner in the New York City real estate market.

Today, according to *Crain's New York Business*, The Trump Organization is the city's third-largest privately held corporation. Its properties include such icons as the Empire State Building; the

General Motors Building at Trump International Plaza; Trump Tower, which is the city's third-most-visited tourist attraction; and the landmark Trump Building on Wall Street.

GREAT REAL ESTATE IN A GREAT CITY

Trump is able to garner a phenomenal 78 percent more profit per square foot for his real estate than any other luxury building in the city. He sees this ability as proof that his projects have a reputation for absolute quality. "People know what to expect from a project that has my name on it. We sold 50 percent of the Trump International Hotel and Tower before anyone even saw it," says Trump.

Trump's imprimatur of quality is also emblazoned on such luxury residential condos and co-op buildings as the Trump Palace, Trump Parc, and Trump Plaza. In addition, the restoration of the former Mayfair Hotel on Park Avenue and the construction of Trump World Tower stand as testament to Trump's high standards in the real estate market.

Still, the pièce de résistance of his real estate empire is Trump Place on the West Side. When this 92-acre property—which fronts the Hudson River from 59th street to 72nd street—is completed, it will offer 5,700 residen-

tial units in 16 buildings, more than 2 million square feet of commercial space, and a magnificently landscaped waterfront park.

From his offices high above Fifth Avenue in Trump Tower, Trump observes some of his most spectacular successes located in what he proclaims to be the greatest comeback city in the world. "There is a revival going on in New York, and it is greater than anything I have ever seen," says Trump. "The city has now become the hottest location anywhere in the world."

Being the number one developer in the Big Apple is a spot Donald Trump likes to occupy. "New York has been very good to me," Trump says, "and I've been very good to New York."

"THERE IS A REVIVAL GOING ON IN NEW YORK, AND IT IS GREATER THAN ANYTHING I HAVE EVER SEEN," SAYS DONALD TRUMP, CHAIRMAN AND PRESIDENT OF THE TRUMP ORGANIZATION. "THE CITY HAS NOW BECOME THE HOTTEST LOCATION ANYWHERE IN THE WORLD."

ALL ACROSS THE FAMED NEW YORK CITY SKYLINE, SHORELINE, AND ALMOST ANY OTHER PART OF MANHATTAN, ONE NAME IS HELPING TO REDEFINE THE CITYSCAPE: THE TRUMP ORGANIZATION.

STRUCTURE TONE INC.

OME COMPANIES DEFINE THEIR UNIQUE CHARACTER OVER the years, evolving gradually, shaped by the requirements of their era, their industry, their clients, and their changing management. Structure Tone Inc., however, works in a different way: When it was established in 1971, it knew exactly what it wanted to be

and has remained dedicated to that goal ever since.

A full-service construction management and general contracting firm, Structure Tone does more than build buildings. It builds relationships, not only among its clients, but also within its organization. At Structure Tone, the ability and commitment to address the ongoing needs of clients is critical to any real and sustained success. A key component of that ability is an equally committed attention to the training and support of its employees.

"Our firm is a tightly knit company working in unison toward one common goal—we don't just build buildings, we build relationships," says James K. Donaghy, chairman. "We maintain solid relationships with our clients due to the exceptional level of quality we provide on all our projects. Our international expertise and local experience service our clients, anytime, anywhere."

WHETHER WORKING ON A PROJECT FOR GIORGIO ARMANI IN NEW YORK (TOP) OR FOR ORACLE IN RESTON, VIRGINIA (BOTTOM), THE BUSINESS OF SATISFYING CLIENTS AND WORKING PROACTIVELY IS A HIGH PRIORITY FOR STRUCTURE TONE INC.

The firm's philosophy has created exactly what it intended. Structure Tone has achieved a reputation as one of the preeminent construction firms in the world today, offering a complete scope of construction services ranging from corporate interior renovations to new, out-of-the-ground construction, major building infrastructure upgrades, and modernization.

EXPANDING WITH THE TIMES

From its roots as a New York-based interior construction company, Structure Tone's depth of hands-on experience in interior and base-building construction enabled the company to expand its capabilities to encompass construction management and technical support for clients, both locally and globally.

The Structure Tone organization is now made up of three privately held companies: Structure Tone Inc., Constructors & Associates, and Pavarini Construction Co., Inc. These companies collectively employ more than 1,000 professionals in 17 offices in the United States and around the world, including England, Ireland, Spain, and Puerto Rico. The organization has constructed more than 3 billion square feet of space, and has earned a $1 billion surety commitment.

CLIENT SERVICE FOR THE FUTURE

Customer focus has always defined Structure Tone's business. In its dedication to nurturing effective relationships with its clients, the firm has always been determined to not only listen thoroughly to clients, but to work proactively. Structure Tone begins each project

by ensuring that the client's needs and goals are thoroughly understood so that they can be translated into a high-quality construction project.

One application of this approach is the ability to see industry trends ahead of the curve. Change is inevitable, and nowhere is that more evident than in the tools available for high-tech business operations. It is imperative for any construction company to have a thorough understanding of how to create working environments that accommodate the newest developments of the information age and that adapt to continuous change.

The firm's new group, ST Tech Services, Inc., was formed to respond to their clients' increasingly technical requirements for advanced office environments. Staffed with a team of technology professionals who analyze a client's current and anticipated needs—whether for a new structure, relocation, consolidation, modernization, or expansion program—this division determines the level of technical sophistication appropriate to the particular situation.

The Competitive Difference

This immersive approach to client service is the profound difference Structure Tone sees between itself and its competition. Another is the fact that the firm is privately held; quarterly reports and bottomline pressures to ensure stockholder satisfaction do not take attention away from the construction industry and client services.

Structure Tone is dedicated to maximizing the performance of every one of its professionals. The firm offers extensive employee training programs on every level, including formal classroom settings, off-site seminars, and one-to-one mentoring programs. One very effective program is the Rotational Training Program, which Structure Tone offers to individuals seeking positions in the preconstruction and construction divisions. The program's objective is to give the new employees exposure to all aspects of the construction process. The company rotates each participant through a series of positions throughout Structure Tone's in-house departments, progressively increasing respon-

sibility along the way.

Finally, every aspect of Structure Tone's operations is geared to providing the most intense, sophisticated client service possible. Wide-area networks offer remote dial-in capabilities from project sites, and every project team systematically processes and shares all project control documentation through a universal project-based filing system built into its communications system. Digital cameras are also utilized to capture project photos that can be sent via E-mail to appropriate parties, and Structure Tone has invested in an Océ 9800 blueprint scanner for global, easy-access storage and retrieval of project documents.

This technology and growth extend Structure Tone's vision of total and instantaneous client service into the future, where the organization will have every project managed by a connected computer system for all team members, the client, the architect, and the engineer. Everyone at Structure Tone will be working together for the good of the firm and its clients, making Structure Tone a leader in the industry for decades to come.

The Ford Center for the Performing Arts in New York (left) and the new IBM headquarters in Armonk, New York (right), are two more examples of Structure Tone's unique expertise.

COVENANT HOUSE

CLOCKWISE FROM TOP:
"THE ODDS SEEM TO BE STACKED AGAINST OUR YOUNG PEOPLE," SAYS BRUCE J. HENRY, EXECUTIVE DIRECTOR OF COVENANT HOUSE NEW YORK. "BUT EVERY YEAR AT COVENANT HOUSE NEW YORK, WE SEE KIDS BUILDING A FUTURE FOR THEMSELVES."

COVENANT HOUSE'S FIRST 10 YEARS SAW STEADY GROWTH IN ITS NEW YORK CITY PROGRAM, AND ITS SECOND DECADE SAW ITS SERVICES EXPAND TO 19 OTHER CITIES IN SIX COUNTRIES. IN THE 1980S, NEW SERVICES WERE ADDED TO HELP YOUNG MOTHERS AND THEIR CHILDREN. AND IN THE 1990S, COVENANT HOUSE CONTINUED TO LOOK FOR NEW WAYS TO SERVE THE YOUNG PEOPLE WHO NEED ITS HELP.

COVENANT HOUSE'S MISSION STATEMENT COMMITS THE ORGANIZATION "TO SERVE SUFFERING CHILDREN OF THE STREET, AND TO PROTECT AND SAFEGUARD ALL CHILDREN WITH ABSOLUTE RESPECT AND UNCONDITIONAL LOVE."

city youths from 16 to 22 years of age is unemployed; one-third of the city's children receive some form of public assistance.

These are the challenges that Covenant House faces every day in its efforts to provide help to those too young to know how to help themselves. "The odds seem to be stacked against our young people," says Bruce J. Henry, executive director of Covenant House New York. "But every year at Covenant House New York, we see kids building a future for themselves. They confront their complex problems with resilience and determination, and manage to beat the odds. When given the opportunity, they've shown that they can accomplish great things."

A MISSION OF SERVICE

Covenant House's mission statement commits the organization "to serve suffering children of the street, and to protect and safeguard all children with absolute respect and unconditional love." Covenant House does this by offering creative and accessible programs for children to facilitate their transition to adulthood.

In addition to food, shelter, clothing, and crisis care, Covenant House offers a variety of services to homeless youth, including health care, education, vocational preparation, drug abuse treatment and prevention programs, legal services, recreation, pastoral care, mother/child programs, transitional living programs, street outreach, a national crisis telephone hot line, assistance in finding long-term living accommodations, and aftercare.

Some of the organization's most successful programs include Rights of Passage, a transitional residential program that provides troubled youth a safe place to live while they learn comprehensive life skills, receive job training, and participate in placement programs. Other successful programs are crisis centers; Nineline, a toll-free help line manned by trained staff and volunteers available 24 hours a day, seven days a week to answer questions from teenagers and parents with problems they can't handle alone; and the Outreach program, where counselors and volunteers cruise the streets in vans, bikes, or on foot to offer food, hope, and counseling to at-risk kids.

Last year, the Covenant House system provided residential and nonresidential services to more than 50,000 youth in six countries. Almost 14,000 young people en-

tered Covenant House crisis shelters and Rights of Passage programs, and another 16,000 received help in community service centers or in aftercare and prevention programs. Outreach programs reached another 20,000 youth on the street, and the Covenant House Nineline received more than 84,000 crisis calls.

A HELPING HAND

Covenant House began in 1969, when a Franciscan priest provided a night of shelter in a snow storm for six young runaways in his small apartment on the Lower East Side of Manhattan. From this modest beginning, Covenant House

has grown into the largest shelter program for homeless kids in America.

Incorporated in 1972, the organization grew from its start in the East Village tenements into a group home program in three of New York City's boroughs, and from there to its first crisis center in Times Square in 1977. Two years later, the crisis center moved to its present location on 41st Street and 10th Avenue on Manhattan's West Side. In 1977, a Faith Community was begun, a group of full-time volunteers who give a year of service, living in a simple community based on the example of St. Francis.

Covenant House's first 10 years saw steady growth in its New York City program, and its second decade saw its services expand to 19 other cities in six countries. In the 1980s, new services were added to help young mothers and their children. And in the 1990s, Covenant House continued to look for new ways to serve the young people who need its help.

In a series of planning sessions in 1996, the agency adopted a

vision statement to guide its expansion of services. It reads, in part: "Covenant House will continue to fulfill its mission by providing shelter and services to children and youth who are homeless or at great risk. We will make every effort to reunite kids with their families. We will collaborate with community agencies and associations and actively participate in community

efforts to improve the conditions of families and children. We will advocate with and on behalf of youth to raise awareness in the community about their suffering."

PARTNERS IN SERVICE

The growth of Covenant House has been dramatic. The agency's $100 million budget is supported almost entirely—85 percent—by private contributions from hundreds of thousands of generous donors.

A large part of Covenant House's effectiveness is due to partnerships the organization has established with the corporate community. "Central to our success has been the cooperation and assistance we have received from the business community," says Sister Mary Rose McGeady, D.C., president of Covenant House, "not only in helping us set up the training modules, but in offering internships and jobs as well to our young people as they prepare for independent living. Across the agency, more than 1,000 companies have partnered with us since the Rights of Passage programs began more than a decade ago."

The Covenant House mission is based on the belief that the most effective assistance not only helps people to handle the difficulties of their present situation, but also helps to prepare them for the future. And for the children and youth helped by Covenant House, it is a future filled with hope.

"CENTRAL TO OUR SUCCESS HAS BEEN THE COOPERATION AND ASSISTANCE WE HAVE RECEIVED FROM THE BUSINESS COMMUNITY," SAYS SISTER MARY ROSE McGEADY, D.C., PRESIDENT OF COVENANT HOUSE (TOP).

SOME OF THE ORGANIZATION'S MOST SUCCESSFUL PROGRAMS INCLUDE RIGHTS OF PASSAGE, A TRANSITIONAL RESIDENTIAL PROGRAM THAT PROVIDES TROUBLED YOUTH A SAFE PLACE TO LIVE WHILE THEY LEARN COMPREHENSIVE LIFE SKILLS, RECEIVE JOB TRAINING, AND PARTICIPATE IN PLACEMENT PROGRAMS (BOTTOM).

First American Title Insurance Company of New York

First American Title Insurance Company of New York, a leader in the New York real estate market, is breaking with tradition to capture a more dominant position in the industry. The title insurance products created and marketed by First American Title Insurance Company of New York help owners protect their property interests in real estate transactions—and help lenders protect their financial interests in those same transactions. By changing the way the company does business, First American Title Insurance Company of New York is now able to offer a full range of real-estate-related products and improve the way it meets the needs of its New York metropolitan area customers.

"While our present success is impressive, we are keeping keenly aware of rapid changes now occurring around us," says James M. Orphanides, president. "We must address change and keep up with our customers' expanding needs. This means we cannot simply sell our products on our terms, playing the game by our rules alone. We are in the challenging position of being conformists in an evolving, non-conformist marketplace."

Diversification of Services

First American's core business always has been and still is real estate title insurance. Now more than ever before, however, clients are seeking multifaceted services and value-added products from one source. With the assistance of its parent company—First American Financial Corporation—First American Title Insurance Company of New York is meeting this challenge head-on by widening the scope of its product offering, providing such programs as tax reporting, flood compliance, appraisals, and equity loan services in addition to title insurance. First American Financial is the market leader in most of these areas, and, in fact, touches more than 90 percent of all real estate transactions in the United States with one or more of its services.

Additionally, First American Title Insurance Company of New York has enhanced its communications links throughout the organization to provide quicker response to attorneys, commercial and residential lenders, developers, and Realtors. In fact, the company is currently finalizing its state-of-the-art communications network, assuring that its growing menu of real estate information services is even more accessible to more clients.

Technical innovation is improving productivity at First American Advanced optical scanning and

archival storage systems have been designed to organize and retain documents more efficiently. Field representatives are now equipped with laptop computers and modems that allow them—no matter where they are—to have complete access to First American's data processing systems. This increased connectivity is dramatically improving the way the company assists its clients, putting up-to-the-minute data at the closing table.

First American is utilizing its vast experience and statewide network of independent agents to address the many opportunities these factors have created. The company offers title insurance services that address the needs and requirements of a richly varied market. The company's agency division oversees more than 130 agents located in urban, suburban, and rural areas all over the state. The agents have a thorough knowledge of all the intricacies of their local real estate markets.

"There are several factors that will sustain our growth now and in the future, most importantly the energy of our people," says Orphanides. "Our agency division is the driving force behind the team spirit that defines our partnerships with our agents and approved attorneys, as well as the dedication of our direct operations."

KEEPING PACE WITH CHANGE

For more than a quarter century, First American has expanded its network by providing each agent with a comprehensive assortment of support services, both legal and technical. The company's highly experienced counsels, agency reps, auditors, and clerical staff all work together to keep each agent constantly informed about new developments in real estate law, as well as in the latest changes in underwriting and claim practices.

Key to its success is the company's attention to anticipating and meeting the future requirements of its clients. First American prides itself on listening and responding to clients' demands for faster, better, and more comprehensive services.

CLOCKWISE FROM TOP LEFT: JAMES M. ORPHANIDES IS PRESIDENT OF FIRST AMERICAN TITLE INSURANCE COMPANY OF NEW YORK.

BY USING FIRST AMERICAN'S CD-ROM- AND INTERNET-BASED UNDERWRITING LIBRARY ON THEIR OWN COMPUTERS, CLIENTS CAN INSTANTLY PULL UP STATE-BY-STATE PRACTICES AS WELL AS FIRST AMERICAN'S OWN UNDERWRITING PRACTICES AND PROCEDURES.

ACCOUNT EXECUTIVES SUCH AS SENIOR VICE PRESIDENT JEFFREY MITZNER OFTEN RELY ON LAPTOP TECHNOLOGY TO ACCESS DATA ANYTIME . . . ANYWHERE.

"To keep pace with change, we will continue to invest in training, sales, marketing, and technology," says Orphanides. "Our technology team is experimenting with many new concepts. We will also shed antiquated methods of delivering our services. Our commitments to our customers will include new products, additional services, faster response, and lower costs.

"Through the collaborative efforts of our company and others in the industry, we must speed up the process and proactively address the changes we are now encountering. We must view New York State as a piece of a total market without boundaries or limitations. Above all, we must remember that the change most necessary will be the way we think."

DATA INDUSTRIES LTD.

WHEN CLIENTS ASK WHAT THE COMPANY SPECIALIZES IN, DATA INDUSTRIES LTD. PRESIDENT CHARLES DUVAL REPLIES, "WE SPECIALIZE IN IMPROVING PRODUCTIVITY AND PROFITABILITY BY LEVERAGING TECHNOLOGY. DATA INDUSTRIES ANALYZES CUSTOMER BUSINESS REQUIREMENTS AND RESOURCES TO DETERMINE THE BEST STRATEGY FOR IMPROVEMENT."

Since 1980, Data Industries Ltd. has grown from two employees to more than 400, with $60 million in projected revenues. Data Industries serves Fortune 1,000 and government clients in New York, New Jersey, Florida, the District of Columbia, and Texas. The company is a minority-owned professional services firm that fulfills short- and long-term business and information technology needs. Its success lies in its ability to provide state-of-the-art solutions to complex problems, on-time and on-budget.

Data Industries maintains six divisions to ensure specific attention for every customer requirement: management consulting; PC and client/server systems; networking and data communication; mainframe and midrange technology; Internet and E-business; and help desk solutions. Covering an extensive portfolio of disciplines and expertise, each division is comprised of analysts, network engineers, programmers, application developers, and data modeling analysts. Specialty project teams are assembled to provide strategic planning, business process reengineering, application development, troubleshooting and customer support, quality control, and software

product installation and custom configuration.

THE RIGHT APPROACH

When clients ask what the company specializes in, Data Industries President Charles Duval replies, "We specialize in improving productivity and profitability by leveraging technology. Data Industries analyzes customer business requirements and resources to determine the best strategy for improvement. This may involve upgrading existing systems, engineering and install-

ing new platforms, or a combination of both. The end result of our planning and development improves productivity, thereby yielding significant cost savings."

But Data Industries' commitment doesn't end there. Says Duval, "Project managers, documentation analysts, and technical trainers provide the proper turnover to ensure the customers can take ownership and fully leverage their new or enhanced systems."

Data Industries' success is based on understanding the client's culture and offering the appropriate services. After detailed assessment, including budget and personnel issues, Data Industries delivers a confidential white paper that addresses the advantages and disadvantages of current systems, and points to ways to optimize technology and make it more cost effective.

"To bring all those pieces together takes tremendous effort. We streamline the process," says Duval. "We understand the need for adaptability. We have clients that are entirely self-sufficient within their own operations and develop their own requirements analysis. Our job then is to provide the resources to implement their vision."

AT DATA INDUSTRIES, SUCCESS IS MEASURED BY IMPROVEMENTS TO THE CLIENT'S OPERATIONS, INCLUDING LOWER MAINTENANCE COSTS, ENHANCED WORK FLOW, AND IMPROVED DATA ACCESS AND INTEGRITY.

Data Industries considers an extensive range of issues to determine functionality, dependability, supporting applications, projections for future needs, networking, remote access, and security, among others. The company can answer questions for its clients, provide expert opinions, or develop sophisticated programs for implementation. Success is measured by improvements to the client's operations, including lower maintenance costs, enhanced work flow, and improved data access and integrity.

Duval credits the company's success to its employees and their keen knowledge of the latest technology: "Our employees are the most qualified in the industry. The people we hire are the best in the business and when we complete our tasks, our clients are satisfied. Eighty-five percent of our business is repeat business. This has been our model for more than 20 years."

Evidence of the company's success is in the number of honors and awards it has received from local, regional, and national institutions. Duval won the 1997 U.S. Department of Commerce National Minority Male Entrepreneur of the Year award, as well as its 1999 Commerce Information Technology Solution (COMMITS) award. He was a finalist in the Ernst & Young 1998 and 1999

Entrepreneur of the Year awards, and is a charter member of the Business Hall of Fame. Data Industries received the City of New York Department of Business Services Outstanding Business Award for 1998, and the National Minority Business Council (NMBC) Outstanding Minority Business Award for 1995.

CREATING NEW OPPORTUNITIES

Data Industries is an excellent example of entrepreneurial energy put to work for the betterment of business and the community. The company has developed an internship program that enables young people to learn from seasoned professionals. Duval extended this philosophy last year by donating a computer lab to Wadleigh High School, located in Harlem. "I believe business should partner with the schools to help educate our children," says Duval. "I have always wanted to give back to my community, and these computers will certainly help these children prepare for their future."

Ultimately, Duval guides the company with this philosophy: "Every day is a new experience, and each day presents something new to discover. So if you put your ego to rest and open your mind to new adventures and opportunities every day, you learn from the past and grow."

BLOOMBERG L.P.

NOWLEDGE IS POWER. SO IT'S NO SURPRISE THAT NEW York, one of the most powerful cities in the world, considers information, the root of knowledge, to be a kind of currency. Divining, digging, mining, researching, and reporting information—effectively, efficiently, and accurately—and delivering it to those

who need it, in real time, are the cornerstones of Bloomberg L.P. What is a surprise is that in the media and financial capital of the world, those services did not exist prior to 1981. It was then that Michael Bloomberg, a partner at Salomon Brothers, found himself unemployed with a $10 million cash buyout in his pocket.

Bloomberg was faced not with the challenge of how to support his family, but with what to do with the rest of his life. Within days of his departure from Salomon Brothers, he resolved to start his own business. His company would provide clear, concise, unbiased, and unbeholden information to the financial world.

With $10 million in seed money to nurture this idea, Bloomberg and four associates began a year of work consisting largely of long days, late nights, and cold pizza. In the end, the team carved out their cornerstone and set it in concrete. In a tiny office in midtown Manhattan, the BLOOMBERG® service was born.

Custom-designed computer terminals were built, debugged, and rebuilt until the seminal Bloomberg terminal was ready for installation. Soon, Bloomberg began broadening the scope of the terminals: focusing on real-time prices and analytics, and expanding to include commodities and globally traded securities. The

terminal also began providing investors with myriad what-if scenarios for major markets, essentially leveling the playing field between buyer and seller. Bloomberg soon became the neutral arbiter of price information for institutional investors and securities dealers alike.

TRANSMITTING DATA WORLDWIDE

The crowded, one-room office in Midtown has given way to a suite of floors on Park Avenue. Here, in addition to coalescing the printed word, the Internet, and the service data, Bloomberg television and radio broadcasts are created for worldwide dissemination. Installed at every reporter's desk, microphones feed reports that can be accessed, expanded, modified, or localized at any Bloomberg bureau and broadcast via 150 affiliates to a vast constituency of listeners worldwide.

Bloomberg radio also reports for diverse business markets. The firm's *Negocios Bloomberg*, the nation's first Spanish language business and financial report, airs three times daily and covers financial, business, cultural, economic, and social issues pertaining specifically to the Hispanic community. The *Bloomberg Urban Business Report*, the first national African-American business radio report, focuses on financial and business news of interest to this community. Broadcast globally in nine languages, Bloomberg Television is a 24-hour news and information channel emphasizing business and financial news. Its multiscreen format of anchored video reports and text updates gives viewers the flexibility to get news on demand.

The centerpiece of the Bloomberg network remains the BLOOMBERG® service on-line system. Accessed by more than 300,000 users around the world, the Bloomberg service reaches

GREGORY HEISLER

IN 1981, MICHAEL R. BLOOMBERG ESTABLISHED BLOOMBERG L.P., A COMPANY THAT HAS BECOME THE WORLD'S PREMIER MULTIMEDIA INFORMATION AND ANALYSIS FIRM.

virtually every central bank, investment institution, corporation, government, and newspaper of consequence from Atlanta to Wellington. The system's specialty is providing statistics, indices, and research covering the gamut of investment instruments. These are listed as yellow keys on the customized Bloomberg keyboard: equities, money markets, currencies, municipal bonds, corporate bonds, mortgage bonds, preferred stock, commodities, index-related investments, and client portfolios. ▶

Bloomberg delivers radio, television, magazine, newspaper, and electronic-screen-based products to clients in more than 100 countries. Responsible for this enormous, continuous feed of information is a 24-hour news gathering staff of 1,000 reporters and editors at 78 news bureaus. These reporters and editors file some 4,000 stories every day. Another 4,100 data collectors and sales, service, and programming specialists round out the Bloomberg family.

The consumer Web site www.bloomberg.com is accessible free of charge to anyone with a computer. It is one of the most comprehensive sites on the Web and is ranked in the top five sites for business and finance. The traffic to the site has doubled every three months, resulting in 5 million unique users a month.

Bloomberg is also the publisher of several highly valued magazines that provide in-depth analysis and perspectives on business and investment trends. Published as part of the Bloomberg service package, *Bloomberg Magazine* provides insights into financial markets, informs about financial products, and details the new functions in the BLOOMBERG® service. *Bloomberg Personal Finance* targets sophisticated individual investors with actionable investment strategies, in-depth features, and savvy insights from leading Wall Street experts. The newest offering, *Bloomberg Wealth Manager*, provides perspectives and information for financial advisers.

COMMUNITY RESPONSIBILITY

With knowledge comes power and with power comes responsibility. Bloomberg assumes that responsibility with an open hand. Whether it is by making donations to numerous worthy causes or by taking a paintbrush in hand to help brighten the walls of a school in the Bronx, the Bloomberg philosophy is one of participation and public service. Bloomberg's contributions have helped a variety of organizations in the New York community, including the Central Park Conservancy, New York Police and Fire Widows' and Children's Benefit Fund, Lincoln Center for the Performing Arts, Jewish Museum, Metropolitan Museum of Art, and Randall's Island Sports Foundation.

This commitment to the community, combined with a history of innovation and a dedication to providing the financial world the information it needs, makes Bloomberg a powerhouse in the financial world and global society for decades to come.

FROM ITS HEADQUARTERS ON PARK AVENUE, BLOOMBERG DELIVERS RADIO, TELEVISION, MAGAZINE, NEWSPAPER, AND ELECTRONIC-SCREEN-BASED PRODUCTS PRODUCED BY A 24-HOUR NEWS GATHERING STAFF OF 1,000 REPORTERS AND EDITORS AND 4,100 DATA COLLECTORS AND SALES, SERVICE, AND PROGRAMMING SPECIALISTS IN 78 CITIES AROUND THE GLOBE.

DUANE BERGER

THERE WAS A TIME WHEN DEALS WERE MADE WITH A handshake, the good guys wore white hats, and old-fashioned values like integrity, trust, commitment, quality, and hard work were alive and well. York Hunter strives in its daily business to keep these values alive. ⚲ For example, a handshake cemented

a $9.5 million construction management project for New York's former Chemist Club, and the white hats—actually OSHA-approved construction hard hats made to look like western Stetsons—were worn by the York Hunter crew.

York Hunter is a construction firm that provides a broad range of services, including general contracting, construction management, design/build, and consulting. The employees at York Hunter believe in doing business the old-fashioned way, but they still maintain the zeal of a dynamic New York firm that believes time is money.

"We owe it to ourselves, our employees, and our clients to uphold our own code of ethics, and we hope these construction hats will help foster a sense of pride for what we do," says Kenneth M. Colao, president and CEO of York Hunter. "In short, we want these hats to symbolize our commitment to integrity on the job."

This combination of values and performance has paid off for York Hunter. The company has become one of the most recognized and respected firms in the business.

STARTING WITH EXPERTISE

In 1983, Colao co-founded York Hunter on a very simple philosophy: 100 percent client satisfaction. "We pursue clients," says Colao, "not projects." This unique approach to old-line business has led to long-term working relationships with clients, and is responsible for York Hunter's dramatic record of growth. With a steady increase in business every year since its founding, the company has experienced 400 percent growth in the last three years.

When Colao opened York Hunter's doors with only a small personal loan, no employees, and no clients, consulting work was the focus. The company developed a very personalized, hands-on approach that quickly generated more and more work. As building revenues rose, York Hunter began to offer construction management and general contracting services.

Colao saw an opportunity to make a unique position for the company by coupling its client-first philosophy with a strategy of diversification of services for equally diverse markets—from private developer, corporate, and retail to high-tech and public-use facilities. In time, York Hunter gained a reputation for its willingness to tackle extremely difficult assignments and a highly successful track record.

For example, just 15 months after the building's official groundbreaking ceremony, the 32-story Courtyard by Marriott Times Square South opened for business. This was the result of York Hunter's record pace on the project; the company's crews often poured a concrete floor a day. The company's major renovation of the dramatic Whitney Museum of Art took place while the renowned facility remained fully operational. In addition, after completing a total renovation of a wing dedicated to rare books and manuscripts in the New York Public Library's central branch, York Hunter is now working on a 121,000-square-foot renovation of the New York Public Library for

CLOCKWISE FROM TOP: LEADING YORK HUNTER INTO THE NEW MILLENNIUM ARE (FROM LEFT) DENNIS PRUDE, EXECUTIVE VICE PRESIDENT; KENNETH M. COLAO, PRESIDENT AND CEO; WILLIAM M. COTE, EXECUTIVE VICE PRESIDENT; THEODORE DOMURACKI, PRESIDENT; AND ALAN REICH, SENIOR VICE PRESIDENT.

YORK HUNTER CREATED THE HIGH-TECH LAW SCHOOL FOR COLUMBIA UNIVERSITY.

THE COMPANY'S MAJOR RENOVATION OF THE DRAMATIC WHITNEY MUSEUM OF ART TOOK PLACE WHILE THE RENOWNED FACILITY REMAINED FULLY OPERATIONAL.

BERNSTEIN ASSOCIATES

ESTO PHOTOGRAPHICS

the Performing Arts at Lincoln Center, which will house the library's collection of music, film, video, books, and other materials.

The firm built Wall Street's first new hotel in eight years, the 17-floor, high-tech Holiday Inn—sometimes referred to as Wall Street's virtual hotel—offering New York's first fully wired hotel, with high-speed T1 Internet connections in each room. It also created the high-tech law school for Columbia University, and is now executing the very challenging sliver building construction of a luxury boutique hotel in SoHo.

York Hunter even erected a 10-story, steel frame in a weekend for the landmark Association of the Bar Building, a project that required a special jib, 140-ton crane to maneuver steel and materials blindly over two existing buildings and into a rear courtyard guided only by hand signals and radio.

BUILDING A TRADITION

Colao says York Hunter's enviable track record is a result of a company philosophy that finds balance and motivation in the desire to do the best and be the best. The company's motto, Building a Tradition™, is also its goal, and that's how it approaches every project: with technical excellence, timely performance, and quality construction.

Most important, York Hunter approaches every project with the attitude that no matter how challenging the task, if it can

possibly be done at all, it is the firm to do it—York Hunter knows how to build in the face of tremendous obstacles and constraints. It is this innovation and tenacity that makes York Hunter the construction company of choice for the kinds of demanding projects that force the competition to take a deep breath.

This kind of track record is made possible in large part because of York Hunter's intense focus on entrepreneurial team building. According to one of its vision statements: "We believe we can add quality and value to our projects by effectively partnering with our clients and the design team. We are committed to client focus, team support, trust and mutual respect, honest communication, accountability, and win-win situations. We utilize facilitators to help forge a cooperative team spirit and long-lasting relationships among all project 'stakeholders' including clients, architects, consultants, vendors, trade contractors and our project team."

In keeping with one of its founding principles of building better buildings through better education, York Hunter goes to great lengths to ensure each employee is thoroughly trained and educated in the latest state-of-the-art methodologies at its company-run York Hunter University. And, to foster the greatest effort among its internal teams, the company conducts working retreats, hosts special events,

and celebrates achievements through awards and performance-based incentive systems.

INTEGRITY AND VALUE

Finally, the York Hunter work ethic is fierce and hands-on, involving everyone in the company. Colao recently took a cross section of 30 people from the firm—both upper management and support personnel—to an off-site location to discuss the company's mission. During the course of the meeting, these employees were asked to rank by secret ballot three reasons for working at York Hunter. The number one reason given by all 30 employees was the integrity of the firm. The number two reason was its values.

With its dedication to integrity, trust, commitment, quality, and hard work, it is little wonder York Hunter wears white hats on the job—just like the heroes of yesteryear who rode into town, tackled the tough problems no one else would touch, and then rode off into the sunset, leaving behind streets made safe for the townspeople.

YORK HUNTER CONSTRUCTED THIS NEW FACILITY ON THE CORNER OF MULBERRY AND CANAL STREETS—FROM THE FOUNDATION UP—FOR THE BANK OF EAST ASIA (LEFT).

JUST 15 MONTHS AFTER THE BUILDING'S OFFICIAL GROUND-BREAKING CEREMONY, THE 32-STORY COURTYARD BY MARRIOTT TIMES SQUARE SOUTH OPENED FOR BUSINESS—THE RESULT OF YORK HUNTER'S RECORD PACE ON THE PROJECT (RIGHT).

COMPUTER GENERATED SOLUTIONS, INC.

SITUATED ONLY A FEW BLOCKS NORTH OF THE DIVERSE crowds of people in New York City's Times Square district, Computer Generated Solutions, Inc. (CGS) is perhaps a product of the melting pot it resides in. ◣ Originally founded as a systems integration and management consulting firm to the apparel

and fashion industries, CGS' New York headquarters is not surprisingly planted in the midst of the largest fashion district in the nation. And, while CGS now services an international clientele coming from a variety of industries, most of those industries also are largely situated in New York—including the financial, entertainment, telecommunications, retail, and government markets.

UNIQUELY NEW YORK

What makes CGS most representative of its surroundings, however, is the uniqueness of its foundation. CGS Founder, President, and CEO Phil Friedman is an entrepreneur who immigrated to New York City in 1976 from the former Soviet Union. When Friedman arrived in the United States, he had de-

grees in electrical engineering, economics, and accounting, but spoke no English, not unlike many native New Yorkers today. After intensive training in English and computer technology, he landed a job with an apparel

MICHAEL DARTER

company in the garment district. Friedman gained experience with the installation of a specialized IBM computer system made for the garment industry. A few short and extremely busy years later, in 1984, he began CGS with only five employees.

At that time, CGS began an IT consulting practice dedicated to the apparel industry that was the foundation for its success with an enterprisewide software solution it later acquired, called ACS Optima™. The product has become the leading ERP solution in the sewn products industry, and has garnered more than 500 installations at apparel and footwear manufacturing companies.

AS DIVERSE AS THE CITY

Today, CGS is a privately held organization that utilizes more than 1,300 professionals in 11 locations around the nation in Atlanta; Chicago; Dallas; Detroit; Edison, New Jersey; Los Angeles; New York; Philadelphia; Raleigh; Tampa; and Washington, D.C. But the culture of the company remains steadfast to its New York philosophy. "CGS is a company that remains true to its entrepreneurial foundation," says Friedman. "CGS values speed over bureaucracy, and innovation over what's commonplace. It's a company with objectives directly aligned with its customers' needs—a dynamic, responsive, quality-driven firm that continually goes beyond the expected.

"CGS has a culture that encourages each staff member to participate in every level of client service and quality control. It prides itself on the diversity of its employees, believing that a diverse staff is a creative staff," says Friedman.

Diversity, not just of employees, but of offerings, is perhaps what distinguishes CGS from most of its competitors in the technology industry. While many organizations focus on narrow areas of

COMPUTER GENERATED SOLUTIONS, INC. (CGS) FOUNDER, PRESIDENT, AND CEO PHIL FRIEDMAN IMMIGRATED TO NEW YORK CITY IN 1976 FROM THE FORMER SOVIET UNION.

MICHAEL DARTER

CGS IS HEADQUARTERED HIGH ABOVE NEW YORK'S FAST-PACED TIMES SQUARE DISTRICT.

expertise, CGS has found success in offering a full range of state-of-the-art computer solutions that can be custom designed to fit a particular organization's size, budget, and objectives. The benefit to the client is the accessibility of multiple services under one convenient contract, eliminating the need to hire and manage additional vendors. CGS can manage all of the client's computer-related services, thus freeing the firm to focus on its core business.

The Composite Solution

To help its clients enhance their productivity, CGS has created several discrete technology practices that can be used individually, as components, or combined into one complete solution for extra value. The Composite Solution™ is an integrated suite of services that include network services such as

remote and on-site help desk solutions; systems integration; application outsourcing; technical training; document management; professional staffing; call center management; Y2K services; and application development.

Complementing this solution is CGS' ability to provide cost-effective computer hardware and services to its clients. This is largely a result of CGS' designation as an IBM Premier Business Partner, which enables it to offer mainframe, AS/400, RS/6000, Netfinity, and S/390 systems. The designation as a premier-level partner is an honor for CGS because IBM only awards its Premier status to top performers whose quality measures up to IBM's arduous standards. Only 5 percent of IBM's business partners qualified for this special recognition during the past year.

IBM is not the only one to laud CGS' accomplishments. In 1995, CGS was named to *Inc.* magazine's Top 500 list of the fastest-growing companies; and in 1996, Friedman was named Entrepreneur of the Year for New York by Ernst & Young. This year, Deloitte & Touche named CGS as part of its New York Fast 50, one of the fastest-growing technology-related companies in the New York area.

And Friedman expects that growth will continue. "As we enter the new millennium, CGS is poised not only for continued growth, but a renewed commitment—to our customers, to our employees, and to the entrepreneurial spirit that also has been our trademark," says Friedman. "If the past is truly prologue, then the future holds the promise of even greater success for all of us."

▸ MICHAEL DARTER

HEN VISITORS OR EXECUTIVES ARE LOOKING FOR A SPE-cial place to stay in New York City for extended periods of time, the city offers a remarkable choice for discerning tastes: Bristol Plaza, an elegant and convenient alternative to traditional hotels and rental apartments. Designed for individuals who enjoy luxury and personal service, Bristol Plaza offers a warm and welcoming atmosphere, a feeling of home for the people staying there. It provides the comforts and ambience of relaxing residential living, combined with the flexibility and benefits of five-star services.

Within minutes of Midtown and Central Park, on a manicured street in the heart of Manhattan's Upper East Side, Bristol Plaza is part of 200-210 East 65th Street, a premier luxury condominium complex. Bristol Plaza can fill the needs of the executive who must be in New York for an extended stay, the new arrival who has not yet found a permanent home, or the frequent visitor who wants a part-time residence. And it is perfect for the company that is looking for standout corporate apartments for its honored executives, or for people whose lives are in flux and who want the sense of belonging that comes from living in a home with the luxurious amenities of a truly exceptional hotel. The facility is so successful in its efforts to make its guests feel pampered and welcome that the people who have stayed there repeatedly say they would never consider staying anywhere else.

BRISTOL PLAZA CAN FILL THE NEEDS OF THE EXECUTIVE WHO IS IN NEW YORK FOR AN EXTENDED STAY, THE NEW ARRIVAL WHO HAS NOT YET FOUND A PERMANENT HOME, OR THE FREQUENT VISITOR WHO WANTS A PART-TIME RESIDENCE.

Equipped for Convenience

The apartments at Bristol Plaza have been designed and furnished with the exceptional style and attention to detail that would certainly be expected in an elegant New York City residence. Kitchens are fully equipped for entertaining,

WHEN VISITORS OR EXECUTIVES ARE LOOKING FOR A SPECIAL PLACE TO STAY IN NEW YORK CITY FOR EXTENDED PERIODS OF TIME, THE CITY OFFERS A REMARKABLE CHOICE FOR DISCERNING TASTES: BRISTOL PLAZA, AN ELEGANT AND CONVENIENT ALTERNATIVE TO TRADITIONAL HOTELS AND RENTAL APARTMENTS (TOP).

RESIDENTS OF BRISTOL PLAZA SHARE IN ALL OF THE ADJACENT CONDOMINIUM'S SUPERB AMENITIES: A FULLY EQUIPPED ROOFTOP HEALTH CLUB OFFERING A 50-FOOT POOL WITH RETRACTABLE DOME ROOF AND OPEN SUN DECK; STATE-OF-THE-ART EXERCISE EQUIPMENT; MASSAGE AND STEAM ROOMS; A SAUNA; A LOUNGE; AND A 24-HOUR, ATTENDED GARAGE (BOTTOM).

including a gas range with microwave oven, refrigerator with ice maker, dishwasher, coffeemaker, cooking utensils, and full dinner service. Italian Carrera marble baths are stocked with fine towels and toiletries. The bedrooms have generous closets, king-size beds with goose down pillows, and fine quality linens. All apartments have color televisions in living rooms and bedrooms, cable television, and VCRs, as well as a state-of-the art telephone system with individual telephone numbers for direct in- and -out usage.

The services provided at Bristol Plaza also attest to the facility's uncompromising commitment to excellence, where willing and gracious staff members take a personal interest in the well-being of their guests and are always ready to assist the residents in enhancing their stay in New York. Bristol Plaza offers the kinds of amenities expected of a luxury accommodation: daily maid service, with fresh towels and quality linens; 24-hour doorman and concierge; arrangements for everything from theater tickets to limousines and car rental; 24-hour telephone message service, fax, and photocopying equipment; and full valet service offering dry cleaning and tailoring, shoe and luggage repair, and personal laundry.

Residents of Bristol Plaza share in all of the adjacent condominium's superb amenities: a fully equipped rooftop health club offering a 50-foot pool with retractable dome roof and open sun deck; state-of-the-art exercise equipment; massage and steam rooms; a sauna; a lounge; and a 24-hour, attended garage. Studios and one-bedroom apartments range from $5,200 to $8,000 per month. Two-bedroom apartments are priced at $8,100 and $8,400 per month.

Bristol Plaza is a pioneer in creating luxury accommodations for longer stays in New York City. The facility's innovation and success have served to stimulate growth of this industry citywide, and its development has been a positive influence in the gentrification of the surrounding area, benefiting property values for local residents, retailers, and businesses. Whenever an extended stay is in order, Bristol Plaza is the place.

JLC Environmental Consultants, Inc.

over the years: the need to ensure that public buildings are safe, particularly in regard to the use of materials that may be hazardous to health. One company dedicated to protecting the environment and the health of the public—by delivering a wide range of reliable, cost-effective testing services—is JLC Environmental Consultants, Inc.

Commitment to the Environment

JLC is the result of one woman's commitment to environmental safety. Jennifer L. Carey, company president, and her staff of professionals believe that environmental safety is an issue that needs to be addressed in every building—especially school buildings, where the health and well-being of children are at stake. In 1987, this belief inspired Carey to found her own construction-support company. In the ensuing years, her firm's knowledge, professionalism, and attention to quality service have achieved

considerable respect in this traditionally male-dominated industry, as well as an impressive growth rate for the company—more than 20 percent annually since its founding.

The growth and success of JLC have sparked acquisition proposals from several larger companies, but Carey's commitment to helping create a safe and healthy environment has inspired her to maintain control of the company. Dedicated to offering the best service available, she wants to be sure that the quality of JLC's services is not compromised. But as proud as she is of her company's success, Carey is most proud of the fact that her work with more than 400 New York City school buildings has helped to protect thousands of children from environmental hazards. JLC has also worked with many Fortune 500 companies to ensure safe work environments for employees.

Testing for Safety

"Service is what sets us apart from our competition," says Carey. "You can call us 24 hours a day, seven days a week and we will be there." The company's reliable service is important to both the construction and the real estate industries in New York, because delays can be extremely costly in these fields.

JLC offers two primary categories of services. The first is asbestos and lead services, which are divided into three phases: investigation, architectural design, and construction monitoring. In-house laboratory services support every step of this process.

The second service category is industrial hygiene management, which involves air, water, and soil testing to determine possible health hazards due to contamination. For example, sick building syndrome (SBS) can sometimes be dealt with by a thorough analysis of the heating, ventilating, and air-conditioning systems—including airflow patterns and temperatures—in occupied buildings.

Headquartered in New York City, JLC also has offices in Freeport and Albany, and has recently expanded its service through acquisitions to provide environmental training. These training programs have been taught as far away as Asia. Says Carey, "We're dealing with contaminants that are destructive in a very real sense. Our mission is to keep the environment safe for people. The more they know, the safer they are." JLC Environmental Consultants' commitment to this mission ensures its continuing success for many years to come.

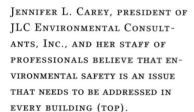

Jennifer L. Carey, president of JLC Environmental Consultants, Inc., and her staff of professionals believe that environmental safety is an issue that needs to be addressed in every building (top).

Dedicated to offering the best service available, Carey wants to be sure that the quality of JLC's services is not compromised (bottom).

▲ © JONATHAN POSTAL / TOWERY PUBLISHING, INC.

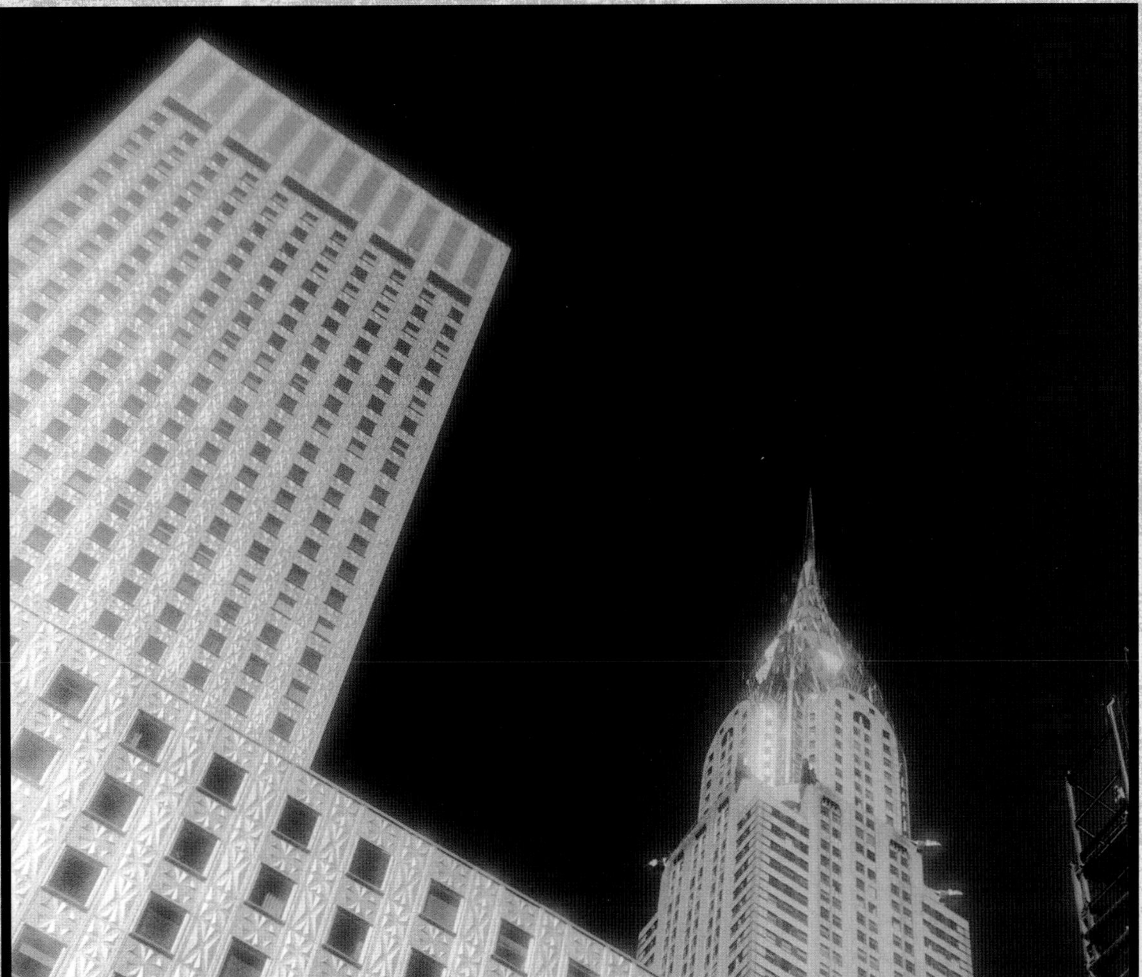

1991 CITIPOST

1991 VIATEL, INC.

1993 HEALTH CAPITAL

1993 THE WILLIAMS CAPITAL GROUP, L.P.

1994 EARTHWEB

1994 GOTHAM, INC.

1995 ALLTEL INFORMATION SERVICES

1995 DOCUMENT EXPRESS, INC.

1995 INTIMATE BRANDS, INC.

1996 BLUESTONE CAPITAL PARTNERS, L.P.

1996 BRIDGE INFORMATION SYSTEMS

1996 FITZMAURICE & COMPANY, LLC

1997 PLATINUM TELEVISION GROUP

CITIPOST

CITIPOST TAKES THE GLOBAL MARKETPLACE VERY SERIously. In less than a decade, Citipost has become the private global post office for large, multinational companies in 17 major cities, including Los Angeles, Hong Kong, London, Frankfurt, Toronto, Chicago, and San Francisco. ▲ Citipost was founded in 1991 by Richard Trayford and Hugh Fitzwilliam-Lay, two Englishmen who hand delivered packages to record and publishing businesses around Manhattan. Their idea was simple: identify the high-volume delivery areas, target specific addresses within those areas, and deliver a high volume of packages for a fraction of normal delivery fees.

By 1993, Citipost had opened additional offices in Boston and Los Angeles. In 1997, the company went global, with offices in London, Frankfurt, Paris, and Hong Kong. Currently, Citipost employs 400 people and works closely with local government agencies to provide jobs for people from disadvantaged backgrounds and those with physical and mental difficulties.

KEEPING COSTS LOW

Citipost's niche is somewhere between a next-day courier service and mail/ground services. It focuses primarily on the delivery of business-to-business materials that are exempt from postal statutes, including small parcels, extremely urgent letters, books, magazines, catalogs, periodicals, newspapers, and reports. The company offers morning delivery, next-day delivery, and two- to three-day delivery to locations around the globe. True to its founding principle, Citipost focuses its operations in a city's central business district, relying on a high volume of pickups and deliveries in a limited area to save time and keep prices low.

Citipost couriers in each city use a unique, hand-pushed tri-cart the company developed to help its employees shorten delivery times. There's also a bicycle version to help couriers weave their way through tangled downtown traffic. For overseas deliveries, Citipost rents space on commercial flights already headed to a targeted destination—a huge cost savings that Citipost passes on to its customers.

OFFERING SOLUTIONS

Trayford and Fitzwilliam-Lay see Citipost as a data and marketing partner for its customers and as a champion against the monopolistic practices and statutes of national post offices around the world. Citipost is able to compete with major post offices because it is the only company in its field with an extensive international network of wholly owned subsidiaries. This means all mail traffic flows through Citipost's own network and is delivered by Citipost employees. The benefits include greater cost control, aggressive pricing, faster and easier package tracking, and international consolidation for customer deliveries.

Citipost boasts an annual growth rate of at least 100 percent over the past five years, and *Inc.* magazine has ranked the company as one of its 500 fastest-growing private companies in the United States for the past four consecutive years. But Citipost isn't resting on its laurels. Its officers have used the company's success to invest in systems and technologies aimed at improving service and accountability, and bringing Web-based technology to the distribution business. The most recent purchase is a global positioning system (GPS) that provides real-time tracking for its worldwide fleet of vehicles and its pushcarts. The GPS allows Citipost to respond more quickly and with more accuracy to customer requests—another step that keeps the company well in front of the pack.

RICHARD TRAYFORD FOUNDED CITIPOST IN NEW YORK CITY IN 1991. TODAY, IT HAS OFFICES IN 17 MAJOR CITIES AROUND THE WORLD.

EALTH CAPITAL WAS FOUNDED IN 1993 BY ENTREPRENEUR Steven Nitsberg, who realized that a successful health care practice depends as much on effective financial management as it does on quality care. For this reason, an increasing number of health care providers are looking for companies that can help

them handle their cash flow requirements. Nitsberg created Health Capital specifically to handle this unusual financial niche market.

Nitsberg, a member of Governor George Pataki's Healthcare Finance and Reform Committee for New York State and a graduate of West Point, started brokering transactions in the health care industry soon after his graduation from the Harvard Business School. He became adept at matching the right funding sources for the right clients from the financial experience he received during his years at Morgan Stanley. Through dedication to his goal, Nitsberg was able to establish his own credit line and open his own company.

Today, Health Capital provides capital based on accounts receivable to a wide range of health care providers, including doctors, medical practices, nursing homes, hospitals, MRI and radiology centers, rehab clinics, and home health care companies.

HEALTHY FINANCING

Health Capital provides flexible, asset-based loans and/or accounts receivable purchase fundings at highly competitive rates through its Working Capital, Acquisition, and Accounts Receivable Financing programs. The company has created a special position in doing smaller deals along with the big ones, and has been successful by tailoring the deals it offers to individual clients.

Today, Health Capital is considered one of the premier funding companies that manage accounts receivable funding for clients whose funding needs range from $100,000 to $100 million. The clients tend to fall into three broad financial segments of the health care industry: companies that are too new to get traditional bank financing; companies that depend on payments from Medicaid, Medicare, and private

insurance, which sometimes takes up to six months; and companies that are looking for mergers and acquisitions, and seek to create funding by using the acquired company's accounts receivable to fund the transaction.

A NONTRADITIONAL APPROACH TO SUCCESS

Traditional banks and finance companies often do not understand the unique health care environment. Medical receivables are difficult for most factors to work with because they are never paid at face value.

As an expert in the health care industry, Health Capital can effectively evaluate the worth of an invoice with a knowledge that is unmatched by commercial banks or other finance or factoring companies. Health Capital is thoroughly familiar with the laws and limits for Medicare, Medicaid, and insurance companies, and

it knows how to leverage the accounts receivable for these clients in order to provide a reliable, consistent cash flow.

Health Capital's mission is "to offer the capital necessary to fuel the growth of the smaller national health care provider community, helping enable the provider to continue delivering high quality health care services, while providing for a sustainable return on investment to Health Capital's shareholders."

Health Capital is also valued for its straightforward approach, integrity, and quality of service. The company prides itself on becoming familiar with each client's unique circumstances, being able to give prudent and effective advice, and helping each client meet its particular goals. These attributes, as well as a general commitment to each client, have created a success story for Health Capital within the health care industry.

HEALTH CAPITAL WAS FOUNDED IN 1993 BY ENTREPRENEUR STEVEN NITSBERG, WHO REALIZED THAT A SUCCESSFUL HEALTH CARE PRACTICE DEPENDS AS MUCH ON EFFECTIVE FINANCIAL MANAGEMENT AS IT DOES ON QUALITY CARE.

VIATEL, INC.

EW YORK-HEADQUARTERED VIATEL, INC., IS AMONG the world's fastest-growing providers of telecommunications services. The company offers a panoply of competitively priced voice and data services to a variety of customers— including individual consumers, businesses, and other carriers—in more than

230 countries and territories worldwide. It also provides high-quality, high-speed, high-capacity bandwidth to companies, carriers, and Internet service providers.

Viatel's principal market focus is western Europe, where it currently operates one of the largest pan-European networks. The company has international gateways in New York and London; international network operations centers in Egham, England, and Somerset, New Jersey; and network points of presence in more than 78 European cities. It also has an impressive sales force, with direct presence

in more than 12 western European cities and indirect sales outlets in more than 180 additional locations on the continent.

Viatel has recorded impressive growth. In 1998, annualized revenues surpassed the $100 million barrier; the company expects to exceed $300 million in revenues in 1999.

THE EUROPEAN CHALLENGE

In the United States today, the availability of affordable telecommunications services is often taken for granted. Since the breakup of Ma Bell, competition

has led to dramatic reductions in the cost of voice calls, a proliferation of varied service options, and perhaps, most important, the development of the infrastructure that supports networks of every size and type. From the explosion of the Internet and E-commerce to the transformation of rudimentary business computing into advanced global networks, telecommunications technology has changed the daily lives and work patterns of virtually every person in America.

The situation in western Europe, however, has been dramatically different. Europe has been disadvantaged by aging voice networks, most of which were built by the same government-affiliated organizations that exercised monopolistic control over rates, service, and supply. Despite the general movement toward telecommunications deregulation and the initiatives taken by the European Union since 1998 to accelerate this process, Europe has lacked the cross-border, fiber-optic network necessary to support advanced telecommunications applications and services, and advance the information revolution.

It is against this backdrop that Viatel—one of the earliest new entrants into the liberalized markets of western Europe— made the decision to engineer, build, and operate the Circe Pan-European Network. "The premise behind Circe is simple," said Michael J. Mahoney, Viatel's president and chief executive officer. "We wanted to bring to western Europe an advanced, cross-border, fiber network that can deliver a wide range of services—from voice telephony and data to advanced multimedia applications and E-commerce— at the lowest possible cost, but with the highest levels of quality and reliability."

"THE PREMISE BEHIND CIRCE IS SIMPLE," SAYS MICHAEL J. MAHONEY, VIATEL'S PRESIDENT AND CHIEF EXECUTIVE OFFICER. "WE WANTED TO BRING TO WESTERN EUROPE AN ADVANCED, CROSS-BORDER, FIBER NETWORK THAT CAN DELIVER A WIDE RANGE OF SERVICES AT THE LOWEST POSSIBLE COST, BUT WITH THE HIGHEST LEVELS OF QUALITY AND RELIABILITY."

CIRCE PAN-EUROPEAN NETWORK

Viatel is investing more than $700 million in the development, construction, and operation of the Circe Pan-European Network. This freshly-built, state-of-the-art, cross-border, fiber-optic network will soon link more than 40 major cities in western Europe. More than 3,000 of the 8,700 route kilometers that make up this superior broadband infrastructure were in service and carrying commercial traffic by mid-year 1999. So far, Circe links London in the United Kingdom; Amsterdam and Rotterdam in the Netherlands; Brussels and Antwerp in Belgium; Paris, Amiens, Nancy, and Strasbourg in France; and Düsseldorf, Frankfurt, and Mannheim in Germany. Construction of the remaining 5,700 route kilometers—

linking other major cities in Germany, France, and Switzerland—should be completed by mid-2000.

The Circe network employs the latest in optical technology, including reduced-slope fiber, dense wave-division multiplexing equipment, and synchronous digital hierarchy, providing high capacity, flexibility, and reliability for the network. Circe, on average, has 65 strands of fiber throughout. But, currently, only a single pair is lit, the amount needed to carry 20 gigabits of information per second. It should be noted, though, that this single pair of fiber can be expanded anytime in the future to deliver 320 gigabits per second without adding any more optronics and without interrupting service. And, given recent advances in optronics, Circe should be able to deliver more than six terabits

of capacity on a single pair of fiber in the very near future.

"Circe is truly the future of Viatel and marks our official transition from a switched-based reseller to a facilities-based, integrated provider of telecommunications services," says Mahoney.

LOWER RATES AND BETTER SERVICE

"By allowing us to control our costs, control our quality, and control our service offerings," says Mahoney, "Circe enables Viatel to maintain its position as the value leader in telecommunications."

By forming an alliance between a new generation of entrepreneurial skills and a customer-oriented focus, with the most advanced and radical technology yet developed, Viatel is paving the way for a new age of communications possibilities for Europe and the world at large.

VIATEL'S INTERNATIONAL NETWORK OPERATIONS CENTER IS LOCATED IN EGHAM, SURREY, ENGLAND.

THE WILLIAMS CAPITAL GROUP, L.P.

WITH A STRONG CLIENT ROSTER THAT INCLUDES A WIDE variety of Fortune 500 corporations, it would be easy to think that the people at The Williams Capital Group, L.P. (WCG) would lose their hunger for new business. But one look at the bustling Fifth Avenue offices of the boutique investment bank

and it becomes evident that complacency is nowhere to be found. According to founder and CEO Chris Williams, "No one owes us anything, so we have to go out there and earn our way by working harder, being smarter, and doing as much as possible to ensure that our clients win on every transaction they entrust to our care."

With an attitude such as this, it is little surprise that in 1999 alone, Ford Motor Credit, Wal-Mart, Sprint Corporation, and many other companies included WCG in their multibillion-dollar financings. This is the story of an organization that has grown despite being handicapped at inception with a small staff and limited capital.

PROSPERITY THROUGH PERSISTENCE

Back in 1993, the year Williams got WCG off the ground, the firm specialized in developing complex, structured transactions. It was a very good business, and the firm prospered. Subsequent market turmoil offered up challenges that tested the mettle of the fledgling company. Hard work and the confidence of several invaluable client relationships enabled the firm to thrive during the unpredictable bull market of the middle and late 1990s.

Today, The Williams Capital Group is considered a solid player in domestic and international equities, as well as in money market, government agency, and corporate bond trading. In the fixed-income markets, WCG is the only boutique firm formally serving as a commercial paper dealer for a dozen blue-chip corporations. In this role, Williams Capital is integral to the daily financing of these corporations by placing hundreds of millions of dollars in commercial paper with investors every single day.

In the equity markets, WCG serves as a formal stock buyback

agent for many large corporations, repurchasing stock for the firm's clients on the floor of the New York Stock Exchange. For the firm's asset management clients, WCG acts as agent by buying blocks of stock, both domestically and internationally, in 36 foreign markets. The Williams Capital Group provides equity execution services to clients 24 hours a day out of the firm's New York and London offices.

In addition, the firm has established a strong reputation as an underwriter of public stock and bond offerings. Williams Capital is one of the very few firms, excluding national brokerages and commercial banks, to

serve as a dealer who assists in the financings of numerous major corporations. WCG's role in the commercial paper markets provided a platform for the firm to expand into the underwriting of corporate bonds and government agency securities. In this arena, the firm serves as comanager or co-lead-manager on bond transactions, adding value to clients by placing the securities with small and mid-sized institutional investors.

EMPLOYEE-OWNED EXCELLENCE

WCG's desire to win is evidenced by the fact that the firm's revenues more than doubled between 1997 and 1998. Employees, who along

TODAY, THE WILLIAMS CAPITAL
GROUP IS CONSIDERED A SOLID
PLAYER IN DOMESTIC AND INTER-
NATIONAL EQUITIES, AS WELL AS
IN MONEY MARKET, GOVERNMENT
AGENCY, AND CORPORATE BOND
TRADING.

with Williams own equity stakes in the business, demonstrated their belief in the firm's future by buying back—well ahead of schedule—the equity held by outside investors, and making WCG a 100 percent employee-owned firm. "Sharing ownership helps to strengthen the commitment employees have to the firm," Williams notes. "People will always work harder and stay longer if they own the business and have a real say in its future.

The opportunity to own equity in our firm has also enabled us to consistently attract the level of talent we require to compete effectively against larger firms."

Far from resting on any laurels, The Williams Capital Group continues to expand, recently opening a London office and applying for membership on the New York Stock Exchange. "If we're going to continue to be successful in this business—and we intend to—we must have the capabilities

that our domestic and international clients demand," says Williams. "One of these is a London base for our international equity and fixed income businesses. Another is highly effective trade execution, which membership on the New York Stock Exchange will enable us to provide. Beyond this, we'll listen to our clients and let them tell us what we need to do to get and keep their business. For us, success is as simple and as elegant as that."

OR INFORMATION TECHNOLOGY (IT) PROFESSIONALS, the goal is not only to access the needed resource, but to do so as quickly and accurately as possible. The challenge is to marshal the pertinent and exclude the extraneous. This is where EarthWeb (Nasdaq: EWBX) excels, designed to fulfill the informa-

tion and business-to-business services needs of the IT industry.

EarthWeb was founded in 1994 to provide a refined, on-line resource targeted to the audience who needs it most—the IT professionals. Agile, intelligent, and aggressive, EarthWeb has emerged victorious from the multitude of competitors crowding the Internet over the past few years. While others have folded, this company is now considered an old-timer in Internet years, and is the largest on-line knowledge base for IT professionals worldwide. With more than 200 employees, EarthWeb serves professionals in more than 100 countries in multiple languages—including one-third of its business from outside the United States—and had more than 200 million page views during the third quarter of 1999 alone.

ON-LINE KNOWLEDGE
Through its network of on-line services, EarthWeb gives technology professionals access to the knowledge base of technical information and services. It has the framework to act as an essential business-to-business intermediary between IT professionals

and vendors of IT products and services. EarthWeb's Internet sites and services provide practical, impartial technical knowledge in multiple, interconnected sites that make it easy for IT professionals to find exactly what they need.

EarthWeb answers the needs of more than 1.4 million unique visitors each month through its various sites. Its sites include Datamation, which provides comprehensive coverage of business and technology issues; ITKnowledge.com, which is a rapidly growing and up-to-date

on-line collection of technical books, tutorials, and source code—all cross-indexed and fully searchable; Developer.com and related sites that address the enterprise developer and Internet developer sectors; and HTML Goodies and related sites, which focus on utilizing the most from emerging Web technologies.

Dice.com, part of the EarthWeb network, provides on-line career management and recruiting services. The site lists more than 130,000 high-tech jobs on-line and offers many value-added services to assist job seekers as well as HR managers and recruiters. Dice.com was recently ranked number one in San Francisco, New York, Boston, and Austin, Texas, for IT jobs by Dynamic Logic, an on-line research company.

With all these easily available resources, it is little wonder that EarthWeb's network of on-line services has earned the company the reputation of being the leading provider of business-to-business on-line services to the global IT industry. And it's no surprise that EarthWeb was ranked the third-fastest-growing company in *Business Week*'s Info Tech 100.

JACK HIDARY SERVES AS PRESIDENT AND CEO OF EARTHWEB (TOP).

EARTHWEB PRODUCES SUCH WEB SITES AS DATAMATION, DEVELOPER.COM, DICE.COM, AND ITKNOWLEDGE.COM (BOTTOM).

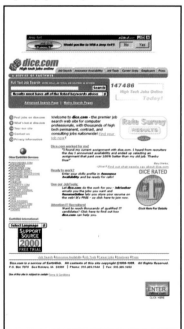

DOCUMENT EXPRESS, INC. HAS ONE VERY IMPORTANT goal: to make its clients look good. According to customer response, the reprographics and digital printing company is meeting that goal by providing fast, reliable document copying, printing, and mailing services to businesses throughout Manhattan.

The company was founded in 1995 by Fred Levine, a 20-year veteran of the reprographics business. Levine had previously cofounded and managed The Copy Exchange, another large copying and duplicating service in Manhattan. He capitalized on his reputation within the New York City marketplace to launch his new enterprise.

With Levine as chief executive officer, the company now occupies a 10,000-square-foot facility on Ninth Avenue and generates significant sales revenue each year. All work is done on-site, under the supervision of Levine and his production manager, who coordinates and oversees the day-to-day operations.

ONE-STOP SHOPPING

Document Express provides convenient, high-quality services for businesses wanting to do large-quantity copying presentations, reports, or mailings. The first step is the reprographics department, which provides pagination; litigation copying; high-quality laser printing; large-quantity, high-speed copying; color laser copying; electronic on-demand printing; and computer label printing.

Projects that require high-quality printing are sent to the electronic on-demand printing department, which includes document transfer by diskette, high-quality output resolution, and document storage and retrieval capabilities. The binding department then puts the documents together with stapling, three-hole punching, saddle stitching, tape binding, GBC VeloBinding, fully automated folding, or automatic collating.

Once the document is created and put together, Document Express provides document distribution services, including envelope inserting, postage application, and mailing, as well as post office or alternate location shipping.

"The key to our success is our commitment to providing superior quality work, on time, at a competitive price," Levine says. "We also develop strong, personal relationships with our customers. I stand behind all the work that we do."

AN INDEPENDENT COMPANY

Levine credits the firm's personalized service to the fact that Document Express is not a national chain, but an independent company. It was founded in Manhattan specifically for Manhattan businesses that often operate day and night, so it is not surprising that 75 percent of its business comes from the legal community. The company caters to an around-the-clock schedule by operating 24 hours a day, seven days a week, with pickup and delivery available at no extra charge. Features like these, coupled with outstanding quality control, keep customers coming back, according to Levine. In addition, employees are loyal, thanks to the company's family-like environment.

"Our exceptional staff reflects the diversity and talents of New York City," Levine says. "They're terrific team players who work to get the job done right. Our business grows because our employees are committed to doing a great job."

Levine was born and raised in New York, and furthered his commitment to the city by taking part in the David Rockefeller Fellows program. The program enables private sector leaders to deepen their understanding of the public needs of New York City and to take an active role in shaping the city's future. With businesses like Document Express and its customer-driven philosophy, the city's future looks very bright.

◀ JULIANA THOMAS PHOTOGRAPHY

DOCUMENT EXPRESS, INC. WAS FOUNDED IN 1995 BY FRED LEVINE, A 20-YEAR VETERAN OF THE REPROGRAPHICS BUSINESS.

GOTHAM, INC.

NIKI TAYLOR HAS BEEN FEATURED IN GOTHAM, INC.'S LIZ CLAIBORNE ADVERTISING CAMPAIGN (LEFT).

GOTHAM'S EXECUTIVE TEAM INCLUDES (FROM LEFT) LARRY DUNST, SHERI BARON, STONE ROBERTS, MARTY SMITH, AND LYNN GIORDANO (RIGHT).

city, New York is a place to invent, refine, execute, and dream.

So, what better place than New York to house a factory of ideas? And that is what Gotham, Inc. is all about: ideas. Without the big agency attitude and infrastructure, Gotham is uniquely suited to deliver bold, creative work even faster. Gotham knows how to create a stir, deliver a message, and build an image. In short, Gotham offers advertising without indulgence—emphasizing ideas graced with humor, insight, and intelligence.

THE EDGE

Gotham's edge comes from a company culture where people trade disciplines easily. Walking into a Gotham meeting, it's difficult to identify the media person from the planner or the art director. The firm believes in holistic advertising people, who, while trained in a discipline, apply their brainpower to every aspect of communication.

Gotham operates on the belief that if people are challenged and comfortable (no ties, no dress codes), they will solve problems beyond the limits of nine to five. As a result, the staff puts in long hours—but also has fun. For this reason, Gotham searches for talented individuals who value team building and open communications, as well as a good idea and a dose of humor.

THE PLAYERS

Gotham's five-partner management team prefers solving problems to dealing with bureaucracy. With a hands-on philosophy, Gotham takes an entrepreneurial approach with an emphasis on advertising results.

Stone Roberts, co-chairman and CEO (and once a president of Lintas USA), has been the point man for clients such as Johnson & Johnson, Cover Girl, Coca-Cola, and Lego. Not only did he suc-

cessfully manage the brand of the decade, Diet Coke, but he also led the way into the age of the supermodel for Cover Girl.

Larry Dunst, co-chairman and CEO, was, at age 28, the youngest president ever of an ad agency, and was CEO of a top 50 agency by age 39.

Sheri Baron, president and chief strategic officer, was one of the youngest on a board of directors at an agency, as well as one of the first inductees into the Advertising Agency Federation's Hall of Achievement.

Lynn Giordano, chief creative officer, has won virtually every creative honor in the advertising business and was named one of the 100 Best and Brightest by *Advertising Age*.

Marty Smith, vice chairman, has his roots in account management, from initial strategic planning to guiding the creative execution for a diversity of products, from analgesics to luxury automobiles.

THE RESULTS

Gotham's new business record has been excellent. With current billings of $370 million, the agency gained clients between 1996 and 1998 that included America Online, CompuServe, Meredith Publishing's *Ladies' Home Journal* and *MORE* magazines, Redken Salon Products, Fidelity Invest-

ments, Global Crossing and Knight/Trimark Group Inc., Helena Rubinstein, SunCom/AT&T Wireless, Pfizer Inc., and an increase in global work for Maybelline, which is now selling mascara from Malaysia to Moscow. As a wholly owned subsidiary of the Interpublic Group of Companies, Gotham's menu of resources provides these and future clients with resources that can compete with the largest agencies in the world.

For the Maybelline account, it has in part been Roberts' leadership in recommending models and actresses for beauty brands that steered the company in the 1990s to create a "face" for Maybelline in Christy Turlington, as well as to incorporate a sense of attainable aspiration. The agency has been innovative in handling Maybelline's full-service needs and modernizing the image of the brand to strengthen its relevance to women. Gotham also established the famous "Maybe she's born with it, maybe it's Maybelline" slogan.

For America Online (AOL), the effectiveness of Gotham's strategic marketing has supported the on-line leader during business bumps and helped to reinforce positive perceptions of the company. The agency also developed more cost-effective marketing initiatives, which remain in place

as part of AOL's fundamental marketing mode. And what line could better describe and sell the ubiquitous AOL than Gotham's concise "So easy to use, no wonder it's number one."

As Roberts points out, "Partnership is fundamental to developing great advertising that builds brands. Created over time with clients, partnerships establish a foundation of trust and teamwork essential for advertising excellence. There must also be respect for good ideas in this business and a willingness to see things differently—many people believe they want something groundbreaking when, in fact, they prefer remaining comfortable with the old."

One of New York's claims to fame is that it is the center of the media and advertising industries. "There was a time in the late '80s and early '90s that industry focus was on the talent in cities like Minneapolis, Seattle, and Miami," says Roberts. "Certainly, all over the country there is creativity in the smallest corners and tired

repetition from metropolitan giants. New York never 'lost it'—and never could—but there's been a new energy, an attitudinal shift back in this city, that says we drive the vitality of advertising and the future of the business.

"We are exquisitely jaded in New York, bombarded by a sea of stimuli," adds Roberts. "But despite that, ad people still find sharp approaches for cutting through the clutter. It never ceases to amaze me how much pure talent, wit, and professionalism New York attracts and nurtures every day."

No wonder there's no time to sleep.

SOME OF GOTHAM'S WELL-KNOWN PRINT ADVERTISEMENTS INCLUDE WORK FOR POWERSTREET, FIDELITY'S ON-LINE TRADING COMPANY; MAYBELLINE; PFIZER; HELENA RUBINSTEIN; AND KNIGHT TRIMARK.

ALLTEL
INFORMATION SERVICES

ALLTEL INFORMATION SERVICES IS ONE OF THE WORLD'S leading information technology companies for the financial, mortgage, and telecommunications industries. ALLTEL provides information processing management, outsourcing services, professional consulting services, electronic commerce solutions,

and application software to customers in more than 50 countries and territories.

The company was founded in 1968 as Systematics and in 1990 became a part of ALLTEL Corporation, a telecommunications and information services company. Since that time, ALLTEL Information Services has become an important ingredient in ALLTEL's balanced business mix, which also includes residential telephone, wireless and paging, long-distance and Internet services, and product distribution.

ALLTEL's headquarters are in Little Rock, with offices in New York City and 10 foreign countries. More than 8,000 people are employed by ALLTEL Information Services.

The company's systems and supporting business processes are at the foundation of some of the world's most successful financial services organizations.

ALLTEL's experience in mergers and acquisitions is a direct result of experience in core account processing—10 of the top 25 U.S. banks rely on ALLTEL's systems for this mission critical effort.

ALLTEL is the leading provider in the United States of software and data processing services to the real estate industry, providing technology solutions that help mortgage banking professionals improve the way

ALLTEL INFORMATION SERVICES WAS FOUNDED IN 1968 AS SYSTEMATICS AND IN 1990 BECAME A PART OF ALLTEL CORPORATION.

TEN OF THE TOP 25 U.S. BANKS RELY ON ALLTEL'S EXPERIENCE IN MERGERS AND ACQUISITIONS.

they originate, sell, and service loans. Roughly 57 percent of outstanding mortgage loans in the United States are processed using ALLTEL software and/or ALLTEL computing systems. ALLTEL is used by 19 of the top 25 U.S. mortgage servicers, including Bank of America, Norwest Mortgage Inc., and Chase Manhattan Mortgage— the number one, two, and four mortgage servicers, respectively, in terms of volume.

ALLTEL's sophisticated Advanced Loan System (ALS) is the retail lending application chosen by more of the top 100 U.S. banks than any other single vendor application, and is installed in 14 major international banks. Global financial powerhouses that have chosen ALS include Barclays, National Australia Group, Bank of America, Ford Credit, and Chrysler Credit.

Some of the world's largest financial organizations—including many large, regional and private banks, as well as 17 of the largest 50 global banks—run ALLTEL's Advanced Commercial Banking System (ACBS). ACBS is the first multiplatform, multilingual, multicurrency application geared to managing the entire life cycle of commercial loans—prospecting, deal origination, deal closing, deal servicing, credit/portfolio management, and loan trading.

No other provider approaches ALLTEL's leadership in core account processing. Thirty-four percent of the total dollar volume of U.S. consumer debt excluding credit cards—more than $2 trillion—runs on ALLTEL systems.

ALLTEL has spent more than 30 years working in partnership with financial institutions delivering end-to-end, top-to-bottom services for organizations ranging from small community banks to the world's largest financial services organizations, and from mortgage lenders to consumer finance companies.

ALLTEL is listed on the New York Stock Exchange (NYSE: AT) and is included in the Forbes 500, Fortune 500, and Standard & Poor's 500 indexes.

SOME OF THE WORLD'S LARGEST FINANCIAL ORGANIZATIONS RUN ALLTEL'S ADVANCED COMMERCIAL BANKING SYSTEM (ACBS).

ALLTEL INFORMATION SERVICES IS ONE OF THE WORLD'S LEADING INFORMATION TECHNOLOGY COMPANIES FOR THE FINANCIAL, MORTGAGE, AND TELECOMMUNICATIONS INDUSTRIES.

Intimate Brands, Inc.

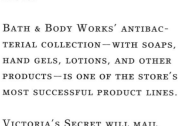
ON FEBRUARY 3, 1999, INTIMATE BRANDS, INC. MADE history in the fields of fashion, advertising, and public relations—all in one bold stroke. This feat was accomplished when one of the company's businesses, Victoria's Secret, held the first-ever live lingerie fashion show on the Internet. Viewed by an

estimated 2 million people via Web cast, the show was the most-watched Internet event in history.

Intimate Brands, which is listed on the New York Stock Exchange under the symbol IBI, is made up of two of the world's best-known brands: Victoria's Secret and Bath & Body Works. Intimate Brands became a public company in 1995 when it was spun off from specialty retailer Limited Inc. Intimate Brands is headed by Chairman and CEO Les Wexner, who began by creating the Limited brand of modern American sportswear for women in 1963.

In the Beginning

In the 1980s, Les Wexner had a simple strategy: Turn the American underwear category into glamorous lingerie in the European fashion, and turn Victoria's Secret into the ultimate lingerie brand. He succeeded in doing this by expanding design resources and focusing the entire organization—from marketing to finance—on that goal. Wexner also began featuring top supermodels in the Victoria's Secret Catalogue and advertising, and expanded the company's products to include a bath and fragrance line.

Two seasoned fashion professionals led Victoria's Secret: Cynthia Fields, president and CEO of Victoria's Secret Catalogue, and Grace Nichols, president and

CEO of Victoria's Secret stores. Together with Les Wexner, they have turned Victoria's Secret into one of the world's best-known brands. A recent recognized brand survey compiled by a management consulting and market research firm shows Victoria's Secret moving from the 26th-most-recognized brand to ninth in just two years. Today, the Victoria's Secret brand boasts more than 800 stores, a catalog circulation of more than 400 million, and annual sales of some $2.6 billion.

More Than Just Another Pretty Face

Bath & Body Works makes up the other business within Intimate Brands. Created in 1990, Bath & Body Works develops and sells personal care products "made from wholesome ingredients grown in

America's heartland." In 1991, expert marketer Beth Pritchard was hired as president and CEO. Under her tenure, Bath & Body Works has grown from 95 stores to more than 1,000. In 1998, sales reached more than $1.2 billion.

Bath & Body Works partners with New York City-based Gryphon, one of the world's leading producers of personal care and beauty products, and a wholly owned subsidiary of Intimate Brands, Inc. Gryphon ensures that Bath & Body Works constantly provides customers with a wide array of new products. At any given time, more than 30 percent of the products in Bath & Body Works stores are brand new, a strategy that Pritchard and Wexner believe is vital to the stores' success.

In 1999, Bath & Body Works launched its newest brand—the

White Barn Candle Company. This new venture, which offers a line of scented candles, home fragrances, and other items, operates both within Bath & Body Works stores, and independently through more than 50 freestanding stores.

Intimate Brands, Inc. is continuing its global focus by expanding and enhancing the Victoria's Secret E-commerce site (www.VictoriasSecret.com) and planning more live lingerie and swimwear Web shows in the future. E-commerce is proving successful for the company, which counted 500 million hits to its Web site in its first 10 weeks of operation. In addition, Victoria's Secret says international visits have run as high as 20 percent of the daily total.

Intimate Brands in NYC

Today, the rapid success of both Victoria's Secret and Bath & Body Works has made Intimate Brands one of the leading specialty retailers of intimate apparel, beauty, and personal care products in the world. While

headquartered in Columbus, Ohio, Intimate Brands has a strong New York presence, with Victoria's Secret marketing, design, and catalog offices all based in the city.

"As the recognized center of the fashion and advertising worlds, New York City was a natural choice for the location of Intimate Brands' design, development, marketing, and beauty groups," says Debbie Mitchell, vice president of Intimate Brands' communications and investor relations. Executives in the Columbus headquarters work closely with New York teams to share ideas and strategies, making the New York operation an integral part of the company's commitment to the development of fashion-forward products.

In 1999, Intimate Brands created and based another major business in New York City: Intimate Beauty Corporation. The business was formed to develop and build a portfolio of distinct beauty businesses, each to

be sold through its own unique venue.

Intimate Beauty Corporation is headed by President Robin Burns, who joined Intimate Brands, Inc. from cosmetics giant Estée Lauder. Burns says the cosmetics arm of Intimate Brands was created to go head-to-head with department store staples such as Clinique and Lancôme. "We expect to create and build a dynamic portfolio of branded beauty business," Burns states. "Our first focus is Victoria's Secret Beauty."

"Through a base of operations in both Columbus, Ohio, and New York City, Intimate Brands draws upon the huge base of expertise in New York City to stay in touch with the needs and preferences of consumers, and remains on top of new trends, marketing strategies, and fashions," says Mitchell. "This powerful dynamic ensures that Intimate Brands will continue to offer the best in design and fashion to its customers in New York, and throughout the world."

CLOCKWISE FROM TOP: BATH & BODY WORKS PRODUCTS ARE AVAILABLE IN MORE THAN 1,100 STORES NATIONWIDE, AS WELL AS THROUGH ITS NEW CATALOG (TOP LEFT).

THE WHITE BARN CANDLE COMPANY IS THE NEWEST ADDITION TO THE INTIMATE BRANDS, INC. PORTFOLIO OF BRANDS. THE BUSINESS WILL HAVE BETWEEN 130 AND 135 STORES NATIONWIDE BY END OF 2000 (TOP RIGHT).

VICTORIA'S SECRET PRODUCTS ARE AVAILABLE THROUGH MORE THAN 880 LINGERIE, BEAUTY, AND HOSIERY STORES NATIONWIDE; THE VICTORIA'S SECRET CATALOGUE; AND WWW.VICTORIASSECRET.COM (BOTTOM LEFT AND RIGHT).

BlueStone Capital Partners, L.P.

INVESTMENT BANKING IS ONE OF THE FEW INDUSTRIES that must continuously cope with the conflicting pressures and changing environments of today's world. On one hand, there are prudent, time-honored principles and practices to be followed. On the other, the Internet impacts every aspect of the industry both directly through investment portfolio management, initial public offerings (IPOs) and stock trading, and indirectly from productivity to the latest interest rate changes of the federal government.

BlueStone Capital Partners, L.P. is one company that has mastered the new reality, helping investors in the search for opportunity among the old bears and the new E-bulls, aiding emerging companies navigating the treacherous path to public offerings, and trading stock on-line using the best technology and some of the brightest advisers.

Global Investment Banking Expertise

BlueStone Capital is a full-service investment banking and brokerage firm that delivers the high-level corporate financial products and services expected by Wall Street giants to the small- and mid-cap market. With more than 300 professional bankers, brokers, and analysts throughout the United States and Europe, its mission is simple: to assist small and emerging companies in maximizing their growth by providing sophisticated financing solutions and strategic advice tailored to meet the short- and long-term goals of each client.

BlueStone Capital has always measured its success on its ability to assist clients during their critical growth stages. The firm provides a broad range of services—ranging from IPOs, mergers and acquisitions, debt financing, private placements of debt and equity, corporate reorganizations, leveraged management buyouts, takeover defenses, and advisory services, including sales and divestitures—as well as strong corporate finance expertise and a global distribution network.

BlueStone Capital's distinguished team of experienced bankers, all of whom are licensed professionals dedicated to providing timely information and investment ideas, combine their own in-depth knowledge of financial markets with the firm's proprietary, value-added research to ensure that all clients fully understand the potential risks and rewards of investment opportunities. This exemplifies the firm's commitment to respond to a wide spectrum of client needs and its intention to develop long-term relationships with clients.

Broad Investment Opportunities

Working closely with investors, BlueStone Capital remains sensitive to their changing needs as it assists them in designing and managing their investment portfolio. At BlueStone Capital, clients can invest in initial and secondary public offerings, private placements, bridge financings, mutual funds, IRAs, profit-sharing plans, and corporate, government, and municipal bonds. In addition, BlueStone provides clients full trading access to any type of security on all of the major exchanges.

The extensive and diverse experience of BlueStone Capital's management team has enabled them to service companies in a wide range of industries, including health care, technology, E-commerce, manufacturing, retail, and financial services. By evaluating and carefully choosing investment opportunities among companies with exceptional growth capability, BlueStone Capital offers knowledgeable investors the

potential for obtaining above-average returns.

WHERE THE INTERNET COMES TO INVEST

BlueStone Capital was founded in 1996, when Kamal Mustafa and six Wall Street veterans created an organization designed to show that small companies can grow using the same sophisticated financial instruments that were once the preserve of merchant banks and their large clients. BlueStone Capital started as one of the few full-service investment banks devoted to emerging growth companies, and given the phenomenal rise of Internet stocks, it has proved to be a crucial decision.

BlueStone recognized very early on that its investment banking products and services had to be complemented by a strong emphasis on innovative technology and on-line capabilities. BlueStone's strong international distribution network provided the platform to develop, launch,

and market a comprehensive, global on-line financial system reinforced by secure, reliable, and superior technology. BlueStone's new system is Trade.com. From the beginning, Trade.com was developed as a truly global, high-quality system, superior to the current offerings, including the top five competitors in the marketplace.

As a total trading system, Trade.com does not merely focus on the equity day trader, but also captures both domestic and global market offerings of equities, bonds, currencies, commodities, and venture and private equity offerings. A full range of product offerings is available, ranging from global insurance to real estate and mortgages. It is crucial to note that Trade.com is truly a global destination with not only its offerings, but also the ability to buy and sell on both domestic and global fronts, which places BlueStone and Trade.com on the path of rapid growth and expansion.

Knowing that even the most advanced system cannot deliver customer service, Trade.com expands upon the BlueStone retail group's strengths. A support system has been established so that Trade.com is proactive, reactive, and highly personalized. In short, a new broker of the future has been created that is not only trained in global securities, but is also familiar with computers, and operates in a customer support/educational role with the customer.

As the Internet's financial supermarket, Trade.com provides the most global and diverse selection of products and services in the on-line financial services industry, demonstrating BlueStone Capital's mission to offer the highest level of services to all clients, whether they are individuals, companies, or institutions. Obviously, Trade.com places BlueStone in a unique position: providing extraordinary global distribution capabilities and control over a powerful financial portal.

BRIDGE INFORMATION SYSTEMS

ACH DAY, MORE THAN A QUARTER MILLION FINANCIAL professionals in more than 100 countries receive market data, news, quotes, statistics, and analytics on global financial and commodity markets through Bridge Information Systems. With annual sales of more than $1 billion, Bridge is the largest pro-

vider of financial information services in North America and the fastest growing in the world.

Through use of advanced technology and a series of strategic acquisitions, Bridge has helped redefine a rapidly changing industry with a business model that serves clients and supports products through a unified processing, delivery, and display architecture. As a result, Bridge is able to offer professional and individual investors the industry's most complete range of products—all at the lowest operating cost for the customer. Bridge's three main business lines include financial information and news, trading and transaction services, and high-speed Internet services.

"Bridge is facilitating a market that is changing dramatically," says Tom Wendel, chairman and CEO. "By offering a wide range of information, news, transaction, and datafeed products powered by our high-speed network, we are able to adapt to this change and serve many clients with many different products through one network."

A HISTORY OF RAPID GROWTH

Bridge was founded in 1974 in St. Louis as a full-service stock trading firm, servicing professional money managers with the highest quality trading execution, electronic market data, and in-depth research and analysis. During the 1980s, Bridge pioneered a number of products, including a local area network (LAN)-based broker's workstation, an electronic trade order entry and routing system, and a computer-based order indication system.

Bridge Trading Company was also established in 1974 to provide quality agency execution of stock trades in listed and OTC markets worldwide, and today operates one of the largest floor brokerage networks on the New York Stock Exchange, with similar networks

TOM WENDEL IS PRESIDENT AND CEO OF BRIDGE INFORMATION SYSTEMS.

on AMEX, Nasdaq, U.S. regional stock and options exchanges, and markets worldwide. Bridge's suite of proprietary transaction services products provides professional investors with a quick and transparent means to execute trades, route orders, investigate order activity, or advertise trades, and offers access to one of the industry's largest broker-neutral networks for secure client-to-client connectivity.

Between 1994 and 1999, Bridge grew nearly 10 times, merging with seven independent market data and technology companies—including MarketVision, EJV Partners, Knight-Ridder Financial, Telesphere, and Telerate, Inc. (previously Dow Jones Markets)—and expanding its services to include data, analytics, and news for the fixed-income, foreign exchange, money, derivative, and energy markets. In 1998, Bridge acquired the brokerage information business of Automatic Data Processing, which strengthened its position in the retail stockbroker market.

In April 1999, Bridge announced another acquisition: SAVVIS Communications Corporation. A leading national service provider of Internet access, SAVVIS offers high-performance communications

solutions to the corporate and wholesale markets. Its network has been consistently rated number one for performance and reliability by Keynote Systems, Inc., a leading industry analyst. By combining with Bridge, SAVVIS has become the largest non-telco ISP in the world, offering service in 40 countries.

Bridge today has more than 5,000 employees in more than 65 sales and marketing offices located in the Americas, Europe, the Middle East, Africa, and Asia/Pacific.

SYSTEMS FOR INFORMED DECISIONS

BridgeNews, Bridge's proprietary newswire service, is among the world's largest financial news organizations. A global network of more than 600 journalists breaks economic, government, financial, and commodity news that affects major and emerging markets. It generates more than 7,000 stories and statistical items each day from around the world.

Bridge provides its financial information to customers through various delivery platforms: workstations, datafeeds, and Web solutions all built on a common infrastructure. The company uses the full range of technology, including Unix, Microsoft Windows, Windows NT, and Java, each carefully crafted to maximize data delivery and functionality.

Bridge operates one of the most powerful communications networks in the industry. This network utilizes a broadband backbone and powerful switches, capable of processing thousands of transactions per second, to deliver data to anywhere on the planet. Together with SAVVIS, Bridge has created one of the world's largest providers of ATM-managed Internet protocol networks, with more than 150 ATM switches worldwide owned and operated by Bridge. Bridge's data processing center has scalable architecture that ensures virtually limitless capacity.

BRIDGE OPERATES ONE OF THE MOST POWERFUL COMMUNICATIONS NETWORKS IN THE INDUSTRY.

NEW FEATURES FOR THE FUTURE

Recently, Bridge unveiled several enhancements to its existing product lines, which feature fully integrated, open-architecture systems. BridgeStation offers the industry's most comprehensive packages of market data, analytics, advanced charting capabilities, and news that use state-of-the-art technology and standard industry protocols. BridgeFeed is an interactive digital datafeed that delivers global market information using advanced data management and delivery technology. BridgeActive1 is a revolutionary decision-support tool, based on open standards, which gives total control to customize, integrate, and manage financial information. The Bridge Trading Room System tackles one of the industry's greatest problems: seamlessly integrating data and applications from multiple sources throughout the trading enterprise.

Telerate, the largest company under the Bridge umbrella, provides the world's most complete source of capital markets information. A range of package options are available, including Telerate Plus, which covers all the world securities markets, and Telerate Energy, the real-time, one-stop energy platform.

Reaching out to clients on the Web, Bridge offers a complete financial information solution available through an Internet

browser. BridgeChannel provides Internet access to data through real-time applets. This high-performance solution incorporates data and analytic tools into an easily accessible platform. Utilizing Java-based technologies, BridgeChannel's streaming data provides dynamic updates to the PC or laptop, giving serious investors play-by-play coverage of the markets. The functionality of BridgeChannel, combined with Bridge's order routing and management tools, is available in BridgeTrader, a total trading solution that operates through an Internet browser, creating the perfect tool for institutions that require a strategic trading tool in a cost-effective platform. Bridge's network also interacts with the array of portable communications devices on the market, including digital cellular phones and palmtop computers, giving mobile investors access to financial information while on the go.

Bridge continues to offer its products and services to a wider audience, affording high-speed access to information in versatile,

cost-effective delivery options. For example, individual investors can take advantage of Bridge's data, news, and charts on the Bridge Web site, bridge.com, or PersonalBridge, a subscription service offering the most content-rich financial information individual investors can access on the Internet.

As the volume of financial information continues to grow, Bridge is using its technology advantage to improve performance and lower costs for its users in the future. In doing so, the company strives to become the world leader in the global financial data distribution business. "Bridge is geared to servicing the financial world, providing financial information and news, trading and transaction services, and network services that will lead market professionals into the new millennium and beyond," adds Wendel.

IN ORDER TO BE COMPETITIVE IN TODAY'S MARKET, companies must find ways to effectively recruit and retain talent. Comprehensive employee benefit programs—including health, welfare, and retirement plans—have become increasingly important in meeting this objective. In today's increasingly com-

plex benefits marketplace, it is becoming a challenge to determine which options are best for a company, the impact they will have on operations, and the associated costs.

Fitzmaurice & Company, LLC (F&C), a rapidly growing strategic benefits planning firm supporting the needs of midsize companies (generally those with 100 to 5,000 employees), partners with its clients, helping them assess their benefits programs, delivering strategic recommendations, and monitoring solutions on a daily basis.

REVOLUTIONIZING AN INDUSTRY
F&C has developed a distinctive, consultative approach to providing benefits advice that sets it apart from the prevailing model of sales/commission-oriented brokerage firms. Each F&C client is assigned to one of the firm's highly skilled, professional consulting teams. Led by a benefits

consultant and supported by a team leader and other professionals, the benefits consultant has complete accountability for the firm's efforts on behalf of the client.

"Our consulting model emphasizes the key person in our work with our clients—the benefits consultant," says Stan Sokolski, vice president. "One hundred percent of our resources, financially and otherwise, are invested in our benefits consultants. They focus all their attention on clients who therefore have full access to, and full attention from, all levels of our staff at all times."

A PARTNER IN THE TRENCHES
F&C's team of dedicated, professional consultants advises clients on the entire spectrum of health and welfare benefits—from the big picture to the day-to-day execution of administrative issues. The firm's consultants are charged with focusing their attention and expertise on client

matters. They pride themselves on creating innovative ideas and solutions that are unique for each client, and they act in total partnership with their clients. With health care costs escalating, industry trends shifting, and companies focusing on controlling costs to remain competitive in a global economy, it is more important than ever for employers to have a partner actively managing this critical component of compensation.

F&C has transformed the way benefits costs are evaluated: How much does the company spend on health and welfare benefits? What percentage of payroll are health and welfare costs? Does the company's plan provide ample choice to employees while, at the same time, leveraging down the company's net cost? How effectively have the total benefit costs been managed over time, and more important, what are they likely to be in the future? These are the types of strategic

JIM BERRY

questions that F&C consultants proactively address and encourage clients to consider on a regular basis.

In addition to the firm's strategic planning and consultative efforts, quite a bit of detail work is required. F&C consultants painstakingly sift through all the pertinent details to develop the best possible program and ensure a successful outcome. The establishment of the benefits plan is only the beginning of an F&C benefit consultant's responsibility. The ongoing management of the client's health and welfare dynamic includes F&C's serving as the facilitator of administrative issues; the advocate in the event of disputed claims; the negotiator with significant leverage throughout the industry; the manager of claims data in order to provide projections and/or make adjustments during the plan year; the auditor, analyzer, and negotiator of all plan renewals and plan financial settlements; and the consultant for benefit-related trends and compliance and regulatory issues.

"Our service starts with providing perspective—getting the employers to clearly define and understand the role of health and welfare benefits in their overall compensation scheme—and then translating that into a plan design that meets their goals," says Robert Fitzmaurice, president. "Once accomplished, we're there day-

to-day in the trenches to make sure the employer is getting its money's worth."

THE MERGERS AND ACQUISITIONS EXPERTS

F&C is a pioneer in the provision of employee benefits evaluation services for mergers and acquisitions, assisting the buyer in the strategic and financial assessment of the health and welfare component during the due diligence phase of the transaction. Since companies rarely, if ever, aggregate

their employee benefit costs in a comprehensive and verifiable fashion, and because there is no separate line item on the financial statement that specifically identifies this expense, the acquirer needs to be protected from any potential land mines. Numerous buyers have discovered that when it comes to the employee benefits area, they can count on F&C to put them in position to shift previously undiscovered liabilities back to the seller, negotiate a reduced purchase price, and smooth transition issues for the company's employees at a time when employees may feel vulnerable.

AN EYE TO THE FUTURE

The employee benefits industry remains one of the most highly fragmented industries in America today. With few barriers to entry and a delivery system of benefits advice and products that is radically out of step with most other professional service businesses, the industry as a whole is primed for a leader to emerge and transform the system. Fitzmaurice & Company's structure and model for providing employee benefits advice uniquely positions the firm to lead the revolution and subsequent consolidation of this industry.

F&C's HEADQUARTERS IS CONVENIENTLY LOCATED IN THE HEART OF MIDTOWN MANHATTAN.

F&C CONSULTANT TEAMS ACT IN TOTAL PARTNERSHIP WITH THE FIRM'S CLIENTS.

PLATINUM TELEVISION GROUP

N THE MARKETPLACE, TIMING CAN BE EVERYTHING. Walter Burton and Doug Scott appear to have perfect timing in the founding and development of their young company, Platinum Television Group. Conceived in 1997, the media services company produces national television shows, corporate training programs, demo products, and other fee-based media services. It has expanded rapidly into Internet services, instructional videos on CD-ROM, direct mail, and publication marketing.

As Burton, who serves as vice president of the company, says, "Virtually anything a client can conceive, Platinum Television can achieve." The approach has paid off. The company's revenues have skyrocketed more than 250 percent each quarter since it was established.

NICHE MARKETING
Currently, the company's largest segment of business is its highly successful consumer educational TV programming under the umbrella of its American Lifestyle Series. *New Home Journal*, *This Week in Real Estate*, and *The Auto Report* are half-hour shows that have achieved almost 100 percent penetration in the top 200 markets across the country via cable, local networks, and major affiliates in all 50 states and in much of Canada. The shows are designed on a national platform that includes

advice and tips from high-profile experts in the field. On the local level, *New Home Journal* and *This Week in Real Estate* feature a wealth of information on communities, mortgage rates, property taxes, pricing, building specs, how to negotiate buying or selling a home, and moving companies. Shows such as *The Auto Report* instruct car buyers on issues such as dealerships, guarantees, and

BY KEEPING PRODUCTION IN-HOUSE, PLATINUM TELEVISION GROUP CAN BETTER CONTROL THE QUALITY OF ITS PRODUCTS.

ALTHOUGH HEADQUARTERED IN FLORIDA, PLATINUM TELEVISION'S PROGRAMS CAN BE SEEN IN ALL 50 STATES AND MUCH OF CANADA.

rebates. Notes Scott, Platinum Television Group president, "We have found a niche to bring the local consumer up to date with the latest information in his or her city, town, and community."

Real estate and auto sales are truly local. While there may be broad national trends, each market has its own personality and its own needs. Platinum Television identifies those local trends and incorporates them into each show. In addition, sponsors and advertisers include large national companies as well as local advertisers. In preparing the show for each market, the company's in-house TV crews cover each city and town thoroughly.

Platinum has developed its own full-time staff in production, editing, research, script writing, and other necessary areas. "We do our own shooting and editing," says Burton, adding that the company does work with local agencies for acting talent. "By keeping our production in-house, we have control over quality, and we think it is important to maintain our reputation in the eyes of viewers, show participants, and advertisers."

Those advertisers are vital to the company's TV success. Platinum advertises its shows extensively in national and local media, usually with four-color ads. According to Scott, the company has more than $7.5 million in advertising in the printed press, primarily through trade-out arrangements. The exposure both in advertising and to TV viewers continues to draw big-name experts to participate in the shows.

A VAST, NEW MARKET

Scott and Burton, who first met when they both worked for the same TV production company, are broadening Platinum's reach beyond television channels to the Internet. In a joint venture with, Quatro Systems, Inc., an established Internet development company in Philadelphia, the duo has formed icasttv.com to bring television programming to the Internet. Launched in September 1999, icasttv.com is targeting various industries, beginning with new home construction. "Essentially, through the Internet, we are offering 24-hour programming to an audience that is absolutely exploding in numbers," says Scott. "We are marrying the cutting edge of technology in the Internet with educational programming to link consumers to industries vital to their everyday lives."

Scott and Burton, both in their early thirties, are children of the technological age, and their vi-

sion is unlimited. "The incredible possibilities of the Internet have barely been touched, especially as it becomes interactive through the consumer's television," says Burton. "We believe that we are on the leading edge of this huge new market." The future promises exciting opportunities for the rapidly growing company.

IN THE AIR

Platinum Television Group's newest division, Inflight Entertainment Network, targets consumer- and industry-driven video news release (VNR) programming for all United Airlines domestic and international flights. Specializing in flights to and from New York, companies chosen for the network are given the opportunity to relay their messages for 17,000 flights and 2.4 million passengers monthly.

"We look for good stories and solutions to issues and topics for today's consumer," says Scott. This division exemplifies how diversified this young company has become. "We started as a production company specializing in a few television programs and have expanded to a full-service new media company with various types of programs, as well as CD-ROM development and E-commerce capabilities," says Scott.

TOWERY PUBLISHING, INC.

Beginning as a small publisher of local newspapers in the 1930s, Towery Publishing, Inc. today produces a wide range of community-oriented materials, including books (Urban Tapestry Series), business directories, magazines, and Internet publications. Building on its long heritage of excellence, the company has become global in scope, with cities from San Diego to Sydney represented by Towery products. In all its endeavors, this Memphis-based company strives to be synonymous with service, utility, and quality.

A DIVERSITY OF COMMUNITY-BASED PRODUCTS

Over the years, Towery has become the largest producer of published materials for North American chambers of commerce. From membership directories that enhance business-to-business communication to visitor and relocation guides tailored to reflect the unique qualities of the communities they cover, the company's chamber-oriented materials offer comprehensive information on dozens of topics, including housing, education, leisure activities, health care, and local government.

In 1998, the company acquired Cincinnati-based Target Marketing, an established provider of detailed city street maps to more than 300 chambers of commerce throughout the United States and Canada. Now a division of Towery, Target offers full-color maps that include local landmarks and points of interest, such as parks, shopping centers, golf courses, schools, industrial parks, city and county limits, subdivision names, public buildings, and even block numbers on most streets.

In 1990, Towery launched the Urban Tapestry Series, an award-winning collection of oversized, hardbound photojournals detailing the people, history, culture, environment, and commerce of various metropolitan areas. These coffee-table books highlight a community through three basic elements: an introductory essay by a noted local individual; an exquisite collection of four-color photographs; and profiles of the companies and organizations that animate the area's business life.

To date, more than 80 Urban Tapestry Series editions have been published in cities around the world, from New York to Vancouver to Sydney. Authors of the books' introductory essays include former U.S. President Gerald Ford (Grand Rapids), former Alberta Premier Peter Lougheed (Calgary), CBS anchor Dan Rather (Austin), ABC anchor Hugh Downs (Phoenix), best-selling mystery author Robert B. Parker (Boston), American Movie Classics host Nick Clooney (Cincinnati), Senator Richard Lugar (Indianapolis), and Challenger Center founder Dr. June Scobee Rodgers (Chattanooga).

To maintain hands-on quality in all of its periodicals and books, Towery has long used the latest production methods available. The company was the first production environment in the United States to combine desktop publishing with color separations and image scanning to produce finished film suitable for burning plates for four-color printing. Today, Towery relies on state-of-the-art digital prepress services to produce more than 8,000 pages each year, containing well over 30,000 high-quality color images.

AN INTERNET PIONEER

By combining its long-standing expertise in community-oriented published materials with advanced production capabilities, a global sales force, and extensive data management expertise, Towery has emerged as a significant provider of Internet-based city information. In keeping with its overall focus on community resources, the company's

STEVE DAVIS

TOWERY PUBLISHING PRESIDENT AND CEO J. ROBERT TOWERY HAS EXPANDED THE BUSINESS HIS PARENTS STARTED IN THE 1930S TO INCLUDE A GROWING ARRAY OF TRADITIONAL AND ELECTRONIC PUBLISHED MATERIALS, AS WELL AS INTERNET AND MULTIMEDIA SERVICES, THAT ARE MARKETED LOCALLY, NATIONALLY, AND INTERNATIONALLY.

Internet efforts represent a natural step in the evolution of the business.

The primary product lines within the Internet division are the introCity™ sites. Towery's introCity sites introduce newcomers, visitors, and longtime residents to every facet of a particular community, while simultaneously placing the local chamber of commerce at the forefront of the city's Internet activity. The sites include newcomer information, calendars, photos, citywide business listings with everything from nightlife to shopping to family fun, and online maps pinpointing the exact location of businesses, schools, attractions, and much more.

DECADES OF PUBLISHING EXPERTISE

In 1972, current President and CEO J. Robert Towery succeeded his parents in managing the printing and publishing business they had founded nearly four decades earlier. Soon thereafter, he expanded the scope of the company's published materials to include *Memphis* magazine and other successful regional and national publications. In 1985, after selling its locally focused

assets, Towery began the trajectory on which it continues today, creating community-oriented materials that are often produced in conjunction with chambers of commerce and other business organizations.

Despite the decades of change, Towery himself follows a long-standing family philosophy of unmatched service and unflinching quality. That approach extends throughout the entire organization to include more than 130 employees at the Memphis headquarters, another 60 located in Northern Kentucky outside Cincinnati, and more than 50 sales, marketing, and editorial staff traveling to and working in a growing list of client cities. All of its products, and more information about the company, are featured on the Internet at www.towery.com.

In summing up his company's steady growth, Towery restates the essential formula that has propelled the business since its first pages were published: "The creative energies of our staff drive us toward innovation and invention. Our people make the highest possible demands on themselves, so I know that our future is secure if the ingredients for success remain a focus on service and quality."

TOWERY PUBLISHING WAS THE FIRST PRODUCTION ENVIRONMENT IN THE UNITED STATES TO COMBINE DESKTOP PUBLISHING WITH COLOR SEPARATIONS AND IMAGE SCANNING TO PRODUCE FINISHED FILM SUITABLE FOR BURNING PLATES FOR FOUR-COLOR PRINTING. TODAY, THE COMPANY'S STATE-OF-THE-ART NETWORK OF MACINTOSH AND WINDOWS WORKSTATIONS ALLOWS IT TO PRODUCE MORE THAN 8,000 PAGES EACH YEAR, CONTAINING WELL OVER 30,000 HIGH-QUALITY COLOR IMAGES (TOP).

THE TOWERY FAMILY'S PUBLISHING ROOTS CAN BE TRACED TO 1935, WHEN R.W. TOWERY (FAR LEFT) BEGAN PRODUCING A SERIES OF COMMUNITY HISTORIES IN TENNESSEE, MISSISSIPPI, AND TEXAS. THROUGHOUT THE COMPANY'S HISTORY, THE FOUNDING FAMILY HAS CONSISTENTLY EXHIBITED A COMMITMENT TO CLARITY, PRECISION, INNOVATION, AND VISION (BOTTOM).

LIBRARY OF CONGRESS
CATALOGING-IN-PUBLICATION
DATA   Koch, Edward I., 1924-
New York: a state of mind / Edward I. Koch.
p.   cm. — (Urban tapestry series)
Includes index.
ISBN 1-881096-76-9 (alk. paper)
1. New York Region—Civilization.   2. New York Region—
Pictorial works.   3. New York Region—Economic conditions.
4. Business enterprises—New York Region.   I. Title.
II. Series.
F128.55.K64   1999
974.7—dc21   99-054412

Printed in Canada

TOWERY PUBLISHING, INC.
THE TOWERY BUILDING
1835 UNION AVENUE
MEMPHIS, TN 38104

PUBLISHER: J. Robert Towery
EXECUTIVE PUBLISHER: Jenny McDowell
NATIONAL SALES MANAGER: Stephen Hung
MARKETING DIRECTOR: Carol Culpepper
PROJECT DIRECTORS: Dawn Park-Donegan, Jim Tomlinson, Mary Whelan

EXECUTIVE EDITOR: David B. Dawson
MANAGING EDITOR: Lynn Conlee
SENIOR EDITOR: Carlisle Hacker
EDITOR/PROFILE MANAGER: Brian Johnston
EDITORS: Stephen Deusner, Jana Files, Brian Johnston, Ginny Reeves,
Sunni Thompson
ASSISTANT EDITOR: Rebecca Green
EDITORIAL ASSISTANT: Emily Haire
EDITORIAL CONTRIBUTORS: Jennifer Bowers Bahney, Laura Bajkowski, Michelle Malina Duarte,
Bill Egbert, Lorene Fong, Catherine McMenamin, Margaret McMenamin
PROFILE WRITER: Regina McMenamin
CAPTION WRITER: Robert J. O'Connor

CREATIVE DIRECTOR: Brian Groppe
PHOTOGRAPHY EDITOR: Jonathan Postal
PHOTOGRAPHIC CONSULTANT: Heidi Volpe
PHOTOGRAPHY COORDINATOR: Robin Lankford
PROFILE DESIGNERS: Laurie Beck, Melissa Ellis, Ann Ward
PRODUCTION ASSISTANT: Loretta Drew
PRODUCTION RESOURCES MANAGER: Dave Dunlap Jr.
PRODUCTION MANAGER: Brenda Pattat
DIGITAL COLOR SUPERVISOR: Darin Ipema
DIGITAL COLOR TECHNICIANS: Eric Friedl, Deidre Kesler, Brent Salazar, Mark Svetz
PRINT COORDINATOR: Beverly Timmons

© ROBERT GALBRAITH

A STATE OF MIND

CHRISTOPHE AGOU is a self-taught photographer living in New York City. His work is part of private collections and has appeared in newspapers and *New York Magazine.* Agou is currently working on two books.

ALLSPORT was founded the moment freelance photographer Tony Duffy captured the now-famous picture of Bob Beamon breaking the world long-jump record at the Mexico City Olympics in 1968. Originally headquartered in London, Allsport has expanded to include offices in New York and Los Angeles. Its pictures have appeared in every major publication in the world, and the best of its portfolio has been displayed at elite photographic exhibitions at the Royal Photographic Society and the Olympic Museum in Lausanne.

HOWARD E. ANDE, a self-taught photographer from Oakville, Connecticut, specializes in agricultural and industrial photography, as well as his passion, railroad photography. In addition to appearing in calendars and greeting cards, his images have been used in numerous trade publications, children's books, magazines, and coffee-table photojournals such as Towery Publishing's *Chicago: Heart and Soul of America.* Ande lives in Streamwood with his wife and an Airedale terrier.

DAVID ANDERSON, originally from Lincoln, Nebraska, specializes in architectural photography. His images have appeared in *Architectural Digest* and *Architectural Record*, and are in the collections of the Brooklyn Museum of Art, Canadian Centre for Architecture, Museum of the City of New York, and University of Nebraska.

DAVID ARCOS received a bachelor of fine arts degree in photography from Parsons School of Design. He specializes in urban photography and environmental portraiture.

STEVE BAKER is an international photographer who has contributed to more than 100 publications. With a degree in journalism from Indiana University, he is the proprietor of Highlight Photography, specializing in assignments for clients such as Eastman Kodak, Nike, Budweiser, the U.S. Olympic Committee, and Mobil Oil, which has commissioned seven exhibitions of his work since 1994. Baker is author and photographer of *Racing Is Everything*, and he has contributed to Towery Publishing's *Baltimore: Charm City; Celebrating a Triangle Millennium; Chicago: Heart and Soul of America; Dayton: The Cradle of Creativity; Indianapolis: Crossroads of the American Dream; Jackson: The Good Life; Los Angeles: City of Dreams; Nashville: City of Note;* and *St. Louis: For the Record.* Currently, Baker resides in Indianapolis.

PATRICK BATCHELDER was born and raised in New York City. His areas of specialty are editorial and stock travel photography, as well as scenic and documentary photography. He is a graduate of the University of Colorado, having received a bachelor's degree in both geography and French, and he also studied at the University of Bordeaux in France. As the owner and operator of Patrick Batchelder Photography, he has had work published in *Islands* and *Inline* magazines, *Sporting News*, and the *New York Daily News*, as well as in Towery Publishing's *New York: Metropolis of the American Dream.* Batchelder's interests include languages, geography, traveling, mapmaking, skiing, and fine wines.

MARION BERNSTEIN has had photographs exhibited in galleries and museums throughout New York. A freelance veteran, she has covered events in the United States, Central America, Europe, and Asia. Bernstein's work also has appeared in publications by Harcourt, HarperCollins, Houghton Mifflin, Random House, Macmillan, Scholastic, and Prentice Hall.

JIM BERRY is a graduate film student at New York University. Before coming to New York, he worked as a newspaper photographer for the *Seattle Times, Philadelphia Inquirer, Albuquerque Tribune*, and *Daily World* (Aberdeen, Washington). He has also worked for the Seattle SuperSonics, Goodwill Games, and *Rolling Stone.*

BRUCE YUAN-YUE BI has traveled extensively in the United States, Canada, and Central and South America. He just finished the World Heritage Series for Jingshu Publishing in Taiwan, and is currently working on the World Traveler Series for the same company. Bi is

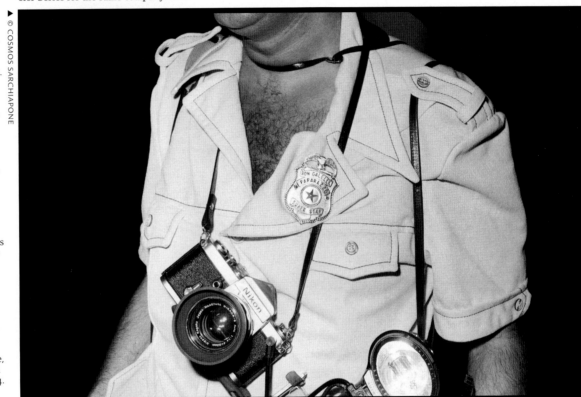

MARK DOWNEY has covered half the countries of the world for clients such as *Time, Geo,* and *National Geographic.* He has photographed everything from riots in Los Angeles to elections in Cambodia.

DAN DRY, who lives in Louisville, is the recipient of more than 300 national and international photography, advertising, and annual report awards. In 1981, Dry received the top prize in his field: the Photographer of the Year award given by the National Press Photographers Association. For eight years, Dry traveled the globe on assignment for *National Geographic,* and his photographs have appeared in almost every domestic magazine, as well as Towery Publishing's *St. Louis: For the Record.* Dry now runs a successful advertising, corporate stock, and editorial studio, with a library that includes more than 250,000 images from around the world. He is married and has two young daughters.

also a regular contributor to the *Earth Geographic Monthly* (Taiwan) and *Photo Pictorial Magazine* (Hong Kong).

PHYLLIS BOBB has attended Brooklyn College, Germaine School of Photography, and Parsons School of Design. Her photographs have appeared on CD covers, brochures, and newsletters, and have been exhibited at the Gallery at Cedar Hollow, the Alfred Lowenhertz Gallery, and the Biggar Gallery in Scotland.

RON BOSZKO is a native of New York.

JOHN CARUCCI, originally from Brooklyn, specializes in night photography and new media. He has published two books: *Capturing the Night with Your Camera* and *The New Media Guide to Creative Photography.*

MICHAEL DARTER received a bachelor of arts degree in photography from the Brooks Institute of Photography in Santa Barbara. His images have appeared in *Bike Magazine, Runner's World, Working Woman, Bicycling Magazine,* and *Champion.* An avid cyclist, Darter also enjoys traveling and photographing different locations.

DAVID FORBERT, originally from Hattiesburg, attended the New York School of Modern Photography and the Caulk School of Photography. Currently a freelance photographer, he was a naval photographer during World War II. Forbert's client list includes IBM, Texaco, and Goodyear.

ROBERT GALBRAITH received a bachelor of arts degree from New York University. Originally from Indianapolis, he moved to Port Washington, New York, in 1945.

ARVIND GARG was born in India, where he taught English until he moved to the United States in 1976. His photographs are included in the permanent collections of the New York Public Library, Brooklyn Museum of Art, and American Museum of Natural History. Garg's images have appeared in *Audubon* and *Saveur Magazine*, as well as in textbooks, encyclopedias, and CD-ROMs.

GERARD GASKIN, a freelance photographer specializing in picture stories, has done work for *Eye Board* and *Emerge* magazines, as well as Sony Records. His photographs have also appeared in Towery Publishing's *New York: Me-*

tropolis of the American Dream. Originally from Trinidad and Tobago, Gaskin received a liberal arts degree from Queensborough Community College and a bachelor's degree in fine arts from Hunter College. He enjoys bike riding, traveling, and many different kinds of music.

CATHERINE GEHM attended the School of Visual Arts in New York. Her photographs have been published through Ariel Books, Random House, and McGraw-Hill. Gehm specializes in travel, nature, landscape, fine art, and commercial photography.

LARS GELFAN, a native of Washington, D.C., has called New York City home since 1991. Having earned degrees in both journalism and sociology from the University of Maryland-College Park, Gelfan won the Award of Excellence for magazine photography in both the 1991 and 1993 Picture of the Year competitions. His photographs have appeared in *Audubon*, the *Chicago Tribune*, the *Los Angeles Times*, *Men's Journal*, *Newsweek*, *French Photo*, *Runner's World*, *Sports Illustrated*, the *Washington Post*, and *USA Today*, as well as in Towery Publishing's *New York: Metropolis of the American Dream*. Gelfan recently returned from a photo shoot in Vietnam.

STEPHEN GRAHAM's background includes a two-year stint at a Georgia daily, an inspiring workshop with Sam Able of *National Geographic*, and an impressive array of shows and exhibitions. He currently focuses on shooting assignment and stock photography, and providing video and cinematography lighting services. Graham specializes in architectural, people, travel, product, and location images.

RICHARD GROSS specializes in corporate, advertising, and stock photography for Fortune 500 companies.

GENEVIEVE HAFNER was born in France and moved to New York City in 1986. She is a graduate of the EFET School of Photography in Lyons, and currently works for Concrete Jungle Images, Inc. Hafner's work has been published internationally—in the *French City Magazine International*, *New York Magazine*, the *Toronto Globe and Mail*, and the *Irish Sunday Tribune*. She won the Merit Award and the Award of Excellence—both for the 1993 annual report of Herman Miller—from the Art Directors Club and *Communication Arts* magazine, respectively. Her photographs have also appeared in Towery Publishing's *New York: Metropolis of the American Dream*. Hafner's specialties are photojournalism and shooting images for New York postcards, and her favorite subjects include street scenes, architecture, urbanism, street art, and New York in general.

STACEY HALPER received a bachelor of fine arts degree in photography from the State University of New York (SUNY)-Purchase College. Her work has been exhibited in galleries in New York, Connecticut, and Arizona, and she recently participated in a group show at the Kodak Gallery in Seoul. Halper is also in the process of finishing her first short film, *Bread and Bones*.

HAZEL HANKIN is a fine-art documentary photographer and teacher, and a native of Brooklyn. Her freelance clients include book publishers, magazines, newspapers, and corporate and non-profit organizations. Hankin received a master of fine arts degree in photography from Brooklyn College, and has been an instructor of photography at the City College of New York since 1986.

TED HARDIN, a self-employed photographer, specializes in portraiture, interiors, cityscapes, fashion, and travel photography. Originally from Washington, D.C., Hardin graduated from Washington and Lee University, and moved to New York in the late 1960s. His photographs can be seen in catalogs for Montgomery Ward, Abraham and Straus, and Konettes, as well as in *Essence*, *Glamour*, *Money*, *Fortune*, *Newsweek*, *New York*, *Town & Country*, *Redbook*, and *Good Housekeeping* magazines. His photographs were also used in Towery Publishing's *New York: Metropolis of the American Dream*. Hardin enjoys doing environmental portraits and working on his ongoing project of photographing New York City at night.

STEPHEN F. HARMON is a self-taught photographer whose areas of specialty

include street scenes, pastoral images, and general natural light photography. A native of New York City, he attended both Queens College and Brooklyn College Law School. Harmon's work can be seen at the New York Historical Society, Museum of the City of New York, and Brooklyn Museum, as well as in Towery Publishing's *Cleveland: Continuing the Renaissance*.

BLAINE HARRINGTON III calls Colorado home when he is not traveling around the globe. For 10 weeks in the fall of 1996, he journeyed 36,000 air miles to 11 countries on photo shoots. In addition, he has contributed to a variety of magazines, including *Business Week*,

Forbes, *Time*, *Newsweek*, *National Geographic Traveler*, and *Ski*. Harrington has worked assignments for the National Geographic Society and Time Life, and has taken cover photos for such travel guides as *Fodor's*, *Frommer's*, *Insight Guides*, and *Real Guides*. His photographs have also appeared in Towery Publishing's *Chicago: Heart and Soul of America* and *Boston: History in the Making*.

PHILIP HILDEN attended the Pratt Institute's Phoenix School of Design, the School of Visual Arts, and SUNY-Old Westbury. As owner of Quality Images, he specializes in natural light portraits and stock images. Hilden is a native of Long Island.

THE IMAGE FINDERS, founded by Jim Baron in 1986, is a stock photography

company located in Cleveland, Ohio. Its files cover a broad range of subjects, including agriculture, animals, butterflies, families, food, sports, transportation, travel, trees, and the western United States.

DARIN IPEMA, originally from Chicago, received a bachelor of fine arts degree in communication from the University of Memphis. He specializes in cinematography, and has shot two independent feature films, as well as several music videos. Ipema's photographs have also appeared in Towery Publishing's *Phoenix: The Desert in Bloom* and *St. Louis: For the Record*.

LOUIS JAWITZ, a native of Long Beach, specializes in travel and location photography. His work has been published in *Nikon World Portfolio*.

BUD LEE studied at the Columbia University School of Fine Arts in New York and the National Academy of Fine Arts before moving to the Orlando area more than 20 years ago. A self-employed photojournalist, he founded both the Florida Photographers Workshop and the Iowa Photographers Workshop. Lee's work can be seen in *Esquire*, *Life*, *Travel & Leisure*, *Rolling Stone*, the *Washington Post*, and the *New York Times*, as well as in Towery Publishing's *Greater Syracuse: Center of an Empire*; *Jacksonville: Reflections of Excellence*; *Los Angeles: City of Dreams*; *Orlando: The City Beautiful*; *St. Louis: For the Record*; and *Treasures on Tampa Bay: Tampa, St. Petersburg, Clearwater*.

FREDA LEINWAND's photographs have appeared in major newspapers and magazines including the *New York Times*, *Forbes*, *Ms.*, *Popular Photography*, and *Family Health*. Her work has also been published in many books and has been seen on national television. Leinwand's photographs have been exhibited in the United States and Canada, and are included in collections at Radcliffe College and the Women's Rights National Historical Park in Seneca Falls.

JAMES LEMASS studied art in his native Ireland before moving to Cambridge, Massachusetts, in 1987. His areas of specialty include people and travel photography, and his work can be seen in publications by Aer Lingus, British Airways, and USAir, as well as the Nynex Yellow Pages. Lemass has also worked for the Massachusetts Office of Travel and Tourism, and his photographs have appeared in several other Towery publications, including *Greater Phoenix: The Desert in Bloom*; *New York: Metropolis of the American Dream*; *Orlando: The City Beautiful*; *San Diego: World-Class City*; *Treasures on Tampa Bay: Tampa, St. Petersburg, Clearwater*; and *Washington: City on a Hill*.

RON LEVINE, owner of Montreal-based Ron Levine Photography, is a 20-year veteran of commercial and editorial photography. His images have appeared in numerous international publications, including *Time*, *Business Week*, *Travel & Leisure*, *Forbes*, *Fortune*, *ESPN: The Magazine*, *Saturday Night*, and Air Canada's *En Route*. Levine's photographs of the southern United States, the Canadian Maritime Provinces, and Poland have been exhibited in museums and galleries internationally, including Colombia's Museo de la Universidad de Antioquia, Germany's Linhof Gallery, Mexico's Centro Cultural el Nigromante, and Poland's Stara Galeria. Levine served as the photography editor for Towery Publishing's *Montréal: la joie de vivre*, and his photographs also appeared in Towery's *Greater Des Moines: Iowa's Commercial Center*.

STEVEN HANS LINDNER, who was born in Manhattan, grew up in New Jersey and moved back to New York City in 1971. Specializing in celebrity portraits, computer imaging, and panoramas, Lindner has worked for Korg International, Allied Signal, Ogilvey & Mather, Warren Kremer Advertising, *EM (Ebony Man)*, *Cosmopolitan*, and Earthstone, Inc. His photographs also can be seen in Towery Publishing's *New York: Metropolis of the American Dream*. Lindner loves to travel and uses his travel opportunities to take photographs. He graduated from Pratt Institute with a bachelor of fine arts degree.

ODETTE LUPIS was born in Istria, and came to the United States as a child refugee from Marshal Tito's regime. Her photography focuses on the multiethnic, multiracial, interdenominational, and interfaith aspects of the American experience. Lupis speaks Italian, French, Spanish, and Greek, as well as English, and her work has been exhibited in the United States, Italy, England, and Japan.

ALAN MALLAMS is an organic chemist working in the pharmaceutical industry and has a keen interest in all aspects of photography. He has been active in photography for 35 years, and has had numerous photographs published in books, calendars, catalogs, textbooks, and postcards, as well as for editorial uses. Mallams has had many years of experience putting on multimedia shows for nature groups and camera clubs.

TOM AND SALLY MYERS have been full-time freelance photographers for 30 years, and have been published in many national magazines, including *National Geographic, National Wildlife, Newsweek,* and *Animals* (London), as well as in Towery Publishing's *Sacramento Tapestry.* Their photos appear in books and educational CD-ROM materials throughout the world, advertisements, album covers, and Hallmark cards and calendars. With their son, Jeff Myers, the family has more than 400,000 color images in their files, covering a variety of geographic areas, including Europe and the Pacific Coast from Mexico to Alaska and inland to Colorado.

Y. NAGASAKI is a graduate of both Aoyama Gakuin University in Tokyo and Long Island University. He received a master of fine arts degree in photography from the City University of New York. Nagasaki was a finalist for the Taiyo-sho Award, Japan's award for the most promising documentary photographer of the year. His body of work includes *He/She: The Third Sex; Stars & Bars: New Glimpses of Old Glory;* and *Pix Stars: Celebrities behind the Lens.*

GREG PEASE is a Baltimore-based photographer specializing in corporate and industrial photography. Having begun his career as a commercial photographer in 1974, he has won numerous awards, and his images have been published in books, magazines, and advertisements, as well as in Towery Publishing's *Baltimore: Charm City.* Best known for his regional landscape and maritime photographs, Pease is coprincipal of Greg Pease & Associates with his wife, Kelly.

PHOTOPHILE, established in San Diego in 1967, is owned and operated by Nancy Likins-Masten. An internationally known stock photography agency, the company houses more than a million color images, and represents more than 90 contributing local and international photographers. Subjects include extensive coverage of the West Coast, business/industry, people/lifestyles, health/medicine, travel, scenics, wildlife, and adventure sports, plus 200 additional categories.

ROBBIE POPE, owner of Park Studio in New York, specializes in marketing. His clients include *Computerworld,* the *New York Post,* the Associated Press, Wallace Enterprise, and thatguitarman.com.

STAN RIES, a specialist in architectural and aerial interior photography, has traveled to Russia on location for ABC-TV and to China to photograph for the Metropolitan Museum of Art. He received a bachelor of arts degree from the University of Kansas.

MIRIAM ROMAIS, a native of Brazil, graduated from Rutgers University with a bachelor of fine arts degree. She is the managing director of En Foco, Inc., a nonprofit photography organization that exhibits and publishes the works of photographers from a variety of ethnic backgrounds. Romais has received grants and awards from organizations such as the Puffin Foundation, and she recently published a book titled *Americanos.*

LINDA RUTENBERG graduated from Concordia University with a master of fine arts degree in photography. Her areas of specialty include portraits and illustrations for books, and her photographs have appeared in Towery Publishing's *Montréal: la joie de vivre.* Rutenberg devotes her spare time to her photography gallery.

© JONATHAN POSTAL / TOWERY PUBLISHING, INC.

COSMOS ANDREW SARCHIAPONE was raised in New Plymouth, Idaho. He attended Fiorello H. LaGuardia High School of Music & Art and Performing Arts at Lincoln Center, received a bachelor of arts degree in music composition from Syracuse University, and has studied under Meyer Shapiro of Columbia University, John Cage of New School University, Milton Glaser of the School of Visual Arts, and Eric Feinblatt of Push Pin Studios.

JAMES D. SCHERLIS, a lifelong Baltimorean, studied at the University of Maryland and the University of Baltimore School of Law. The owner of James Scherlis Photography, he specializes in editorial/feature, performing arts, and stock photography, as well as teaching and mentoring budding photographers. An internationally recognized cameraman, he is the official photographer for the National Symphony, Peabody Conservatory of Music, and Library of Congress Music Division. Scherlis' work has also appeared in Towery Publishing's *Baltimore: Charm City.*

CHARLES SCHISLA, a native of Indianapolis, received a bachelor of science degree in radio from Butler University. As owner of Schisla Communications, he specializes in public relations. Schisla's photography has appeared in *Islands, Gourmet,* and *St. Anthony Messenger,* as well as in Towery Publishing's *St. Louis: For the Record.* Active in the promotion and coordination of many state, national, and international events, Schisla always carries his camera to capture the sights he sees.

SHARON SELDEN, originally from Oakland, has studied at Tisch School of the Arts and SUNY-Purchase. As owner of Sharon Selden Photography, she focuses primarily on offbeat and wacky subjects, as well as automobile-related sports. Selden's clients include Man's Ruin Records, Raygun Publishing, and *Gearhead Magazine.* She is currently writing a book about figure-eight auto racing.

RHODA SIDNEY received a bachelor of arts degree in modern languages from the University of New Mexico. She specializes in photographing people and places. Sidney's work has appeared in the Newark (New Jersey) Museum.

HARVEY STEIN teaches photography at the International Center of Photography, New School University, and Drew University. He specializes in street photography, portraiture, and travel images. A recipient of a 1983 Creative Arts Public Service Grant, Stein has published *Parallels: A Look at Twins; Artists Observed;* and *Coney Island.* His photographs have also appeared in numerous publications, including *Time, Life, Esquire, Smithsonian,* the *New York Times, Glamour,* and *Forbes.*

ERIKA STONE's professional photography career spans the decades from the 1940s until the present. Although mainly self-taught, she has studied with Berenice Abbott and George Tice at New School University. Until 1960, she served as a freelance photojournalist for *Time* and *Der Spiegel.* Stone has also published numerous books, including *ProTechniques of Photographing Children,* four books for babies in a series called Tot Shot, and three children's books in Walker Publishing Company's Open Family series. She was among 20 women photographers whose work was included in the anthology *Women of Vision,* published in 1982.

ROBERT VIZZINI was born and raised in New York City. The owner of Vizzini Design and Photography, he specializes in landscapes. Vizzini's clients include Children's Television Workshop, *Woman's Day, LensWork Quarterly,* and *Popular Photography.*

HARVEY WANG is a lifelong resident of New York City. He specializes in black-and-white portraiture, and photographs from his acclaimed book *Harvey Wang's New York* have been exhibited at the Museum of the City of New York and in the National Museum of American History at the Smithsonian Institution. Wang has published five books and currently films documentaries for National Geographic's *Explorer* television series. He earned a bachelor's degree in anthropology from SUNY-Purchase. Wang's work can also be seen in Towery Publishing's *New York: Metropolis of the American Dream.*

TIM WILLIS, owner of Tim Willis Photo, specializes in travel photography.

DAN WITZ, a native of Chicago, has lived in New York for the last 20 years. He has received several fellowships from the National Endowment for the Arts.

Additional photographers and organizations that contributed to *New York: A State of Mind* include DreamWorks SKG, Jay Kidd, and Greg Probst.

INDEX TO PROFILES

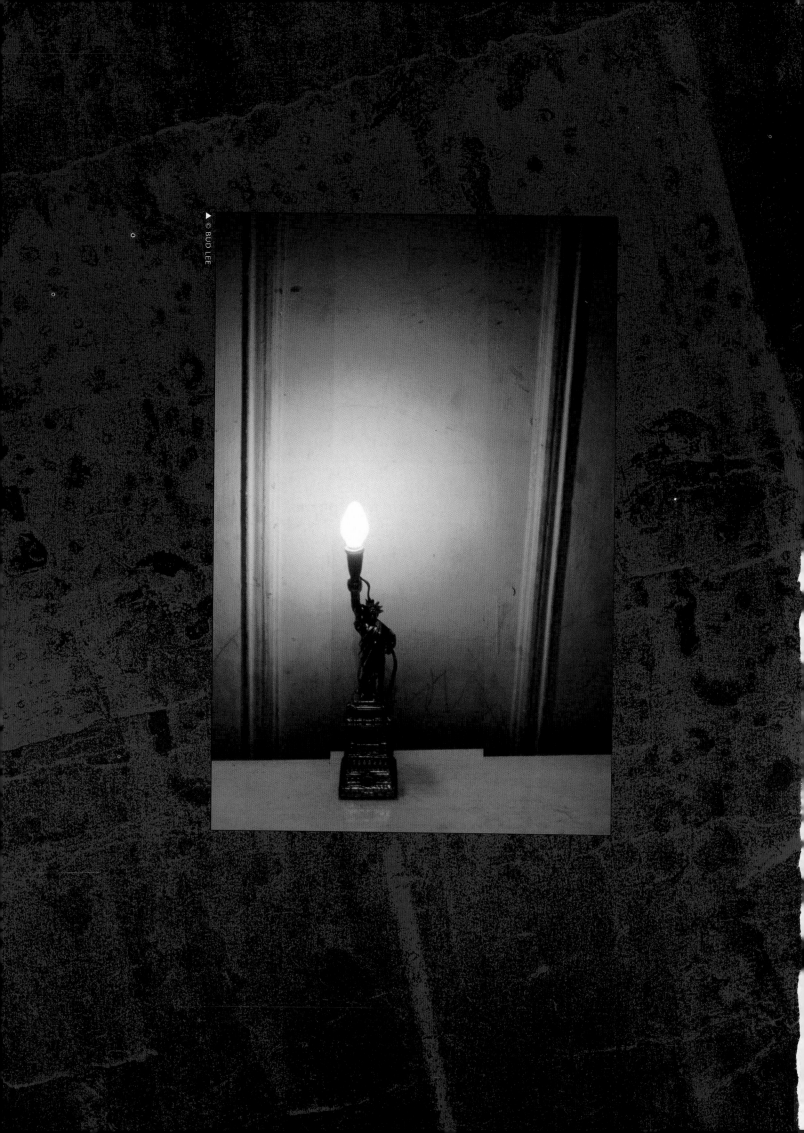